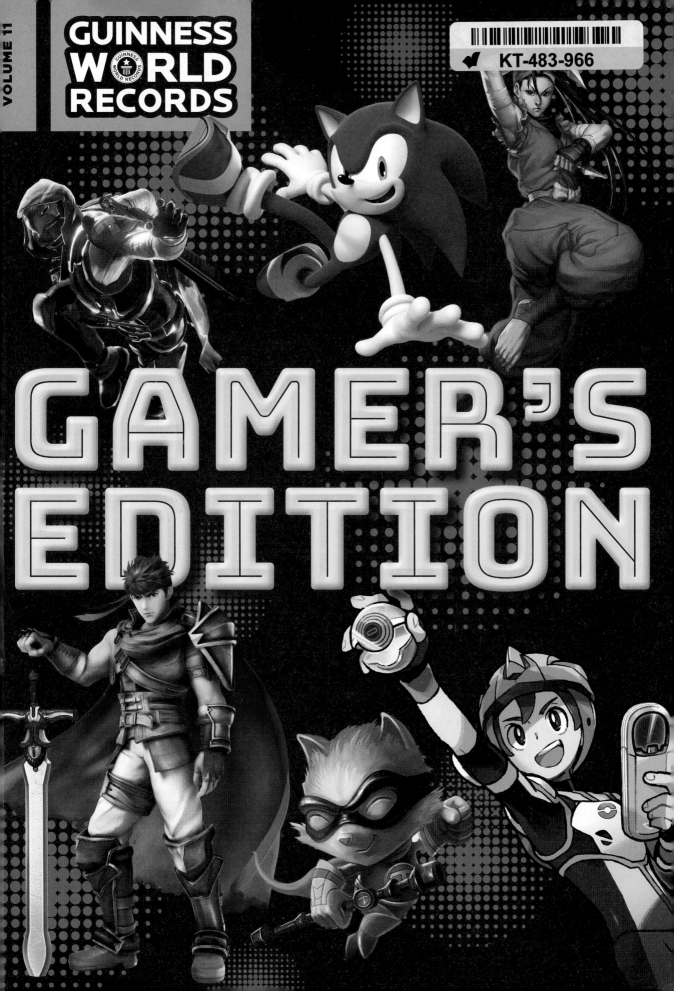

British Library Cataloguing-in-Publication Data: a catalogue record for this book is available from the British Library.

UK: 978-1-910561-73-7
US: 978-1-910561-74-4
US: 978-1-910561-91-1

Check the official website at guinnessworldrecords.com/gamers for more record-breaking gamers.

ACCREDITATION:
Guinness World Records Limited has a very thorough accreditation system for records verification. However, while every effort is made to ensure accuracy, Guinness World Records Limited cannot be held responsible for any errors contained in this work. Feedback from our readers on any point of accuracy is always welcomed.

Guinness World Records Limited does not claim to own any right, title or interest in the trademarks of others reproduced in this book.

© 2017 Guinness World Records Limited, a Jim Pattison Group company

OFFICIALLY AMAZING

THE JIM PATTISON GROUP

GAMER'S EDITION 2018

Editor
Stephen Daultrey

Senior Managing Editor
Stephen Fall

Layout Editor
Bruno MacDonald

Editor-in-Chief
Craig Glenday

Senior Project Editor
Adam Millward

Project Editor
Ben Hollington

Information & Research Manager
Carim Valerio

Proofreading
Matthew White

VP Publishing
Jenny Heller

Head of Pictures & Design
Michael Whitty

Picture Editor
Fran Morales

Picture Researcher
Wilf Matos

Talent Researchers
Jenny Langridge,
Victoria Tweedy

Design
Gary Harrod

Assistant Designer
Calvin North

Artworker
Billy Waqar

Original Illustrations
Maltings Partnership

Production Director
Patricia Magill

Publishing Manager
Jane Boatfield

Production Assistant
Thomas McCurdy

Production Consultants
Roger Hawkins, Dennis Thon,
Tobias Wrona

Reprographics
Res Kahraman at Born Group

Original Photography
Paul Michael Hughes,
Ranald Mackechnie,
Kevin Scott Ramos,
Ryan Schude

Indexer
Marie Lorimer

Printing & Binding
MOHN Media Mohndruck GmbH,
Gütersloh, Germany

GUINNESS WORLD RECORDS

CORPORATE OFFICE
Global President: Alistair Richards

Professional Services
Chief Financial Officer: Alison Ozanne
Financial Controller: Andrew Wood
Accounts Receivable Manager: Lisa Gibbs
Finance Managers: Jaimie-Lee Emrith, Daniel Ralph
Assistant Accountants: Jess Blake, Yusuf Gafar
Accounts Payable Clerk: Tajkiya Sultana
Accounts Receivable Clerk: Jusna Begum
Trading Analysis Manager: Elizabeth Bishop
General Counsel: Raymond Marshall
Legal Counsel: Terence Tsang
Junior Legal Counsel: Xiangyun Rablen
Paralegal: Michelle Phua
Global HR Director: Farrella Ryan-Coker
HR Assistant: Mehreen Saeed
Office Manager: Jackie Angus
Director of IT: Rob Howe
IT Manager: James Edwards
Developers: Cenk Selim, Lewis Ayers
Desktop Administrator: Alpha Serrant-Defoe
Analyst / Tester: Céline Bacon
Global SVP Records: Marco Frigatti
Head of Category Management: Jacqueline Sherlock
Information & Research Manager: Carim Valerio
RMT Training Manager: Alexandra Popistan
Category Managers: Adam Brown, Tripp Yeoman, Victoria Tweedy
Category Executive: Danielle Kirby
Records Consultant: Sam Mason

Global Brand Strategy
SVP Global Brand Strategy: Samantha Fay
Brand Manager: Juliet Dawson
VP Creative: Paul O'Neill
Head of Global Production Delivery: Alan Pixsley

Global Product Marketing
VP Global Product Marketing: Katie Forde
Director of Global TV Content & Sales: Rob Molloy
Senior TV Distribution Manager: Paul Glynn
Senior TV Content Executive & Production Co-ordinator: Jonathan Whitton

Head of Digital: Veronica Irons
Online Editor: Kevin Lynch
Online Writer: Rachel Swatman
Social Media Manager: Dan Thorne
Digital Video Producer: Matt Musson
Junior Video Producer: Cécile Thai
Front-End Developer: Alex Waldu
Brand & Consumer Product Marketing Manager: Lucy Acfield
B2B Product Marketing Manager (Live Events): Louise Toms
B2B Product Marketing Manager (PR & Advertising): Emily Osborn
Product Marketing Executive: Victor Fenes
Designer: Rebecca Buchanan Smith
Junior Designer: Edward Dillon

EMEA & APAC
SVP EMEA APAC: Nadine Causey
Head of Publishing Sales: John Pilley
Key Accounts Manager: Caroline Lake
Publishing Rights and Export Manager: Helene Navarre
Distribution Executive: Alice Oluyitan
Head of Commercial Accounts & Licensing: Sam Prosser
Business Development Managers: Lee Harrison, Alan Southgate
Commercial Account Managers: Jessica Rae, Inga Rasmussen, Sadie Smith, Fay Edwards
Country Representative – Business Development Manager, India: Nikhil Shukla
PR Director: Jakki Lewis
Senior PR Manager: Doug Male
B2B PR Manager: Melanie DeFries
International Press Officer: Amber-Georgina Gill
Head of Marketing: Justine Tommey / Chriscilla Philogene
Senior B2B Marketing Manager: Mawa Rodriguez
B2C Marketing Manager: Christelle Betrong
Content Marketing Executive: Imelda Ekpo
Head of Records Management, APAC: Ben Backhouse
Head of Records Management, Europe: Shantha Chinniah
Records Managers: Mark McKinley, Christopher Lynch, Matilda Hagne, Daniel Kidane, Sheila Mella
Records Executive: Megan Double
Senior Production Manager: Fiona Gruchy-Craven
Project Manager: Cameron Kellow

Country Manager, MENA: Talal Omar
Head of RMT, MENA: Samer Khallouf
Records Manager, MENA: Hoda Khachab
B2B Marketing Manager, MENA: Leila Issa
Commercial Account Managers, MENA: Khalid Yassine, Kamel Yassin
Official Adjudicators: Ahmed Gamal Gabr, Anna Orford, Brian Sobel, Glenn Pollard, Jack Brockbank, Lena Kuhlmann, Lorenzo Veltri, Lucia Sinigagliesi, Paulina Sapinska, Pete Fairbairn, Pravin Patel, Richard Stenning, Kevin Southam, Rishi Nath, Seyda Subasi-Gemici, Sofia Greenacre, Solvej Malouf, Swapnil Dangarikar

AMERICAS
SVP Americas: Peter Harper
VP Marketing & Commercial Sales: Keith Green
VP Publishing Sales, Americas: Walter Weintz
Director of Latin America: Carlos Martinez
Head of Brand Development, West Coast: Kimberly Partrick
Head of Commercial Sales: Nicole Pando
Senior Account Manager: Ralph Hannah
Account Managers: Alex Angert, Giovanni Bruna, Mackenzie Berry
Project Manager: Casey DeSantis
PR Manager: Kristen Ott
Assistant PR Manager: Elizabeth Montoya
PR Coordinator: Sofia Rocher
Digital Coordinator: Kristen Stephenson
Publishing Sales Manager: Lisa Corrado
Marketing Manager: Morgan Kubelka
Consumer Marketing Executive: Tavia Levy
Senior Records Manager, North America: Hannah Ortman
Senior Records Manager, Latin America: Raquel Assis
Records Managers, North America: Michael Furnari, Kaitlin Holl, Kaitlin Vesper
Records Manager, Latin America: Sarah Casson
HR & Office Manager: Kellie Ferrick
Official Adjudicators, North America: Michael Empric, Philip Robertson, Christina Flounders Conlon, Jimmy Coggins, Andrew Glass, Mike Janela
Official Adjudicators, Latin America: Natalia Ramirez Talero, Carlos Tapia Rojas

JAPAN
VP Japan: Erika Ogawa
Office Manager: Fumiko Kitagawa
Director of RMT: Kaoru Ishikawa
Records Managers: Mariko Koike, Yoko Furuya
Records Executive: Koma Satoh
Marketing Director: Hideki Naruse
Designer: Momoko Cunneen
Senior PR & Sales Promotion Manager: Kazami Kamioka
B2B Marketing Manager PR & Advertising: Asumi Funatsu
Project Manager Live Events: Aya McMillan
Digital & Publishing Content Manager: Takafumi Suzuki
Commercial Director: Vihag Kulshrestha
Account Managers: Takuro Maruyama, Masamichi Yazaki
Senior Account Executive: Daisuke Katayama
Account Executive: Minami Ito
Official Adjudicators: Justin Patterson, Mai McMillan, Gulnaz Ukassova, Rei Iwashita

GREATER CHINA
President: Rowan Simons
General Manager, Greater China: Marco Frigatti
VP Commercial, Global & Greater China: Blythe Fitzwiliam
Senior Account Manager: Catherine Gao
Senior Project Manager: Reggy Lu
Account Manager: Chloe Liu
External Relations Manager: Dong Cheng
Digital Business Manager: Jacky Yuan
Head of RMT: Charles Wharton
Records Manager: Alicia Zhao
Records Manager / Project Co-ordinator: Fay Jiang
HR & Office Manager: Tina Shi
Office Assistant: Kate Wang
Head of Marketing: Wendy Wang
B2B Marketing Manager: Iris Hou
Digital Manager: Lily Zeng
Marketing Executive: Tracy Cui
PR Manager: Ada Liu
Content Director: Angela Wu
Official Adjudicators: Brittany Dunn, Joanne Brent, John Garland, Maggie Luo, Peter Yang

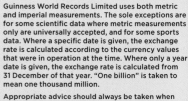

FOREWORD

Hey everyone!

DanTDM here. Welcome back to Guinness World Records' star-studded, action-crammed *Gamer's Edition*... with a special introduction from little old me!

It's amazing that there's a whole book like this one, devoted just to the creative and dedicated people doing weird and wonderful things in the world of gaming. And the last 12 months have been particularly dynamic. Where do I even begin?!? Nintendo launched a new console, the VR revolution is rumbling on, *Pokémon GO* and *Overwatch* smashed all kinds of records, and *LEGO® Worlds* is finally out. Then there's all the gamers and gaming fans – like me! – featured here, who spend thousands of hours setting so many new Guinness World Records titles.

Go on, have a peek inside. You'll find everything from the best-selling games and biggest spaceships to the fastest *FIFA* goal, and even players finishing games with the weirdest of controllers!

What makes this awesome book extra special, of course, is that this is the third year running I've appeared in it! At the time of writing, mine was – and hopefully still is! – the **most viewed *Minecraft* channel on YouTube**. It's had nearly 10 billion views – can you believe it? It's completely mad! So a mega thanks to my fans for tuning in each day and making my dream possible. I would never have believed, when I launched my channel in 2011, that someday I'd hold multiple Guinness World Records titles.

This last year has been big for me in lots of other ways, too. I've been touring the globe on my first world tour, launched my own series on YouTube Red and had a first graphic novel published (left). No rest for us gamers! Maybe I'll set more Guinness World Records titles in the year to come. Anyone want to give me a challenge? You know where to find me.

I hope you enjoy reading this year's *GWR Gamer's Edition*. I love it, and not just because I'm in it!

Bye everybody!

DanTDM

CONTENTS

BE A RECORD-BREAKER

Whether you're an expert gamer, an eSports superstar, a pioneering developer or a collector of gaming memorabilia, Guinness World Records wants to hear from you!

GWR hosts exclusive world record videogame challenges at Twin Galaxies. Head over to www. twingalaxies.com to test your skills in a number of games and fun categories.

1 | MAKE AN APPLICATION

The first stop for any would-be record-breaker should always be **www.guinnessworldrecords.com**. Hit "Set a record" to find out how the process works and how to register an account. Email us to let us know which record you'd like to attempt.

READ THE RULES | 2

It takes six weeks to process an application. If you want to beat an existing record, you'll be sent guidelines. If it's a new record we like the sound of, we'll compile rules for it. Many ideas are turned down at the application stage, but we will explain why. Use this book and the website to see the kinds of records we like, then try again!

3 | PRACTICE MAKES PERFECT

GWR record attempts are just like a sports competition – you need to train hard to make sure you're in peak condition to take them on. The more hours you practise, the greater your chances of success will be.

MAKE YOUR ATTEMPT | 4

Once you're certain that your gaming skills are in prime condition, you're ready to take on the record. Make sure you have everything in place to meet the guidelines – you will need a good-quality video recorder, witnesses and anything else we've specified you require for a valid claim.

5 | SEND YOUR EVIDENCE

Preparation can ensure your potential new record isn't missed or rejected because of technical issues. When filming videos, do a trial run to make sure that the lighting is right and that there are no obstructions. After you've filmed your attempt, package up the evidence and send it to GWR. Easy!

FRAME YOUR CERTIFICATE | 6

You did it! Successful record-breakers will be sent an official certificate to show off to their friends. If you're very lucky, you may even be one of the fortunate few to make it on to these pages next year. And if you've missed out, there's no need to despair – you can always try again.

EDITOR'S LETTER

Welcome to the 2018 volume of the *Guinness World Records Gamer's Edition*. This one's our 11th annual since we began back in 2008, and boy have things changed since then. For a start we didn't have *Minecraft* in 2008, which is almost as unthinkable as a world without cars or light bulbs. Now we have VR, video streaming, eSports championships and YouTube megastars.

I want to kick off this year's book by talking all about SUPERHEROES. Everyone loves a super-powered crime-buster, right? Incredibly, in Dec 2018, it will have been 40 years since the release of the **first official superhero game**, *Superman* for the Atari 2600. That feels like 27 million

First working prosthetic based on a videogame (pp.56–57)

Most subscribed female games broadcaster on YouTube (pp.54–55)

lifetimes ago (!?!) or something. Furthermore, the May 2017 release of DC Comics fighter *Injustice 2* will see Superman extending his record as the **longest-running videogame character**, fending off the threat from that ghost-evading dot-gobbler PAC-Man (who, incidentally, you can find on pp.90–91).

Both of those landmark feats are major reasons why you'll find an entire special chapter dedicated to superhero games on pp.100–119. Fast-foot it over to those pages like DC Comics' The Flash or Marvel's Quicksilver and you'll be besieged by outlandish and incredible records featuring the evil-thwarting likes of Spider-Man, Batman, Iron Man and the X-Men, from the quickest completions to the largest cosplay costumes.

SEARCHING FOR MONSTERS

The biggest success story of 2016 was arguably the launch of *Pokémon GO*. Seriously, it was nigh on impossible to venture out into the streets and not bump into hordes of hunters trying to catch pocket-critters on their phones. Celebrating the months in which the world truly went Poké-potty, we reminisce with some of the most memorable *GO* stories from around the globe. PLUS, we even have a photoshoot with the guy who made a giant, record-breaking Pokémon costume out of balloons (pp.80–81).

Largest Game Boy (pp.122–23)

Highest score on *Donkey Kong* (pp.76–77)

TO THE STARS, BACK, AND BEYOND...

The blockbuster games blast out thick and fast. This year's book has been divided up into special themes. Sci-fi followers should head to pp.54–73, where they'll find futuristic favourites including Star Wars, *Halo*, *DOOM* and *Overwatch* (the **most watched new game on Twitch in 2016**). We also have a feature on something known as "transhumanist gaming" on pp.56–57 (check out my slightly painful arm-wrestle to the left!). I'd like to say the cyborg arm here is out of this world, but it's really not – it's actually part of *this* world. We know – we have the photos to prove it!

For fans of fantasy (pp.18–51), there's an otherworldly array of classic and new franchises, from *Dark Souls* to *Vainglory*. We meet the **oldest games YouTuber**, 81-year-old Shirley Curry (pp.18–19). Over in the real world (or at least one that's a bit more like our own), we attempt to re-tell human history through games (pp.124–27). You'll find everything from deadly plagues and great fires to gold rushes and space missions, all joyfully regaled through the power of pixels.

Largest mechanical wings on a cosplay costume (pp.26-27)

Most tournament victories in *Injustice: Gods Among Us* (pp.100–01)

Sports enthusiasts can get their virtual kick with *FIFA*, *Madden* and *Rocket League* (pp.156–73). Icons such as Mario, Donkey Kong and *Minecraft* are headline acts in our aptly named Legends chapter (pp.76–97). And burly game heavyweights such as *WWE 2K* and *Tekken* flex their muscles in our Fighting chapter (pp.176–89).

As for my personal favourite feature? That'll be our urban legends on pp.20–21. Here, we investigate some bizarre gaming mysteries, from haunted cartridges to mind-control arcade machines. Truly creepy stuff, right?

KEEP ON SPEED-RUNNING...

Finally, before I disappear into the virtual sunset, I'm proud to say that the new *Gamer's Edition* features our first ever tables of speed-run records, all supplied by the good folk at Speedrun.com. Leg it to pp.192–201 to discover the quickest completions in a variety of top titles, from quirky indie games such as *Assault Android Cactus* to time-defying adventures such as *Castlevania*.

Enjoy the book and don't forget: if you want to try to be a record-breaker yourself, we have all the details on p.5. We're now hosting some videogame record challenges at the website of Twin Galaxies – the **longest-running videogames adjudicator** – with plenty of new games to be added in the coming months. It's never been easier to have a crack at breaking a Guinness World Records title for a videogame. Get involved and, who knows, we may even see you in the next book...

Stephen Daultrey
   Editor, *GWR Gamer's Edition*

Largest collection of *The Legend of Zelda* memorabilia (pp.28-29)

YEAR IN GAMING

Part 1: MAY to NOV 2016

Some of the biggest – and strangest – highlights since the last *Gamer's Edition* went to press...

JUL 2016

JUN 2016

HUNGRY FOR NEW TWITCH CONTENT?

Twitch expanded on its gaming coverage by launching "social eating", a service enabling users to watch broadcasters *eat* things. However, owing to some apparent early misuse – basically, users chowing on things far too disgusting to list here – Twitch issued some rather detailed guidelines. Kotaku's headline ran: "Don't eat pet food (and other very serious new Twitch rules)"!

SPEED-RUNNER VS FOOD

In July, Canadian speed-runner "Mitchflowerpower", aka Mitch Fowler, tried the impossible: to finish *Super Mario Bros. 3* before US TV host Stephen Colbert could devour a microwaveable snack! Fowler, who holds the record for the **fastest completion of *Super Mario Bros. 3* (no wrong warp)**, was competing in a televised challenge on *The Late Show* to promote the Summer Games Done Quick event. Perhaps unsurprisingly, Colbert won this particular race.

JUL 2016

SONIC'S BIRTHDAY WHEELS

Super-speedy hedgehog Sonic celebrated turning 25 years old in 2016 and was spoilt rotten with birthday goodies. One of his best presents was this Honda Civic car, which was showcased at the San Diego Comic-Con in July. However, despite the vehicle's sporty stylings, we doubt it's as fast as the hedgehog himself.

AUG 2016

GOLD MEDAL COSPLAY FROM JAPAN'S PM

The closing ceremony of the Rio Olympics in Brazil threw up a gaming surprise – literally – when Japan's prime minister, Shinzō Abe, popped out of a giant green pipe dressed as Mario. The cosplaying governor was promoting his nation's impending hosting of the 2020 Summer Olympics. Not that Mario is a stranger to the sporting showpiece, of course – the podgy plumber has been co-hosting official Olympics videogames with Sonic since 2007.

SEP 2016

GAMERS BEAT BOFFINS

A group of 469 gamers impressed the science world when they discovered the shape of a protein ahead of lab boffins. The gamers made their find while solving puzzles in *Foldit*, an online game created to encourage players to assist in scientific research by collaboratively folding protein molecules. Experts say that their find could help battle Alzheimer's.

SEP 2016

CLIMBING WALL *PONG*

It's not unusual for a retro classic to get a modern makeover, but this AR game of *Pong*, played on a special climbing wall, was so quirky that it went viral. Entitled *Climball*, the exergame – as well as the wall itself – was created by the Finnish company Augmented Climbing Wall.

OCT 2016

LOL CONQUERS TABLE TOPS

Not content with their PC MOBA surpassing 100 million players (see pp.24–25), a crack team of Riot Games employees decided to design a *League of Legends* board game, too. Entitled *Mechs vs. Minions*, the table-bound effort had apparently been in production for three years and was finally released in October.

NOV 2016

AROUND *ELDER SCROLLS* IN 62 HOURS

Bethesda's 1996 RPG *The Elder Scrolls II: Daggerfall* is famed for its gigantic gaming area and once held the GWR title for **largest playable world in a videogame**. That sprawling size was fully evidenced when the Dutch YouTube channel "How Big is the Map?" laboriously walked their avatar from one end of its world to the other, a journey that took 61 hr 54 min. The entire "stroll" can be viewed across 14 videos.

NEWS IN BRIEF

In May 2016, it was revealed that a *Megaman* animated series was in the works for 2017. The show will celebrate the character's 30th anniversary.

Bethesda's E3 2016 press conference was infamous for the screams of one audience member. A compilation video of "Bethesda's Annoying "Woo!" Lady" racked up nearly 50,000 views on YouTube.

In July, two US marines playing *Pokémon GO* called the cops after finding a man behaving suspiciously. It transpired that the man was a murder suspect. (Head to pp.78–79 for more strange *GO* tales).

A pop-up eSports tournament at the Rio Olympics in August was won by Canada. The event was organized by the International eGames Committee and saw gamers competing in Nintendo's *Super Smash Bros. for Wii U*.

Despite often being billed as the "worst game on Steam", the infamous 2009 puzzler *Bad Rats* was treated to a sequel in July. The new game was entitled *Bad Rats Show*.

In November, the co-founder of *Gears of War* studio Epic Games, Tim Sweeney, donated $15 million (£12 million) in order to save a 7,000-acre forest in North Carolina, USA, from destruction.

MECHS MINIONS

DAGGERFALL

I'M AT   DUNGEONS   HOMES   EXIT
           TEMPLES   TOWNS

YEAR IN GAMING

Part 2: DEC 2016 to APR 2017

...and it doesn't stop there. Here's another bunch of fun and crazy highlights from the world of gaming.

DYNASTY WARRIORS 9 TO RECREATE CHINA IN GIANT GAME MAP

Game worlds have been getting ridiculously huge for years now, but gamers still gawped when Omega Force revealed that it was recreating the *whole* of China for *Dynasty Warriors 9*. The incoming title is the first open-world entry to Koei's hack-and-slash series and promises to replicate locations such as Hulao Pass in real detail.

DEC 2016

WILL FERRELL TO FRONT eSPORTS COMEDY

Having sent-up basketball (*Semi-Pro*), ice skating (*Blades of Glory*) and motorsports (*Talladega Nights*), Will Ferrell is now turning his wry eye to eSports. As revealed by the studio Legendary, the comedy actor is working on an as-yet-untitled new flick in which a middle-aged gamer (Ferrell) tries his luck in the highly youthful world of pro gaming.

JAN 2017

FEB 2017

IT'S *DOOM* PLAYED IN A PORSCHE!

In a car-customizing manoeuvre bound to get road-safety experts turning purpler than a *DOOM* demon, YouTuber "vexal" souped-up his sports car so that he can play the shooter while, er, driving. The 1993 classic displays on the dashboard but is controlled by the car's steering wheel, horn and accelerator. "Modding a Porsche 911 to play *DOOM* is absurdly dangerous," rightly warned Gizmodo's headline. At least "vexal" did promise that he wouldn't try it out on public roads...

! **DO NOT TRY AT HOME**

FATHER OF PAC-MAN DIES

On 22 Jan 2017, Masaya Nakamura – the founder of Namco and "father of PAC-Man" – passed away, aged 91. Set up in 1955, Namco made carnival rides before turning to arcade machines in the 1970s. A total of 293,822 *PAC-Man* coin-op machines were built from 1980 to 1987, making it the **most successful coin-op arcade game**.

FEB 2017

"DEMON KING" OF *LOL* SMASHES TWITCH RECORD

On 6 Feb 2017, *League of Legends* megastar Lee "Faker" Sang-hyeok – described by Kotaku as "perhaps the best *League of Legends* player on Earth" – launched his own Twitch channel. Within an hour of going live, the popular player astonishingly smashed a record for the **most watched Twitch stream by an individual**, peaking with 245,000 concurrent viewers. PVP Live championed: "The Demon King of *League of Legends* himself has taken up his throne."

FEB 2017

SPEED-RUNNER COMPLETES ALL 714 NES GAMES

On 26 Feb 2017, Twitcher "The Mexican Runner", aka Piotr Delgado Kusielczuk (MEX), became the **first person to complete every licensed Nintendo Entertainment System game**: a total of 714 titles. Across nearly three years, Piotr spent 3,435 hr 12 min 24 sec smashing through the giant mound of retro oldies. However, not all NES games have clear endings, so some were played for sustained periods. For example, he spent 91 hr on *Miracle Piano Teaching System* – a 1990 "game" that teaches players the piano!

MAR 2017

SWITCH LAUNCHES, GAMES TASTE BAD

Licking game cartridges isn't a wise idea, but that didn't deter gaming journalists from sampling games for the new Nintendo Switch console – and discovering that they taste absolutely disgusting! The reason for the cartridges' vile flavour was a coating of denatonium benzoate – a bittering agent – added to their sticky labels to stop kids and pets from eating them. Licking the games is the "worst thing you can do to your tongue," grimaced Kotaku's Mike Fahey (above). "It was like someone poured a bottle of concentrated [new car scent] into my mouth," spat writer Jeff Gerstmann to the BBC.

APR 2017

MOVIE TREATMENT FOR *WE HAPPY FEW*

Despite still only being in Steam Early Access, Compulsion Games' *We Happy Few* has already been announced for a movie adaptation. The indie oddity – described as a "psychedelic horror" – is set in an alternative 1960s England. The film is being produced by Gold Circle Films, the folk behind *Pitch Perfect*.

AWARDS ROUND-UP

Highlights from the biggest awards ceremonies since the last *Gamer's Edition*...

OVERWATCH
Blizzard's shooter collected an incredible 20 gongs across six major ceremonies.

THAT DRAGON, CANCER
Inspired by personal tragedy, Numinous' arthouse adventure won BAFTA and SXSW awards for innovation.

THE GAME AWARDS 2016
1 Dec 2016, Los Angeles, USA

Award	Game
GAME OF THE YEAR	*Overwatch*
Best studio/Game direction	Blizzard (*Overwatch*)
Best narrative	*Uncharted 4: A Thief's End*
Best art direction	*INSIDE*
Best music/Sound design	*DOOM*
Best performance	Nolan North (Nathan Drake), *Uncharted 4: A Thief's End*
Games for impact	*That Dragon, Cancer*
Best independent game	*INSIDE*
Best mobile/Handheld game	*Pokémon GO*
Best VR game	*Rez Infinite*
Best action game	*DOOM*
Best action/adventure game	*Dishonored 2*
Best role-playing game	*The Witcher III: Wild Hunt – Blood and Wine*
Best fighting game	*Street Fighter V*
Best family game	*Pokémon GO*
Best strategy game	*Sid Meier's Civilization VI*
Best sports/racing game	*Forza Horizon 3*
Best multiplayer game	*Overwatch*
Best eSports player	Marcelo "coldzera" David
Best eSports team	Cloud9
Best eSports game	*Overwatch*

BRITISH ACADEMY GAME AWARDS (BAFTA)
6 Apr 2017, London, UK

Award	Game
BEST GAME	***Uncharted 4: A Thief's End***
Artistic achievement	*INSIDE*
Audio achievement	*The Last Guardian*
British game	*Overcooked*
Debut game	*Firewatch*
Evolving game	*Rocket League*
Family	*Overcooked*
Game design	*INSIDE*
Game innovation	*That Dragon, Cancer*
Mobile	*Pokémon GO*
Multiplayer	*Overwatch*
Music	*Virginia* (Lyndon Holland)
Narrative	*INSIDE*
Original property	*INSIDE*
Performer	Cissy Jones (Delilah), *Firewatch*

GAME DEVELOPERS CHOICE AWARDS
1 Mar 2017, San Francisco, USA

Award	Game
GAME OF THE YEAR	*Overwatch*
Audience award	*Battlefield 1*
Lifetime achievement	Tim Sweeney (developer)
Innovation	*No Man's Sky*
Best audio	*INSIDE*
Best debut	Campo Santo (*Firewatch*)
Best design	*Overwatch*
Best mobile/Handheld game	*Pokémon GO*
Best narrative	*Firewatch*
Best technology	*Uncharted 4: A Thief's End*
Best visual art	*INSIDE*
Best VR/AR game	*Job Simulator: The 2050 Archives*

INSIDE
Playdead's suspenseful puzzler picked up 11 major awards including four BAFTAs.

UNCHARTED 4: A THIEF'S END
Nate Drake's twisty adventure picked up two overall "game of the year" awards.

SXSW GAMING
18 Mar 2017, Austin, USA

Award	Game
GAME OF THE YEAR	**Uncharted 4: A Thief's End**
Excellence in technical achievement	Battlefield 1
Excellence in musical score	DOOM
Excellence in gameplay	DOOM
Excellence in SFX	Battlefield 1
Excellence in visual achievement	Uncharted 4: A Thief's End
Excellence in animation	Uncharted 4: A Thief's End
Most memorable character	Nathan Drake (Uncharted 4: A Thief's End)
Excellence in narrative	Uncharted 4: A Thief's End
Excellence in art	Firewatch
Excellence in convergence	Batman: The Telltale Series
Excellence in multiplayer	Overwatch
Trending game of the year	Overwatch
eSports game of the year	Overwatch
Most promising new IP	Overwatch
Excellence in design	Dishonored 2
Matthew Crump cultural innovation award	That Dragon, Cancer
Mobile game of the year	Pokémon GO

34th GOLDEN JOYSTICK AWARDS
18 Nov 2016, London, UK

Award	Game
ULTIMATE GAME OF THE YEAR	**Dark Souls III**
Best multiplayer game	Overwatch
PC game of the year	Overwatch
Best gaming moment	Play of the game in Overwatch
Competitive game of the year	Overwatch
Best storytelling	The Witcher III: Wild Hunt – Blood and Wine
Best visual design	The Witcher III: Wild Hunt – Blood and Wine
Best audio	Fallout 4
Best indie game	Firewatch
Gaming personality of the year	Sean Plott, aka "Day[9]"
YouTube – Upcoming personality of the year	Jesse Cox
Studio of the year	CD Projekt Red
Innovation of the year	Pokémon GO
Lifetime achievement	Eiji Aonuma (designer) (The Legend of Zelda)
Best gaming platform	Steam
Best original game	Overwatch

DICE 20TH ANNUAL AWARDS
23 Feb 2017, Las Vegas, USA

Award	Game
GAME OF THE YEAR	**Overwatch**
Action game of the year	Overwatch
Outstanding achievement in game design	Overwatch
Outstanding achievement in online gameplay	Overwatch
Outstanding achievement in art direction	INSIDE
Outstanding achievement in game direction	INSIDE
D.I.C.E. sprite award	INSIDE
Immersive reality technical achievement	Eagle Flight
Immersive reality game of the year	Superhot VR
Mobile game of the year	Pokémon GO
Handheld game of the year	Pokémon Sun and Moon
Strategy/simulation game of the year	Sid Meier's Civilization VI
Sports game of the year	Steep
Role-playing/Massively multiplayer game of the year	Dark Souls III
Racing game of the year	Forza Horizon 3
Fighting game of the year	Street Fighter V
Family game of the year	Ratchet & Clank
Adventure game of the year	Uncharted 4: A Thief's End
Outstanding achievement in sound design	Battlefield 1
Outstanding achievement in original music composition	DOOM
Outstanding achievement in character	Trico (The Last Guardian)

DARK SOULS III
The medieval-styled RPG was the "ultimate game of 2016", as voted by the public at the Golden Joysticks.

HARDWARE

Rounding up the big technological tales from 2016 and 2017

There's no question that 2016 and 2017 were productive in terms of new gaming tech. However, two stories have dominated: the ongoing rise of VR and the impact of Nintendo Switch.

There are now multiple major VR headsets available, including the PlayStation VR, HTC Vive and Oculus Rift. According to Euromonitor, the **largest AR/VR headset brand** was Samsung Gear, which debuted earlier (Nov 2015) than its rivals. It had estimated sales of $43,041,400 (£29,031,200) in 2015.

As for the Switch, Nintendo is no stranger to innovation, and the new console certainly underlines that. Launched in Mar 2017, it's designed to function as both a portable device and a home console, so features a 720p, 6.2-in HD screen, yet can connect to TVs and has clip-on controllers. Check out Your New Favourite Games on p.202 for special Switch titles heading your way.

NES MINI MONSTER SALES

In addition to the Switch, Nintendo also launched the NES Classic Mini (or Mini Famicom in Japan) in Nov 2016. Both are small versions of the original 1980s NES console, with 30 games built in. It took just four days for all 262,961 units of Japan's Mini Famicom to sell out. The machines, aimed at retro-heads, were discontinued in Apr 2017, but rumours abound that a SNES Mini could be up next.

SWITCHED-ON SUCCESS

The Switch's success seemed as likely as a release date for *Half-Life 3*. Too expensive, said critics, and not enough must-play games. But demand was huge: half a million sales in its first weekend made it Nintendo's fastest-selling console in the USA, beating the Wii (first-day shoppers in New York pictured right). In Japan, it headed towards 360,000 sales, and Nintendo doubled its first-year production run. As we went to press, *Super Mario Odyssey* looked set to round off a triumphant 2017.

VIRTUALLY REAL VR?

VR's rise has inspired researchers to develop hardware that adds depth and realism to the visual experience. One example, created in China, is the VUE VR Treadmill, a 360-degree platform that allows players to walk, run, crouch and jump in virtual environments. Meanwhile, in the USA, AxonVR is developing a lightweight exoskeleton that enables wearers to experience physical sensations. Thanks to the company's HaptX technology, players might feel the warmth of a virtual coffee mug, or the brush of a butterfly's wings. There are plenty of other exciting developments in the works too – keep your eyes peeled!

KEYCHAIN-SIZED GAME BOY

In Nov 2016, hacker "Sprite_TM" – aka Jeroen Domburg of the Netherlands – completed a fully functional Game Boy that fits on a keychain. Measuring 54 mm (2.1 in) long, it's the **smallest Game Boy** – a tiny cousin to our **largest Game Boy** on p.123. It works from an ESP32 chip, runs games from an emulator and has a built-in speaker. Jeroen created it for 2016's Hackaday SuperConference, and his record was verified in Shanghai, China, on 15 Dec that year.

BEHOLD THE MEGAPROCESSOR

Gamers proud of their huge PC set-ups may cast envious glances at the computer below – dubbed the Megaprocessor by its maker, UK digital electronics engineer James Newman. The giant was born in Newman's Cambridgeshire home, using 42,370 transistors. It measures about 10 m (32 ft 10 in) wide and 2 m (6 ft 8 in) tall, making it the **largest functional microprocessor model**. It also contains 10,500 LED lights and cost more than £40,000 ($58,752) in parts. Newman had used it to run *Tetris*.

THE SIMPSONS IN VR? *MMM...*

"Treehouse of Horror XXVII", the 600th episode of *The Simpsons*, aired in the USA on 16 Oct 2016. Using the low-cost VR technology Google Cardboard, viewers could enjoy the episode's extended opening credits – dubbed "Planet of the Couches", a parody of *Planet of the Apes* – as a 360-degree experience. Woo-hoo!

GAMER TRIBUTES

For gamers, few achievements are more epic than becoming part of the game itself. It's rare, but it happens. Here are fans that forever live on in virtual fame...

MICHAEL MAMARIL

APPEARANCE: *Borderlands 2* (2K Games, 2012)

An NPC who hands out loot in Sanctuary, Michael Mamaril was created in honour of a 22-year-old fan who passed away. Michael's friend contacted Gearbox asking to have a memorial read by the robot Claptrap. The studio not only obliged, but also put Michael in the game.

MATTHEW BRAGG

APPEARANCE: *City of Heroes* (Cryptic Studios, 2004)

Before the official launch of *City of Heroes*, Matthew Bragg had earned a reputation for being one of the most welcoming and helpful "heroes" in the MMO's online community. Unfortunately, however, Bragg died soon after the game was released. In recognition of his contributions, the developer renamed the game's tutorial character after Bragg's forum alter ego, "Kiyotee".

"GOOD GUY" EVAN

APPEARANCE: *Fallout 4* (Bethesda, 2015)

Journey south in *Fallout 4*'s Nuka-World and you'll find a helpful NPC named Evan sitting atop his trailer. The character was modelled and named after a *Fallout* fan who passed away following the sequel's release. Bethesda added him via DLC.

LUKE OLIVER

APPEARANCE: *Batman: Arkham Asylum* (Eidos/Warner Bros., 2009)

Arkham Asylum is home to Gotham's vilest criminals. In Rocksteady's moody hit, Batman fan Luke Oliver joined their ranks after winning a 2008 contest to have his face rendered on an in-game character.

PAUL KEELER

APPEARANCE: *Star Wars: Knights of the Old Republic II: The Sith Lords* (LucasArts, 2004)

Paul Keeler became the envy of Star Wars fans when he joined the cast of the RPG sequel after winning a tour of LucasArts' headquarters. Keeler appears as a pazaak card player called Nikko, who interacts with the player during a murder investigation on the planet Onderon.

EZRA CHATTERTON

APPEARANCE: *World of Warcraft* (Blizzard, 2004)

The Elder Tauren character Ezra Wheathoof was introduced in honour of a boy named Ezra who passed away in 2008. Ezra previously worked with Blizzard in creating the character Ahab Wheathoof, as arranged by the Make-A-Wish Foundation.

WU HONGYU

APPEARANCE: *Overwatch* (Blizzard, 2016)

Wu Hongyu's given name appears on a spacesuit in the Lijiang Tower map. It was added after the Chinese gamer was killed chasing a bike thief; a heroic act that saw him posthumously given a Courageous Citizen award by the Guangzhou government. The character Mercy's catchphrase "Heroes never die" also displays in Chinese characters.

SEAN SMITH

APPEARANCE: *EVE Online* (CCP Games, 2003)

Sean Smith, aka "Vile Rat" (above), was one of *EVE*'s most respected players. So when the IT worker with the US Foreign Service was killed during an attack on the US consulate in Libya in 2012, the space MMO's community had his name emblazoned across the stars in-game.

THE EPSILON PROGRAM CREW

APPEARANCE: *Grand Theft Auto V* (Rockstar Games, 2013)

In *GTA V*, players cross paths with the Epsilon Program, a Los Santos-based cult. Rockstar launched a spin-off site and invited gamers to become members. Five "winners" (below) were picked to appear on the site as characters that had gone missing from the program.

JESSE, USA · JOSCHA, GERMANY · HAYLEE, USA · TIANA, AUSTRALIA · AMEER, USA

DAN EMMERSON

APPEARANCE: *Dead Space 2* (EA, 2011)

In 2010, UK student Dan won a contest designing a melee move for EA's space-horror. His "prize" was a cameo in the game, in which he appears as a doomed space-station resident who is stabbed through the chest by a necromorph. "My mum didn't care much for it," he said.

ERIK WEST

APPEARANCE: *The Elder Scrolls V: Skyrim* (Bethesda, 2011)

Erik West (aka "Immok the Slayer") became the inspiration for Erik the Slayer in *Skyrim* after impressing Bethesda with his knowledge of the *Elder Scrolls* RPG series while touring the developer's studios as part of his Make-A-Wish request. West may no longer be with us, but his Nordic lookalike has a permanent home at Rorikstead's Frostfruit Inn.

SARAH'S "JENNER" MECH

APPEARANCE: *MechWarrior Online* (Piranha Games, 2013)

In 2013, Piranha released a uniquely decorated "Jenner" mech to honour the death of a five-year-old Canadian fan named Sarah. Proceeds from the mech's sale helped raise thousands of dollars for the Canadian Cancer Society.

FANTASY

From *League of Legends* to *Zelda*, fantasy games let us loose in amazing worlds and alternate realities. The gameplay is as varied as the games themselves, from the complexities of *Hearthstone* and *Dota 2* to the simple fun of *Skylanders*.

"I love playing games, especially Skyrim. Getting into Gamer's Edition is pretty cool and amazing!"
Gamer grandma Shirley Curry

Oldest videogames YouTuber
Shirley Curry (USA, b. 2 Apr 1936) – aged 81 years 26 days as of 28 Apr 2017 – has shot hundreds of videos for her self-titled channel, building up an impressive fanbase of 238,449 subscribers and accumulating 6,509,749 views. The Virginia resident, introduced to gaming by her son in the 1990s, mostly streams the action RPG *The Elder Scrolls V: Skyrim* (pictured). She's also played *ARK: Survival Evolved* and *No Man's Sky*. Shirley describes herself as a "grandmother who loves to play, and now record, games".

DRAGON QUEST III

LEGEND: In Japan, it's illegal to release a *Dragon Quest* game during the week.

TRUTH: When *Dragon Quest III* was released in Japan on Wed, 10 Feb 1988, many children played truant and dozens of workers called in sick. Consequently, the publisher, Enix Corporation, decided not to release any other *DQ* games during the working week. This policy stayed until 2012, when *Dragon Quest X* was released on a Thursday, but the restriction was self-imposed and was never government law.

POLYBIUS

LEGEND: Created by the US government as a tool of mind control.

TRUTH: *Polybius* was said to have appeared in arcades in Oregon, USA, in 1981, and players complained of suffering from nightmares and nausea. It was also claimed that gamers were watched by mysterious men in black. However, while tricksters have created fake machines to fuel this tale, no genuine versions of the game have ever been discovered.

SPECIAL FEATURE

GAMING URBAN LEGENDS

Urban myths have become as intrinsic a part of gaming as aggressive aliens and princesses in peril. But which of these seemingly tall tales from the annals of gaming can be dismissed as fanciful nonsense, and which might actually be true? *Gamer's Edition* dons its detective hat...

FINAL FANTASY VII

LEGEND: *FFVII* was the **most returned videogame** when it was released outside Japan for PlayStation in 1997.

TRUTH: Sony in the USA spent $100 million (£62.4 million) marketing one of the first *Final Fantasy* RPGs released outside Japan. Most of this funded flashy TV ads showcasing the game's explosive cutscenes rather than its slow, turn-based gameplay. Consequently, anecdotal evidence suggests that *FFVII* was returned in large numbers by Western gamers who felt misled by the advertising and wanted something more gratifying. In hindsight, how wrong they were...

THE LEGEND OF ZELDA

LEGEND: A *Majora's Mask* cartridge in the USA is haunted by evil spirits.

TRUTH: In 2010, a player obtained a copy of this N64 classic from a creepy old man at a garage sale. When loaded, sinister things happened: a music track played backwards, spooky characters appeared from nowhere, and hero Link randomly burst into flames. Despite finding its way on to a paranormal forum, the footage was later revealed to be the result of some elaborate ROM-hacking and video editing.

BERZERK

LEGEND: In the 1980s, several people died after playing the arcade shooter *Berzerk*.

TRUTH: In Illinois, USA, in 1981, a man died after playing *Berzerk*, but autopsy reports concluded that his death was the result of a heart condition. Years later, in 1988, a man was stabbed after playing *Berzerk* in the same arcade, but his death was not related to the game. Rumour-mongers have tried to attribute other deaths to *Berzerk*, but there's no evidence that any fatalities are actually connected to the game.

FOOTBALL MANAGER 2013

LEGEND: Sports Interactive's management sim is the **most pirated game** of all time.

TRUTH: In 2013, the UK studio revealed that *FM 2013* had been illegally downloaded by more than 10.1 million people. Code hidden in phoney versions enabled SI to track the IP addresses of people playing counterfeits. One illegal copy had been downloaded in the Vatican, home of the Catholic Church!

MADDEN NFL

LEGEND: A curse has struck every cover star in the American football series.

TRUTH: Of the 19 players who've appeared on a *Madden NFL* cover since 1998, 17 have suffered real-life injuries. But while some sports fans have been suckered in by tales of a "Madden curse", and petitioned for their favourite stars to be kept off the front of the game, publisher EA has argued that it's natural for pro athletes to suffer injuries following seasons of peak performance.

KILLSWITCH

LEGEND: A mysterious game deletes itself upon completion and is the **most expensive videogame sold at auction**.

TRUTH: According to internet legend, Russia's Karvina Corporation produced only 5,000 copies of its 1989 horror adventure *Killswitch*. When Japan's Yamamoto Ryuichi purportedly paid $733,000 (£382,029) for the last sealed copy in 2005, the only thing the collector published was a video of himself weeping at his computer after the game had been wiped. However, there's no real evidence that *Killswitch* existed, and footage of Ryuichi crying is nowhere to be found.

FALLOUT 3

LEGEND: Coded messages in Bethesda's RPG predict the future.

TRUTH: In-game radio stations broadcast messages in Morse code that apparently predicted the death of TV actor Gary Coleman and the *Deepwater Horizon* oil disaster, both of which took place in 2010, two years after the game's release. Other messages didn't come true, but as one in-game broadcast suggests Britney Spears will win an Academy Award in 2023, this urban myth isn't dead yet...

POKÉMON TV SERIES

LEGEND: An episode of the hit animated TV show resulted in a wave of seizures.

TRUTH: When "Electric Soldier Porygon" aired in Japan on 16 Dec 1997, a reported 685 child viewers were rushed to hospital suffering from medical ailments, including seizures and nausea. Distraught animators pointed the finger at a rapid strobing effect that had been used to portray an explosion in cyberspace. The episode was never shown again, even in edited form.

DOTA 2

Incepted as a *Warcraft III* map in 2003, *Dota* invented the Massively Online Battle Arena (MOBA) genre. Its 2013 sequel, published by Valve, is now the most lucrative eSports game.

Largest eSports first prize

Despite only forming in 2014, China's Wings Gaming (right) scooped a life-changing $9,139,002 (£7,055,020) when they won The International *Dota 2* Championships on 8–13 Aug 2016 in Seattle, USA.

The tournament's prize pool, raised predominately through the sale of gaming add-ons, totalled $20,770,460 (£16,034,100) – the **largest prize in eSports**.

Youngest gamer to earn $1 million in eSports

On 8 Aug 2015, Pakistan's "Suma1L", aka Syed Sumail Hassan (b. 13 Feb 1999), was just 16 years 176 days old when his team Evil Geniuses won The International.

Victory at the event in Seattle, USA, brought his total pro gaming winnings to $1,639,867 (£1,057,890).

He told GWR: "Winning The International was all that mattered. I proved that I am the best."

Longest *Dota 2* win streak

From 23 Apr to 2 Jun 2013, the Swedish eSports outfit Alliance won 25 pro Dota 2 matches without defeat, according to data compiled by GosuGamers. The team's incredible run was finally ended by Germany's Mousesports.

113

PLAYABLE

heroes in *Dota 2*, each offering unique abilities and strategies.

Most competitive *Dota 2* matches won

Based on pro matches tracked by community portal joinDOTA, Russia's Team Empire (below) had recorded the most victories in Valve's free-to-play PC hit – a total of 1,003 wins as of 27 Feb 2017. By contrast, they were beaten 655 times and were ranked 19th, based on their overall performances across tournaments, leagues and exhibition games. The team's victory tally outnumbered that of 2015's The International champs, Evil Geniuses (812 wins), who were ranked number one on the site.

Most viewed *Dota 2* channel on Twitch

Match broadcasts from the Ukrainian eSports organizer Starladder1 totalled a life-grabbing 337,862,093 views as of 29 Mar 2017.

Theirs was the second most viewed Twitch channel overall, behind Riot Games' official stream for *League of Legends* action. *LoL* is *Dota 2*'s keen rival on the eSports MOBA circuit.

Most actively played game on Steam

Dota 2 continues to be the most played game on Valve's PC distribution service. The battle arena title reported 10,080,377 active players on 30 Mar 2017.

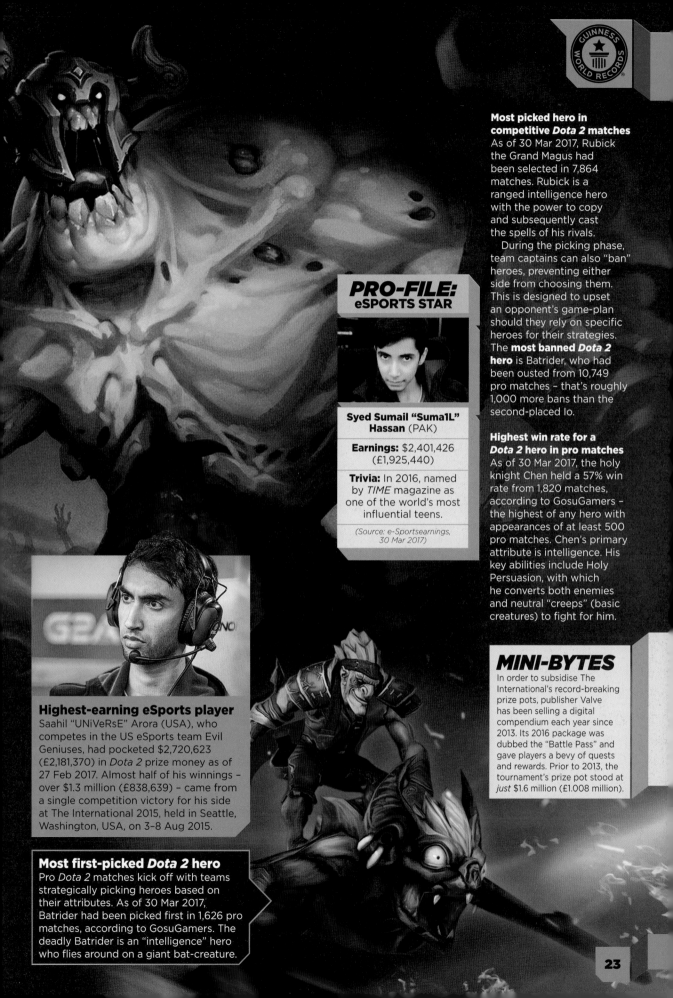

Most picked hero in competitive *Dota 2* matches

As of 30 Mar 2017, Rubick the Grand Magus had been selected in 7,864 matches. Rubick is a ranged intelligence hero with the power to copy and subsequently cast the spells of his rivals.

During the picking phase, team captains can also "ban" heroes, preventing either side from choosing them. This is designed to upset an opponent's game-plan should they rely on specific heroes for their strategies. The **most banned *Dota 2* hero** is Batrider, who had been ousted from 10,749 pro matches – that's roughly 1,000 more bans than the second-placed Io.

Highest win rate for a *Dota 2* hero in pro matches

As of 30 Mar 2017, the holy knight Chen held a 57% win rate from 1,820 matches, according to GosuGamers – the highest of any hero with appearances of at least 500 pro matches. Chen's primary attribute is intelligence. His key abilities include Holy Persuasion, with which he converts both enemies and neutral "creeps" (basic creatures) to fight for him.

PRO-FILE:
eSPORTS STAR

Syed Sumail "Suma1L" Hassan (PAK)

Earnings: $2,401,426 (£1,925,440)

Trivia: In 2016, named by *TIME* magazine as one of the world's most influential teens.

(Source: e-Sportsearnings, 30 Mar 2017)

MINI-BYTES

In order to subsidise The International's record-breaking prize pots, publisher Valve has been selling a digital compendium each year since 2013. Its 2016 package was dubbed the "Battle Pass" and gave players a bevy of quests and rewards. Prior to 2013, the tournament's prize pot stood at *just* $1.6 million (£1.008 million).

Highest-earning eSports player

Saahil "UNiVeRsE" Arora (USA), who competes in the US eSports team Evil Geniuses, had pocketed $2,720,623 (£2,181,370) in *Dota 2* prize money as of 27 Feb 2017. Almost half of his winnings – over $1.3 million (£838,639) – came from a single competition victory for his side at The International 2015, held in Seattle, Washington, USA, on 3–8 Aug 2015.

Most first-picked *Dota 2* hero

Pro *Dota 2* matches kick off with teams strategically picking heroes based on their attributes. As of 30 Mar 2017, Batrider had been picked first in 1,626 pro matches, according to GosuGamers. The deadly Batrider is an "intelligence" hero who flies around on a giant bat-creature.

LEAGUE OF LEGENDS

Released in 2009, Riot Games' team-based MOBA is already one of the most played – and watched – games in history. Its pacey mix of strategy and action has made it an eSports hit, with sponsors investing vast sums into building top teams.

Most wins of the *LOL* World Championship

Inaugurated in 2011, the *League of Legends* (*LoL*) World Championship is one of the most prestigious prizes in eSports. South Korea's SK Telecom T1 has won its Summoner's Cup three times: in 2013, 2015 and 2016.

The team's most recent triumph was in Los Angeles, USA, on 29 Oct 2016 (below). By winning, they bagged a large share of a $5.07-million (£4.1-million) pool – the **largest prize pool for a *LoL* tournament**. The sum was partly funded by gamers buying in-game items.

Highest win rate for a Champion

Based on pro *LoL* matches tracked by GosuGamers, the "master of shadows" Zed had been on the winning team in 57% of the contests in which he had been selected, as of 17 Mar 2017. Zed is a ninja with spinning blades and a physical shadow that mimics his attacks.

> **"We have arrived. eSports are not science fiction, and this is no longer the stuff of the future. This is now."**
> *USA Today* on the 2016 *LoL* World Championship

Most picked Champion

Playable characters in *LoL* are known as Champions. Based on GosuGamers stats, the unearthly Thresh (right) had been picked by pros in 3,555 matches – a total of 34% of all competitive games – as of 17 Mar 2017. Thresh is a cunning, sadistic and restless spirit who takes pride in tormenting mere mortals. His abilities include harvesting the souls of dead enemies.

20
COUNTRIES
represented at the 2016 *LoL* World Championship, including Hong Kong, Canada and Croatia.

First pro sports club to acquire an eSports team

On 20 Jan 2015, Turkish sports organization Beşiktaş Istanbul – owner of the famous Beşiktaş soccer team – acquired the Turkish *League of Legends* side Aces High. In doing so, it set a new trend for other pro clubs to invest in gaming.

Largest attendance for a *League of Legends* match

On 19 Oct 2014, a sell-out crowd of 40,000 fans watched the final of the 2014 *LoL* World Championship, which was staged at the Seoul World Cup Stadium in South Korea.

Most played online multiplayer game (current)

According to SuperData, *League of Legends* was the most played online title throughout 2016, averaging 100.4 million players each month.

The game also grossed $1.9 billion (£1.5 billion) – the **most revenue from digital sales (current)**. *LoL* is a "freemium" title, mostly making its money through microtransactions.

Most subscribed official gaming channel on YouTube

Riot's MOBA is a big hit on YouTube. As of 17 Mar 2017, the game's channel had 7,953,657 subscribers, putting it ahead of official channels for *Clash of Clans* (7,883,897), PlayStation (5,395,517) and *Call of Duty* (4,729,791).

Highest-earning *LoL* player

According to e-Sportsearnings, South Korea's Lee "Faker" Sang-hyeok has earned $897,818 (£718,680) in winnings. The legendary star is simply hailed by fans as "God".

MINI-BYTES

Since 2012, winners of the *LoL* World Championship are presented with the Summoner's Cup (see far left). This giant keepsake was designed by Thomas Lyte in London, UK – the same creators behind the English FA Cup (soccer) and golf's Ryder Cup.

PRO-FILE: eSPORTS STAR

LEE "FAKER" SANG-HYEOK (KOR)

Winnings: $897,818

Trivia: Was aged just 17 when his SK Telecom T1 side won the 2013 *LoL* World Championship. He's now been involved in all three of the team's championship wins (see opposite).

(source: e-Sportsearnings, 17 Mar 2017)

Most popular game in cosplay

Packed with hordes of memorable Champions, *LoL* has inspired a fervent cosplay scene (pictured right is a fan dressed as the bestial huntress Nidalee). As of 13 Feb 2017, 50,265 photos had been uploaded by users to the global community site WorldCosplay.net.

Most viewed Twitch channel

LoL is a dominant force on the Twitch streaming platform. As of 17 Mar 2017, Riot Games' official channel had accrued 890,050,581 views. The *LoL* publisher typically streams live tournament matches.

The **most viewed Twitch individual** is the *LoL* pro "imaqtpie", aka Michael Santana (USA), with 198,367,834 views.

LEAGUE OF LEGENDS COSPLAY

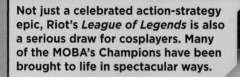

Not just a celebrated action-strategy epic, Riot's *League of Legends* is also a serious draw for cosplayers. Many of the MOBA's Champions have been brought to life in spectacular ways.

Largest mechanical wings on a cosplay costume

Constructed across a period of six months, Leo Simon's (UK) costume of the Champion Aether Wing Kayle made gaming headlines in late 2015. The suit features movable wings that are operated by 10 individual motors. Fully open, the wings measure 4.26 m (13 ft 11 in) – double the length of a king-size bed.

1,000 HOURS
that Leo Simon physically spent making his Kayle wings.

MINI-BYTES

Such has been the cosplay explosion around *LoL*, Riot Games hosted its first "Cosplay Lab" in Los Angeles, USA, in Feb 2017. Fans participated in a three-day workshop, learning both theory and craft. The lab was promised to be the first of many.

Q&A WITH LEO SIMON

Why *League of Legends*' Kayle?
She's very strong and she's one of the few characters that can be played in every role in the game.

How long did the costume take?
Including research, the whole project took me from May 2014 to Oct 2015. So well over a year.

What do fans think?
I've cosplayed Kayle at Insomnia, MCM, London Film & Comic Con [all UK]. Most people are wowed even before the costume moves, but when it does they get their minds blown! Fans come up to me every five seconds so I'm unable to go round, just due to the sheer number of people.

Have you had any accidents?
I must have hit 40 people in the head with the wings! They weigh 16–17 kg [35–37 lb] so I've had to train with a 20-kg [44-lb] backpack, doing power-walks, just to wear them.

Largest walkabout puppet based on a videogame

Commissioned by Riot Games and created by US FX studio Buddy Builds in Jul 2016, a giant puppet of the Champion Thresh stands at just under 13 ft 7 in (4.1 m) tall. The creature is designed to be worn by 6-ft-tall (1.8-m) operators who can effectively walk around in it (acting as the character's legs) while controlling the arms using rods.

Most popular *LoL* character for cosplay

According to WorldCosplay.net, *League of Legends* is the 11th most popular franchise overall for cosplay, predominately behind anime series such as *Black Butler* and *Gintama*. For *LoL* fans, no Champion is more liked than the "Nine-Tailed Fox" Ahri. As of 14 Mar 2017, a total of 6,307 Ahri cosplay photos had been uploaded to the global community site.

THE LEGEND OF ZELDA

For over 30 years, hero Link has been rescuing Zelda in this mystical series. The 2017 Switch adventure *Breath of the Wild* was reported to be Nintendo's fastest-selling launch title.

Rarest *Zelda* game
Videogame memorabilia collector Tom Curtin sold a copy of *The Legend of Zelda* on eBay for $55,000 (£35,483) in Aug 2013. The cartridge – a fully playable, pre-release prototype for the 1986 NES original – is thought to be unique.

Fastest 100% completion of *Ocarina of Time*
The USA's "zfg" completed everything in 1998's classic *Ocarina of Time* in 4 hr 15 min 3 sec on 23 Jun 2016, as verified by Speedrun.com.
   Ocarina – Link's debut for the Nintendo 64 console – is the **best-selling action-adventure game on a Nintendo platform**. It had sold 7.6 million as of 27 Mar 2017. The game also sold 4.73 million when it was ported to the 3DS in 2011.

First first-person *Zelda* virtual reality (VR) port
Randy "Ubiquitron" Bennett created *Zelda VR – The Legend of Zelda* remade as a first-person 3D game for Oculus Rift – on 5 Feb 2014. Using the original graphics and textures, the mod wasn't Zelda's first VR port, but its first-person focus dramatically altered the feel of the game. Bennett promised an update of the beta version in 2015, but this had yet to appear as of Mar 2017.

Largest collection of *The Legend of Zelda* memorabilia
While *Zelda* players gather bomb flowers and boomerangs, Norway's Anne Martha Harnes has collected 1,816 individual items connected with the series. The collection was verified at her parents' home in Molde on 14 Jul 2016.
   Anne began her collection in 2008. Her favourite game in the series is the *Ocarina of Time* sequel *Majora's Mask*, released in 2000.

Most critically acclaimed Switch game
Soon after its release, 2017's open-world *Zelda* game *Breath of the Wild* was GameRankings' best reviewed title for any platform. Even as more reviews emerged and its average dipped, it remained behind only two *Super Mario* titles and *Zelda*'s *Ocarina of Time*. As of 27 Mar 2017, it had a 97.29% average from 57 reviews – the best for a Switch game.

Most viewed fan film based on *The Legend of Zelda*

"THE LEGEND OF ZELDA RAP [MUSIC VIDEO]", by US comedians Smosh, had 68,810,088 YouTube views as of 27 Mar 2017. It's the parodists' second most viewed video after an *Assassin's Creed* song.

First franchise to enter the Spike Video Game Awards Hall of Fame

In 2011, the *Zelda* series was the first to be honoured with the Spike Video Game Awards Hall of Fame award, at a ceremony in Culver City, California, USA. Sadly, it was also the last: the awards show, staged annually from 2003, folded in 2013.

MINI-BYTES

An arcade-museum.com forum member unveiled his self-made *Zelda* arcade cabinet in 2016. "It's an all-wood construction," he wrote. "Inside is a decased 20" CRT [arcade monitor] and an NES wired to the arcade joystick and buttons."

Fastest marathon as a videogame character

John Kelly (USA) achieved two ambitions at the Boston Marathon (Massachusetts, USA) on 18 Apr 2016, which he ran in 2 hr 57 min. He had dreamed of running the marathon and, as a child, wanted to be the heroic Link.

Fastest blindfolded completion of *The Legend of Zelda: A Link to the Past*

Twitcher "parisianplayer" (FRA) streamed himself completing 1991's *A Link to the Past*, while blindfolded, in an incredible 9 hr 5 min 11 sec. He achieved this feat in one sitting on 21 Jan 2017. "Never really got stuck so that's cool," he wrote.

All Bosses, all glitches

Estimate: 12 hours

4:20:50

Most followed game cosplayer on Instagram

Gaming personality Jessica Nigri (USA) – here portraying Link – had 2.3 million Instagram followers as of 27 Mar 2017. Jessica has cosplayed a range of gaming characters as well as providing the voice for the manga and game character Super Sonico.

THE LAST GUARDIAN

Featuring strange worlds inhabited by even stranger beasts, the games of Japan's Fumito Ueda are widely hailed as "art". Minimalist tales and dreamy visuals add to their magic.

Most critically acclaimed PS3 compilation

Featuring remastered HD versions of "Team ICO"'s first two games, *The ICO & Shadow of the Colossus Collection* (Sony, 2011) boasts a GameRankings score of 91.79%, based on 35 reviews. It's the 25th highest-rated release overall for Sony's 7th-gen platform.

Most subscribed Team ICO-themed YouTube channel

The "Nomad Colossus" channel is dedicated to *The Last Guardian* and its spiritual ancestors *ICO* and *Shadow of the Colossus*. As of 24 Mar 2017, it had 29,487 subscribers. Owner Michael Lambert (AUS) says the "games are masterpieces".

Most reviewed PS2 videogame

Shadow of the Colossus (right) and *Grand Theft Auto: San Andreas* each have 94 critic reviews listed on GameRankings.

Despite the numbers of ratings – a factor likely to bring overall averages down – the titles carry enviable average scores of 91.43% and 95.08%, respectively.

Longest development period for an action-adventure

The Last Guardian was in the making at Ueda's Sony Japan studio – nicknamed "Team ICO" after their 2001 adventure *ICO* – for nearly 10 years. Originally planned for the PS3, it hit the PS4 on 6 Dec 2016. The game is a thematic sequel to the studio's *Shadow of the Colossus* (2005) and focuses on the friendship between a boy and the griffin-like Trico (pictured). GameSpot described it as "fascinating".

The Last Guardian's development record has a challenger: Ubisoft's much-desired *Beyond Good & Evil 2*, in and out of production since 2007, still had no release date as of Mar 2017.

Most viewed *Last Guardian* video on YouTube
Referencing the game's lengthy development, "I WAITED 6 YEARS TO PLAY THIS.. The Last Guardian - Demo" – uploaded to YouTube by "PewDiePie" on 12 Oct 2016 – had 13,856,224 views as of 24 Mar 2017. The video had been watched more than double the number of times as the game's official E3 trailer.

Tallest colossus in *Shadow of the Colossus*

In the PS2 classic, players must confront 16 mountainous beings known as colossi. The final one, Malus, is estimated to stand between 48 m (157 ft 5 in) and 66 m (216 ft 6 in) tall. The Team ICO Wiki says a real-life Malus could "look directly into the clock face of London's Big Ben".

Shadow of the Colossus derives some of its emotional weight from the fact that the colossi are essentially peaceful, yet must be fought to complete the game.

Fastest completion of *The Last Guardian*

Testing puzzles and platforming moments didn't stop Japan's "Karekusa" vanquishing *The Last Guardian* in 3 hr 28 min 3 sec. The run was achieved on 11 Feb 2017, as verified by Speedrun.com.

MINI-BYTES

Companions play major roles in "Team ICO" games. In *ICO*, players guide ethereal princess Yorda through a castle. *Shadow of the Colossus* introduces a horse named Agro (above). And in *The Last Guardian*, players interact with Trico – hailed by Game Revolution as the "most believable videogame sidekick".

At the Independent Games Festival Awards in Mar 2017, Fumito Ueda announced that his next game would be... *Madden 2018*: "After many years of game design, I have finally been entrusted with a franchise that is near and dear to my heart." It proved to be a prank!

First game with hand-holding

ICO (2001) features a mechanic with which the player can hold hands with a non-player character. *The New Yorker*'s Chris Suellentrop wrote: "My first time doing it gave me goosebumps."

Largest colossus in *Shadow of the Colossus*

Essentially a flying sandworm, the game's 13th colossus, Phalanx, boasts an estimated body length of between 145 m (475 ft 8 in) and 200 m (656 ft 2 in).

FINAL FANTASY

In Square Enix's role-playing series, powerful stories combine with spectacular worlds. *Final Fantasy* is not only the most globally known of all Japanese RPGs. It's also one of the most revered gaming franchises ever.

Longest development period for an RPG

Released to global acclaim on 29 Nov 2016, *Final Fantasy XV* was created across a period of more than 10 years. The game was initially incepted in May 2006 as the spin-off title *Final Fantasy Versus XIII*, but was later re-envisioned as a main series game at E3 in Jun 2013. Even then, it took more than three years to be fully developed.

However, the RPG's lengthy studio time pales against 2K's FPS *Duke Nukem Forever* (2011). At 14 years, that title had the **longest dev period of any game**.

Longest end credits in an MMO

The credits in the MMO remake *Final Fantasy XIV: A Realm Reborn* (2013) run to 1 hr 38 min – the length of many Hollywood movies. The credits list many players who had also played the previous version of *Final Fantasy XIV* (2010).

FFXIV: A Realm Reborn scored 86.08% on GameRankings compared to the original's 50.27% – the **most improved score for a game remake**.

Q&A WITH NAOKI YOSHIDA – PRODUCER OF *FFXIV: A REALM REBORN*

How much changed between the original *FFXIV* and your remake?
I wasn't involved in the original version but I took over halfway through. It was in a mess so we remade it from scratch.

The game has grown so much it now has its own convention called Fanfest...
Yes, we've had Fanfests in Las Vegas, London, Frankfurt and Tokyo. The US event sold out its 5,000 tickets quickly.

What's been the best *FF* cosplay you've seen at Fanfest?
One Japanese cosplayer dressed up as Garuda, who's a primal, giant bird-looking character. Because the wings are so huge, she couldn't walk by herself! Another fan cosplayed as Demon Wall – a monster in a wall – so they wore a giant cube and a wig! There's always someone turning up in a surprising costume, which I love to see.

Most original pieces of music in a game

As of its patch 3.5 from Nov 2016, the MMORPG *Final Fantasy XIV: A Realm Reborn* featured 384 music pieces that were recorded for the game, including its expansion *Heavensward*. Much of the music was composed by Japan's Masayoshi Soken.

Final Fantasy XV (right) crams in 405 songs, including scores from past games and tracks by Florence + the Machine – the **most songs in an *FF* game**. Players can listen to them while driving the in-game Audi R8 car.

Abbey Road Studios

MINI-BYTES

The Buster Sword from *FFVII* is one of the most iconic weapons in gaming. This inspired YouTuber "michaelcthulhu" to make a scaled replica of it. An epic 51-min video of the master craftsman building this metallic, 5-ft 7.6-in (1.7-m) beast had been viewed 8,730,942 times as of 22 Mar 2017.

Most prolific RPG series

The first *Final Fantasy* game was released in 1987. Since then, no RPG series has been as busy churning out new role-playing titles as *FF*. Following the release of *FFXV* on 29 Nov 2016 (below), Square Enix's franchise had given rise to 87 series titles, including its core series of RPGs and multiple spin-offs. The franchise has also produced many other non-role-playing spin-offs, including a TV series, rhythm games and a racer based on its iconic chocobo creatures.

Highest HP for a boss in a *Final Fantasy* game

The "Superboss" Yiazmat from *FFXII* (2006) has a daunting 50,112,254 hit points (or HP) for players to extinguish. Yiazmat is the final boss in a series of optional post-game hunts and defeating "it" rewards the player with 30,000 gil (the in-game currency) and the "Godslayer" badge.

5M COPIES

of *FFXV* sold globally on day one, according to Square Enix.

Fastest completion of *Final Fantasy VII*

Often hailed by fans as the best *Final Fantasy* story, 1997's PlayStation smash *FFVII* was completed by the Twitcher "Luzbelheim" in 7 hr 25 min 28 sec on 25 Jan 2016, as verified by Speedrun.com.

Most soundtrack albums for a videogame series

There have been at least 180 commercially released albums containing music from or inspired by *Final Fantasy*. These include soundtracks, live orchestral performances, classical guitar renditions, chiptune versions, piano collections and a compilation album designed to be played exclusively in pubs!

Most expensive retail car based on a videogame

Unveiled on 11 Nov 2016, the Audi R8 "Star of Lucis" is a replica of the royal vehicle featured in *Final Fantasy XV* and its CG film *Kingsglaive: Final Fantasy XV*. The one-off car was priced at 50,000,015 yen (£378,567; $471,267), with wannabe punters having to enter a raffle just to win the chance to buy it. According to Audi's website, the supercar boasts "design inherited from the gods".

VAINGLORY

Following a trail blazed by *League of Legends* and *Dota 2*, Super Evil Megacorp's MOBA challenges two opposing teams to destroy each other's base and battle AI-spawned minions. The twist? It's for iOS and Android...

Fastest completion of the *Vainglory* tutorial
"MLGGaryIndiana" (USA) raced through *Vainglory*'s "original initiation" in 1 min 36 sec on 26 Mar 2016, as verified by Speedrun.com.

Most viewed *Vainglory* match on YouTube
A turret-trashing showdown between Invincible Armada (KOR) and Divine Brothers (JPN) at 2015's *Vainglory* World Invitational had 546,423 views as of 25 Apr 2017. Invincible Armada (former members of Phoenix Armada) won every match that they played at the event!

First touchscreen eSport
First unleashed on iOS in Nov 2014, *Vainglory* has been revolutionary in bringing touchscreen gaming to eSports. The MOBA's first global pro tournament was the *Vainglory* World Invitational, held in South Korea in Jul 2015. Prior to that, eSports organizations ESL and VGL had hosted regional cups. On 2–4 Dec 2016, the prestigious first World Championship was held in Hollywood, California, USA, with 12 teams battling for a $60,000 (£47,100) top prize.

25k

PEAK
concurrent viewers on Twitch for the first *Vainglory* World Championship.

Youngest winner of a major *Vainglory* tournament
The USA's Riley Haghian (b. 29 Mar 2003, second from left), aka "Zio"/"DNZio", was aged 13 years 68 days when he led Hammers Velocity to victory at *Vainglory*'s North American Spring Championship on 5 Jun 2016.

Most popular hero in *Vainglory*
"Lane"-class sniper Skye (right) had a pick rate of 55% on the US and European competitive circuit in 2016. She's noted for speed, chasing opponents to deal out damage at close range. Her "unique strafing attacks," says the game's official site, "change the complexion of fights".

Highest margin of victory in the *Vainglory* World Championship
On day two of the 2016 World Championship, on 3 Dec, South Korea's Phoenix Armada beat Japan's DetonatioN Gaming with a crystal-crushing score of 14–0. Phoenix Armada went on to win the tournament without losing a single match along the way.

Most damage dealt in a single hit in *Vainglory*
Singapore's "Gatorrex" inflicted 717,237 damage points in a single strike, as posted to YouTube on 4 Dec 2016. The player used a complex system of in-game mechanics, including the bubble shield (which reflects damage received by the player's hero) and enemy walls (which deal high levels of damage to prevent opponents from reaching a team's Vain Crystal – the primary target of games).

Shortest *Vainglory* World Championship match
South Korea's Phoenix Armada (left) took just 8 min 45 sec to beat the USA's Team SoloMid in the final on 4 Dec 2016.

Oldest player to compete in the *Vainglory* World Championship

China's "Queen", aka Pan Ruo Tian (b. 18 Feb 1987), was aged 29 years 289 days when her team, Hunters, was knocked out in the quarter-finals on 3 Dec 2016. "Queen" – the event's only female – has qualified for every major *Vainglory* competition, domestic and international.

MINI-BYTES

In 2016, the USA's Echo Fox became the first *Vainglory* team to hire a coach. Ben "FooJee" Watley (USA) had been a member of sister *Vainglory* teams GankStars Vega and GankStars Sirius. His role, said one player, was to "let us know what we're doing wrong".

Q&A WITH KRISTIAN SEGERSTRALE – CEO OF SUPER EVIL MEGACORP

What inspired you to make *Vainglory*?
We all grew up as PC gamers and wanted to build the same kind of immersive, strategic and tactical games for the touchscreen generation. And also resurrect the idea that you should get together with friends to play. We used to lug our PCs to friends' houses, looking like dorks, but it was super fun. Now you can just get together with your touchscreens.

How have gamers reacted to it?
One younger player said he heard people play games like this, like *League of Legends*, on a PC. He couldn't understand how you control them with a clunky mouse and keyboard. It's like how [some] people couldn't make the transition from playing shooters on PC to console.

What are your hopes for *Vainglory*'s future?
That it continues to grow rapidly. We're hoping to show the touchscreen generation that there's more to play than three-minute Pay2Win sessions!

Most banned hero in *Vainglory*

At MOBA eSports events, opponents can nominate a hero to "ban". This often means ousting one who counters your team's strategy. Adagio (a healer who causes area-of-effect damage) had a ban rate of 44% on the US and European competitive circuit in 2016.

SKYLANDERS

The multi-million-selling spawn of *The Legend of Spyro*, Activision's fantastical franchise popularized the toys-to-life genre. With puzzles and fighting action, *Skylanders* is pure fun.

Largest videogames hardware accessories brand (retail, current)

Sales of *Skylanders* toys amounted to a massive $466,926,100 (£314,939,000) in 2015 – more than any other gaming accessory or hardware, according to the Euromonitor International Passport database on 16 Jun 2016. The success story continued with that year's *Imaginators*, featuring Starcast (right).

Most viewed *Skylanders* YouTube channel

The YouTube channel of siblings "TheSkylanderBoy AndGirl" (USA) had 1,710,861,622 views as of 18 Apr 2017. The duo's most popular videos include episodes in which their relatives try to draw characters in a set time.

500 TOYS

released for *Skylanders* as of Jan 2017. This includes figurines, vehicles, traps and location pieces.

Fastest completion of *Skylanders: Imaginators*

Polish gamer, programmer and YouTuber "BetaM" completed the PS4 version of *Imaginators* in 2 hr 2 min 27 sec on 30 Oct 2016, as verified by Speedrun.com. This is comfortably ahead of British gamer "XacerB8", who completed the Xbox 360 version in 2 hr 3 min 15 sec on 23 Dec 2016.

The **fastest completion of 2011's *Spyro's Adventure*** was by British gamer "Zeldafan01", who completed the Wii U version in 1 hr 51 min 50 sec on 3 Dec 2016.

First toys-to-life game to enable users to create their own characters

Skylanders: Imaginators allows players to design characters. Then, using the game's Creator app, these can be turned into trading cards or 3D-printed figures (like this one of Sir Hoodington, right), complete with chips containing their creation's data.

Oldest characters in a *Skylanders* game
Having debuted in *Crash Bandicoot* in 1996, Crash (pictured) and his adversary Doctor Neo Cortex would appear 20 years later as playable guests in 2016's *Skylanders: Imaginators*. The later game even features special levels – the Thumpin' Wumpa Islands – that recreate gameplay from the characters' earlier adventures.

Most critically acclaimed toys-to-life game
The Xbox 360 version of 2013's *Skylanders: Swap Force* held a GameRankings score of 84.68%, from 28 reviews, as of 18 Apr 2017. This beat other games that specifically require toys-to-life figurines. (The highest-rated *Infinity* game is scored 80.86%.)

Most videogame characters in fast-food promotions
Seventeen different playable *Skylanders* characters had been included in Happy Meal promotions at McDonald's as of 18 Apr 2017. The full menu was: Chompy, Chop Chop, Crusher, Drobot, Eruptor, Free Ranger, Freeze Blade, Gill Grunt, Ignitor, Jet-Vac, Kaos, Magna Charge, Prism Break, Rattle Shake, Spyro (below), Tree Rex and Wash Buckler.

MINI-BYTES
The free-to-play *Battlecast* (below), launched in 2016, marked *Skylanders'* entry into the trading-card arena. The cards – first packaged with the previous year's *SuperChargers* – feature characters and spells. There were an initial 300 variants to collect.

Largest collection of *Skylanders* memorabilia
Christopher Desaliza of Pace, Florida, USA, owns 4,100 unique items of *Skylanders* memorabilia. The collection – counted on 27 Jan 2015 – includes figurines, trading cards, stickers, covers, lanyards, posters and more. Christopher estimates that his record haul is worth at least $100,000 (£66,541).

Highest-altitude freefall videogame session
For the European launch of *Trap Team* on 10 Oct 2014, Activision hired skydivers – dubbed "Skytrappers" – to put the "sky" in *Skylanders*. The group started playing the game in freefall at a 12,500-ft (3,810-m) altitude.
The skydivers travelled at 122 mph (196 km/h) in freefall – about five times faster than Usain Bolt's top speed – and even managed to trap a villain while playing the game!

HEARTHSTONE

Spinning off from *World of Warcraft*, this fantastical card battler allows gamers to play as one of *WoW*'s nine character classes. Since its 2014 launch, it has racked up millions of fans and become a popular eSport.

Longest pro win streak

German *Hearthstone*r Jan "SuperJJ" Janßen (below) beat the Netherlands' "ThijsNL" at the SeatStory Cup IV on 13 Nov 2015. This kick-started an amazing 18-match win streak, taking in the Time2Win Invitational and WePlay Season 1. The run ended on 27 Nov 2015 when "SuperJJ" lost to Canada's Ryan Murphy-Root at DreamHack Winter 2015.

Most pro wins (single class)

Dutch *Hearthstone* master Thijs "ThijsNL" Molendijk had, as of 24 Feb 2017, won 108 pro matches playing as the Druid, according to GosuGamers. The player was European champion in both 2015 and 2016.

He also set the record for **most pro games played (single class)**: 188 as Warlock.

Most damage dealt by a single spell

On 20 Sep 2015, Romanian *Hearthstone*rs Plank and KaptVoorvel set up a match between Priest and Paladin. Their aim: to deal the most damage possible in a single turn. With seven copies of Prophet Velen on the Paladin side of the field, a spell dealing 1,343,228,898 damage was doubled seven times to become 171,933,298,944 damage.

$250K

PRIZE POOL
available at *Hearthstone*'s 2017 Winter Championship, on 23–26 Mar.

Most viewed *Hearthstone* video on YouTube

The official "Hearthstone -- The Tavern Is Open Trailer", uploaded on 27 Jan 2014, had achieved 4,634,556 views on YouTube as of 11 Apr 2017.

Many of the comments focused on its declaration that "victory requires strategy", accompanied by a visual of a Hunter deck – arguably the least strategic class

Highest class win rate

Narrowly ahead of Hunters and Warriors, the Druids were top of the class as of 11 Apr 2017. Their 6,469 victories equated to a 52% win rate on the GosuGamers boards.

Among the Druid ranks is Cenarius' protégé Malfurion Stormrage (right), who is the leader of the night elf druids. His card was illustrated by revered artist Alex Horley.

Malfurion Stormrage

30

Most copies of a single card in a *Hearthstone* deck

In 2016, there were nine copies of "A Light in the Darkness" in an Arena deck. Its effect: "Discover a minion. Give it +1/+1."

The run featuring this deck ended with a disappointing 3–3 record. To the game's Liquipedia page, however, more troubling was, "If you turn on a light while it's dark, doesn't that mean it's no longer dark?"

Highest-earning *Hearthstone* player

Russia's Pavel Beltiukov had won a total of $286,414 (£231,026) as of 11 Apr 2017. Three major wins in 2016 – including BlizzCon, one of the highlights in the *Hearthstone* calendar – shot him to the top of the prize-winnings leaderboard.

> **"Playing at BlizzCon is an insane experience. It's really hard to describe. You're working all year to get there."**
>
> Thijs "ThijsNL" Molendijk

Most Twitch followers for a *Hearthstone* player

Canadian tournament pro Octavian "Kripparrian" Morosan had attracted 961,120 followers to his "nl_Kripp" Twitch channel as of 11 Apr 2017.

"My goal is to be as respectful and thankful to every viewer," he told Glixel. "The people that stick around are the ones who realize that."

Most 12-win Arena runs

According to figures from developers Blizzard published on us.battle.net, Chinese player "ggcnm" completed 152 Arena runs, each with the maximum 12 wins, in 2016. In contrast, "Kripparrian" (left) led his region with only 95 12-win runs. Over the year, "ggcnm" won 8,378 games of Arena.

MINI-BYTES

Dot eSports diligently ranked all of *Hearthstone*'s emotes in 2016. At number one was "Spectacular!" by Malfurion Stormrage (see far left). "A truly pantheon-level emote," they enthused. "We'll be shouting 'Spectacular!' at bad plays 'til the day we die."

Longest single turn

On 25 Mar 2015, France's Florian "Mamytwink" Henn took 1 day 21 hr 18 min to complete a turn.

The average turn takes around 90 sec. However, "Mamytwink" exploited a loophole that enabled him to fire 28,752 arcane missiles (instead of the usual three). Animation for the move took 45 hr 18 min.

Mamytwink

The player's YouTube channel shows how he set up his epic turn.

Arcane Missiles

Shoot 3 missiles at random enemies for 1 damage each.

39

LORD OF THE RINGS

Written between 1937 and 1949, J R R Tolkien's *LotR* novel almost single-handedly shaped the modern fantasy genre. Many games can now be found inhabited by wily wizards, heroic hobbits and 'orrible orcs...

Fastest completion of *Middle-earth: Shadow of Mordor*

US gamer "FearfulFerret" completed the open-world actioner *Middle-earth: Shadow of Mordor* in 1 hr 56 min 35 sec on 19 Nov 2014. The run was completed on the PC.

Fastest completion of *LotR: The Return of the King*

Australian warrior "Thinks The Clown" slayed his way through EA's 2003 movie tie-in in 1 hr 30 min 55 sec, as verified by Speedrun.com on 14 Mar 2017.

The **fastest completion of *LotR: The Two Towers*** – predecessor to *The Return of the King* – was 57 min, achieved on the GameCube by Sweden's "Blackpod" on 8 Dec 2016. "NEW WORLD RECORRDDD!!!" he rejoiced.

60 YEARS
Gap between the events of the *Hobbit* and *LotR* novels – the time period for *Middle-earth: Shadow of Mordor*.

First licensed multiplayer MOBA

The multiplayer online battle arena is still a young genre, and Monolith's *Guardians of Middle-earth* (2012) was the first based on a non-gaming series. Two teams can choose from various Middle-earth "guardians", including the necromancer Sauron and Frodo (below centre).

Longest-running MMORPG based on a book

Launched on 24 Apr 2007, Daybreak Game Company's *The Lord of the Rings Online* was still casting its magic 9 years 337 days later, as of 27 Mar 2017. Revealingly, earlier MMO hits such as *World of Warcraft* (2004) and *EverQuest* (1999) are indebted to Tolkien's novels.

Best-selling hack-and-slash

Recreating scenes from Peter Jackson's first two *LotR* movies (2001–02), EA's *LotR: The Two Towers* (2002) had sold 6.65 million copies as of 27 Mar 2017, according to VGChartz. The actioner challenges players to slay Sauron's evil hordes using multiple attack combos.

Fastest completion of *LEGO The Hobbit*

On 12 Oct 2015, the US Twitcher Erin "rinimt" Jenison raced through a blocky version of Middle-earth to defeat Smaug the dragon in 3 hr 47 min 24 sec, as verified by Speedrun.com.

Oldest videogame voice actor

Sir Christopher Lee (b. 27 May 1922, d. 7 Jun 2015), who plays the role of narrator and Saruman the White in *LEGO The Hobbit* (Warner Bros. Interactive Entertainment), was aged 91 years 316 days when the game was released on 8 Apr 2014. Movie legend Lee had previously starred as the evil Saruman in Peter Jackson's *LotR* movie trilogy.

Most licences in a single videogame

Following its second year of releases from 27 Sep 2016, TT Games' toys-to-life hit *LEGO® Dimensions* features characters from 28 third-party franchises. Tolkien's *LotR* is shown below with the elf Legolas (left) alongside *Jurassic World* characters.

Most critically acclaimed *LotR* game

As of 27 Mar 2017, the 2007 MMO *The Lord of the Rings Online* (originally subtitled *Shadows of Angmar*) had a GameRankings score of 86.89%. It pipped the 86.55% achieved by *Middle-earth: Shadow of Mordor* in 2014.

MINI-BYTES

Master LEGO builder Jonas Kramm (DEU) has built a fully functional *LotR* pinball machine using 2,000 toy bricks. The machine measures just over 2 ft (0.6 m) long. Its creator – a *LotR* fan – told website The Brothers Brick that it took him 12 hr straight to build.

Most videogames based on one novel

Penned as a sequel to 1937 novel *The Hobbit*, J R R Tolkien's *LotR* established Middle-earth as one of the most amazing – and strangest – places in literary fiction. Since 1982, at least 29 videogames have unfolded inside Tolkien's magical world, each linked to the events of *LotR*. Recent romps include *Middle-earth: Shadow of Mordor* (Warner Bros., 2014, below), the sequel of which, *Shadow of War* (2017), will bring the total to 30 titles.

Tallest LEGO model in a videogame

Every new LEGO game features models that were first built in physical LEGO bricks before being digitally transposed into the game. As of 27 Mar 2017, Sauron's Barad-dûr tower in *LEGO The Lord of the Rings* (TT Games, 2012) is the largest model made for a game. The construction measured 2.5 m (8 ft 2 in) in height and used 53,673 bricks.

WARCRAFT

Spawned in 1994 by Blizzard's *Warcraft: Orcs & Humans*, *Warcraft* is now a vast multimedia franchise. Among its most successful incarnations are 2004's *World of Warcraft*, the game that put the "massive" in MMORPG, and a 2016 movie.

Highest-grossing live-action movie based on a videogame

Beating a burning legion of mixed reviews, 2016's *Warcraft* had grossed $433,125,655 (£325.6 million) at the worldwide box office as of 21 Mar 2017, according to The-Numbers.com.

This made Duncan Jones' epic – with Toby Kebbell as Durotan (right) – the most successful live-action adaptation and the **highest-grossing movie based on a videogame** overall, leaving *Angry Birds* on the second-place perch.

The movie was particularly popular in China, where it grossed an Azerothian $221 million (£170 million).

> ## "I'm equally proud and furious about Warcraft. I love it. I spent so much time on it. I put all my heart into trying to make it work."
> Director Duncan Jones on his *Warcraft* movie

Most viewed *Warcraft* channel on Twitch

As of 31 Mar 2017, veteran adventurer Roberto "Towelliee" Garcia (USA) was the most watched Twitcher dedicated to the fantasy franchise, accruing a mighty 100,131,573 views.

"I have been tanking on a progression level of *WoW* for about 11 years now and loving every second of it," he writes on his YouTube channel. "I strive to be the best at what I do."

Leeroy Jenkins

4

Charge. Battlecry: Summon two 1/1 Whelps for your opponent.

6 / 2

Most viewed *Warcraft* video

"Leeroy Jenkins" – the video that gave gamers a new war cry – had earned 45,962,118 YouTube views as of 31 Mar 2017.

The infamous, bumbling *Warcraft* warrior, after whom the video is named, was immortalized on a *Hearthstone* card (above).

First person to complete *World of Warcraft* (*WoW*)

Chinese Taipei's "Little Gray" completed *WoW*'s available achievements on 27 Nov 2009. The level-80 Tauren Druid – on the Wrathbringer server – scored a full 986 in the vast Armory database.

Largest virtual gathering of gnomes

The Running of the Gnomes – an annual *WoW* event since 2010 – was created by "Skakavaz" and "Dravinna" (aka "Magical Warlock Girl") for breast cancer research. The sixth run, on 24 Oct 2015, saw 2,454 gnomes race in pink tabards.

First videogame pandemic

A deadly virtual plague hit *WoW* in Sep 2005, affecting thousands of players. The "corrupted blood" infection meted out by Hakkar in the Zul'Gurub dungeon was only supposed to affect players close to his corpse. Instead, it transferred to other areas via an in-game pet, then spread from player to player.

The Sims: Livin' Large was hit by a guinea pig disease in 2000, but that proved to have been created by the game's designer. The *WoW* incident was the first accidental digital pandemic and the first to affect entire servers – to the point that it was considered a potential model for behaviour in real-life pandemics.

Highest-earning *Warcraft III* player

South Korea's Jang "Moon" Jae-ho had earned a huge $465,481 (£375,803) from *Warcraft III* events as of 21 Mar 2017, according to e-Sportsearnings.

3.3 m

FIRST-DAY SALES

reported for 2016's *WoW: Legion*, making it the fastest seller in the franchise.

Longest *WoW* marathon

Spanish gamer Hecaterina "Kinumi Cati" Iglesias (above) played *WoW* on a PC for 29 hr 31 min. This epic run, on 29–30 Mar 2014, was also the record for the **longest marathon on an MMORPG**.

Hecaterina had earlier achieved the **longest JRPG marathon**: 38 hr 6 min on *Final Fantasy X*, on 26–28 Jul 2013.

MINI-BYTES

Warcraft-branded beer was produced in China to promote the movie (which may explain its popularity there). The drink was a joint creation by the Tsingtao Brewery and Warner Bros.

Most unique pets collected in *WoW*

European gamer "Ryzølda", playing on the "Hyjal" realm, had collected 884 of *WoW*'s 893 unique pets as of 20 Mar 2017. Of these, 865 were at max level.

First player to reach level 110 in *WoW: Legion*

Within hours of the *WoW* expansion's release on 29 Aug 2016, Sweden's Jimmy "fragNance" Landqvist hit the top level. His progress from level 100 – playing as a Havoc Demon Hunter on the Twisting Nether server – was streamed live on Twitch.

On 24 Nov that year, the Mannoroth server's "Doubleagent" hit level 110 without leaving the Pandaren starting area. This gave the gamer the record for **highest level without choosing a faction** (neither Alliance nor Horde). "Doubleagent" gained experience by mining ore and picking flowers.

DARK SOULS

As unforgiving as they are compulsive, the *Souls* action RPGs from Japan studio FromSoftware are a cult sensation. Brooding, medieval settings combine with the toughest bosses ever battled. You have been warned.

Hardest boss in *Dark Souls III*

According to 12,000 players polled on IGN, the Nameless King is the toughest encounter of all 19 bosses in *Dark Souls III*. The towering war god claimed 5,966 votes – a massive 50.13% of the poll. He rides a flying dragon and brandishes a spear that's even bigger than the player. Fortunately for adventurers, facing him is optional.

Fastest "all bosses, no DLC" completion of *Dark Souls III*

Released in 2016, *Dark Souls III* introduced 19 new bosses, including Soul of Cinder and Curse-Rotted Greatwood. On 22 Oct 2016, "Nemz38" (UK) beat them all in 59 min 24 sec.

The same player also achieved the **fastest any% completion**, in 35 min 44 sec on 7 Oct 2016. This run allows players to side-step any optional boss fights, or skip them using glitches.

> *"I've really been pursuing making games that give players a sense of accomplishment by overcoming tremendous odds."*
>
> *Dark Souls* director Hidetaka Miyazaki

Most alternative controls used to complete *Dark Souls*

Bandai Namco's original *Dark Souls* (2011) can be a torturously tough experience for many lesser gamers, but "bearzly", aka Benjamin Gwin (CAN), managed to finish it with nine different control methods. His roll call of the "most obscure" controllers he could find included a *Donkey Konga* bongo drum, a dance mat, a steering wheel, a guitar peripheral and even a microphone, used with only his voice.

Most popular boss in the *Souls* series

With just over 100 bosses featured across four *Souls* games and 2015's spiritual cousin, *Bloodborne*, fans have readily debated the finest series adversary. The foreboding duo of Dragon Slayer Ornstein and Executioner Smough (right), from 2011's *Dark Souls*, have ranked in the top five of at least 11 critics' choice features, including top spots in Den of Geek's Top 105 and Dorkly's Top 40. The series debuted in 2009 with *Demon's Souls*.

Most money pledged to a Kickstarter board game based on a videogame

On 19 Apr–16 May 2016, the UK-based makers of *Dark Souls – The Board Game* raised £3,771,474 ($5,413,840). Their game, set inside Bandai Namco's *Dark Souls* universe, includes miniatures modelled on the formidable bosses Dragon Slayer Ornstein and Executioner Smough.

The game had briefly held the overall record for **most money pledged to a Kickstarter board game**. That was until *Kingdom Death: Monster 1.5* raised an astonishing $12,393,139 (£10,024,000) on 25 Nov 2016–7 Jan 2017.

Fastest time to defeat the Nameless King without blocking, dodging or parrying in *Dark Souls III*

On 3 May 2016, US Twitcher "TolomeoR" humiliated the game's infamous foe in 2 min 56 sec, despite the obvious handicaps. To add to the achievement, the gamer managed this while at the lowliest "Soul Level 1".

PRO-FILE: YOUTUBER

"VaatiVidya" (AUS)

Subscribers: 917,218

Views: 125,450,818

Trivia: Specializes in lore, gameplay and animation vids for all ...*Souls* games.

(Info correct as of 2 Mar 2017)

Most downloaded mod for *Dark Souls* (2011)

"DSfix" by Austria's Peter "Durante" Thoman had been downloaded 1,489,523 times from nexusmods.com as of 2 Mar 2017. The mod enhances the PC version's graphics, sharpening up the character models and environments. Impressively, "Durante" released the mod only about half an hour after *Dark Souls* came out.

Most invading dark spirits vanquished in *Dark Souls III* (Xbox One)

In *Dark Souls III*, players can "invade" each other's world, seeking to steal the souls that they have attained. According to TrueAchievements, Rebecca "DarkCassa" Cunningham (UK) had defended her world from 1,999 invading rivals, who are disguised as dark spirits.

Most viewed *Dark Souls* "lore" video on YouTube

With minimal storytelling and dialogue in *Dark Souls*, fans speculate on the games' "lore". As of 2 Mar 2017, "*Dark Souls* Story - Solaire and the Sun" by Michael "VaatiVidya" Samuels (AUS, above left) had a total of 1,871,703 views.

MINI-BYTES

Dark Souls III won the "Love/Hate Relationship" gong at the first-ever Steam Awards in Dec 2016, as voted by PC players. The award recognizes a game that can be a lot of fun but also *horribly* punishing.

Fastest time to defeat the Nameless King using only feet in *Dark Souls III*

...*Souls* players have a habit of trying to finish these rock-hard games in unusual ways. In a video uploaded to YouTube on 6 Jun 2016, Philippines gamer "Celesterian Games" (inset) defeated *DS III*'s the Nameless King – voted by players as the game's toughest foe – in 2 min 41 sec. He was using only his bare feet to operate the controller.

FANTASY ROUND-UP

From the otherworldly adventuring of *The Witcher* to the Spartan swordplay of *God of War*, fantasy gaming has inhabited many genres and many realms... and inspired many minds.

Best-selling hack-and-slash series

Featuring grand settings and terrifying monsters straight from Greek mythology, Sony's *God of War* (represented here by 2007's *God of War II*) has long been a must-have for PlayStation action fans. As of 8 Mar 2017, the franchise had sold 24.77 million units, according to VGChartz. That figure will likely swell when its hotly championed, incoming eighth opus, *God of War*, finally rages on to the PS4.

500K

UNITS SOLD

in its first week by *Total War: Warhammer* – making it reportedly the fastest seller in Sega's franchise.

Fastest time to marry in *The Elder Scrolls V: Skyrim*

Canadian romantic "Fivexual" wasted little time hitching himself to an NPC partner in Bethesda's 2011 RPG. The gamer married the Imperial spellcaster Marcurio (below) in 3 min 37.06 sec on 2 Nov 2016. The fastest marriage is one of Speedrun.com's more intriguing niche runs.

Most backers for a Kickstarter videogame

Originally listed with the working title *Double Fine Adventure*, Tim Schafer's quirky point-and-clicker *Broken Age* was backed by 87,142 people on Kickstarter in Feb–Mar 2012. In total, it raised $3,336,371 (£2,129,550) on the crowdfunding platform.

Most users of an MMO

On 12 Sep 2016, *RuneScape* became the first MMO to officially exceed 250 million user accounts. Publisher Jagex celebrated by hosting daily prize draws, in which players could win gold coins – the common in-game currency. *RuneScape* is set in a medieval realm and has been through many updates since its launch in Jan 2001.

Most viewed cover version of a game soundtrack

"Skyrim", by violinist Lindsey Stirling and singer Peter Hollens (both USA), had 64,461,976 views on YouTube as of 8 Mar 2017. It's a cover of Jeremy Soule's theme from *The Elder Scrolls V: Skyrim*.

MINI-BYTES

The Witcher's protagonist Geralt of Rivia was immortalized on a stamp by Poland's state postal service Poczta Polska. A collaboration with publisher CD Projekt, the limited edition of 180,000 was issued in 2016.

A source of pride for Poland – it was name-checked by Barack Obama on a visit to the country – *The Witcher*'s impact has spread far beyond its birthplace. On 7 Aug 2016, Russian sports shooter Vitalina Batsarashkina wore *Witcher*-themed glasses and a game medallion during a silver medal-winning performance at the 2016 Summer Olympics.

Most critically acclaimed videogame reboot

The Xbox version of the supernatural *Prince of Persia: The Sands of Time* (Ubisoft, 2003) held a 92.67% score on GameRankings, from 66 reviews, as of 8 Mar 2017.

The action-adventure is a reboot of Jordan Mechner's *Prince of Persia* platform series, which debuted on the Apple II in 1989.

Longest-running fantasy game series

Predating *Ultima*, *King's Quest* and versions of Tolkien's Middle-earth, *Dungeons & Dragons* has spawned videogames for 38 years, from 1975 to 2013.

Inspired by the table-top RPG conceived in 1974, the first *Dungeons & Dragons* videogame was the dungeon-crawler *dnd*. This was created by Illinois, USA, students Gary Whisenhunt and Ray Wood for the PLATO system in 1975.

The most recent release was Cryptic Studios' free-to-play MMORPG *Neverwinter*, launched for the PC in Jun 2013.

Most Golden Joysticks won

Conceived in 1983, the Golden Joystick Awards is an annual event, with votes cast by the public. Following its 2016 event, held on 18 Nov in London, UK, *The Witcher III: Wild Hunt* (2015) had scooped seven awards across four years, with a further four gongs for its 2016 expansion *Blood and Wine*. According to publisher CD Projekt, the action-RPG has pocketed more than 800 awards overall, making it one of the most decorated games in history.

Longest RPG marathon

On 6–8 May 2012, the five-man US crew "The Great Falls Gamers" delved into *The Elder Scrolls V: Skyrim*'s mystical expanses for 48 hr 14 min. The record was set at the Montana State University College of Technology, Great Falls, USA. The team had previously held the record for the **longest FPS marathon**.

MINI-BYTES

Ultima creator Richard Garriott put a container of his blood on eBay in Jul 2016. The listing lasted less than a week before being pulled, Kotaku speculated, "most likely due to eBay's strict 'Don't Sell Blood' policy".

JAPANESE ROUND-UP

Japan's rich culture and mythology has inspired game design in vibrant, incredible ways. Whether mystical or mischievous, Japanese fantasy games can be filled with mechs, monsters and martial artists...

Longest-serving videogame voice actor

Japanese actress Masako Nozawa voiced *Dragon Ball*'s Son Goku (right and main picture) for 23 years 219 days, from *Dragon Ball Z: Super Butōden*'s release on 20 Mar 1993 to *Dragon Ball: Xenoverse 2* on 25 Oct 2016.

Masako has also performed in *Final Fantasy Type-0*, *Kingdom Hearts* and, since 1986, the *Dragon Ball* TV series.

Most popular game character for cosplay

At the user-generated cosplay community site WorldCosplay.net, 7,967 photographs of fans dressed as Junko Enoshima had been posted as of 29 Mar 2017. Fashionista Junko is a key character from 2010's handheld/mobile mystery adventure *Danganronpa: Trigger Happy Havoc*, which challenges players to investigate a fight club overseen by a robot bear.

Longest-running Japanese RPG series

Dragon Quest celebrated its 30th anniversary in 2016. Pitting a young hero against a Dragonlord, Yuji Horii's series began with Chunsoft's *Dragon Quest*, aka *Dragon Warrior*, in 1986. It's set to continue with the 11th main canon game – *Dragon Quest XI* – in 2017.

The franchise has also spawned spin-offs: the magical *Dragon Quest Monsters* and top-down adventure *Slime*.

Oldest videogame music composer

Composer Koichi Sugiyama (below right) was born in Japan on 11 Apr 1931. Commissioned to write music for *Dragon Quest* in 1986, he was still going strong aged 85 years 46 days, as of 27 May 2016, when *Dragon Quest Heroes II* was released. He has also scored *Dragon Quest XI*, to be released in 2017.

Most hit points for a boss

In the 2015 simulation RPG *Makai Shin Trillion* (Compile Heart), players star as a demon lord trying to save their supernatural realm from destruction. To triumph, they must defeat a main boss called Trillion, who has 1 trillion hit points.

Longest JRPG title in English

Shin Megami Tensei Devil Summoner Raidou Kuzunoha vs The Soulless Army (Atlus, 2006) has 70 characters including spaces. Its sequel, *Shin Megami Tensei Devil Summoner 2 Raidou Kuzunoha vs. King Abaddon* (Atlus, 2008) boasts 68.

Longest-running dedicated cosplay event

Debuting in Nagoya in 2003, the World Cosplay Summit had been staged annually in Japan for 13 years as of its 2016 event, held on 30 Jul–7 Aug. The Summit sees participants from all over the world cosplaying characters from Japanese games, manga, anime and tokusatsu. Since 2005, the event has climaxed with the World Cosplay Championship.

Most viewed concert by videogame characters

Splatoon's pop-star duo the Squid Sisters performed a holographic music concert at Japan's Niconico Tokaigi gaming event on 30 Jan 2016. As of 29 Mar 2017, "Shiokaraibu" ("Squid Sisters Live") had 1,743,971 views on Nintendo's YouTube channel.

This glow-stick-waving debut was followed by performances at Japan's Choongakusai music festival and a Japan Expo in Paris, France, in Apr and Jul 2016.

Most critically acclaimed RPG for an eighth-generation platform

The PS Vita JRPG *Persona 4 Golden* (Atlus, 2012) has a GameRankings score of 94.16%, from 43 reviews. This puts it ahead of other eighth-gen console hits *The Witcher III: Wild Hunt* (92.23%) and *Bloodborne* (90.66%), as of 29 Mar 2017.

In the offbeat game, high-school students track a killer through dungeons. This enhanced version of the PS2 game *Persona 4* is also the **most critically acclaimed PS Vita title**.

Persona 5 – released in Japan in 2016 and due to hit worldwide in 2017 – may well challenge its predecessor: it won a gold prize at 2016's PlayStation Awards.

870,000

WORDS
of story in 3DS *Dragon Quest VII*.

MINI-BYTES

Around the world, the likes of Pokémon and Mario are gaming legends. In Japan, however, many consider *Dragon Quest* to be *the* iconic game. But creator Yuji Horii has admitted it was inspired by elements from two American games: Sir-Tech's *Wizardry* and Origin's *Ultima*.

Also very popular in Japan is the *Monster Hunter* franchise, which began in 2004. There's a Monster Hunter ride at Universal Studios Japan – which, in 2012, hosted a 17-m-wide (55-ft 9-in), 8.59-m-tall (28-ft 2-in) sculpture of the franchise's Silver Rathalos flying wyvern (above).

Most prolific strategy game series

Populated by battling mechs from manga and animes such as *Mobile Suit Gundam* and *Mazinger Z*, Banpresto's *Super Robot Wars* has yielded 64 games since its 1991 debut, according to Giant Bomb. *Super Robot Wars V* appeared in Feb 2017.

HORROR ROUND-UP

The horror genre is alive and well... or should that be undead and kicking?!? Terrifying titles set in the dank swamps of Louisiana or the eerie mountains of Transylvania are sure to chill you to the core...

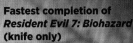

Fastest completion of _Resident Evil 7: Biohazard_ (knife only)
Despite most gamers requiring flame-throwers and firearms to tackle the game's unrelenting bug-hordes (among other monstrosities), France's "Cáelm_Bleidd" finished _Resident Evil 7_, with only a knife, in a time of 1 hr 48 min 8 sec. The gamer achieved this on 22 Feb 2017, as verified by Speedrun.com.

The **fastest completion** overall is 1 hr 29 min 40 sec, achieved by US gamer "xerian" on 17 Mar 2017.

Set in the Louisiana swamps of deep south USA, _RE7_ is a return to the exploratory gameplay of the earlier games – except that it's played in first-person and even VR.

Best-selling survival-horror series
Back with a vengeance for 2017's _Resident Evil 7: Biohazard_ (right), Capcom's _Resident Evil_ series still rules supreme for virtual frights. As of 11 Apr 2017, the (sometimes) slow-burning games had amassed global sales of 63.06 million, according to VGChartz.

Resident Evil is also the **most prolific survival-horror series**. Since its 1996 debut, it has rolled out 32 titles, including spin-offs and mobile games.

Most expensive _Resident Evil_ edition
Available only in Europe and Japan, 2012's _Resident Evil 6: Premium Edition_ retailed for up to £899 ($1,439). In addition to the game itself (for consoles), the package offered an authentic cowhide leather jacket that was a replica of the one worn by Leon Kennedy (left) in the game, plus four tablet cases, extra DLC maps and stickers.

Longest script for a graphic adventure
Released in 2015, Sony's _Until Dawn_ was a plot-driven supernatural adventure in which eight "friends" try to survive a trip in the mountains. The game features multiple branching narratives that theoretically lead to hundreds of possible outcomes. Writers Graham Reznick and Larry Fessenden (both USA) claimed to have written 10,000 pages of dialogue, although only 1,000 pages were used. The huge script was partly due to the adventure's lengthy development period, with the game having originally been mooted as an action title in 2012.

Most crowdfunded videogame based on a movie

Having obtained rights for the 1980s slasher movie franchise of the same name, *Friday the 13th: The Game* (Gun Media, 2017) had raised $2,060,651 (£1,693,760) across the platforms Kickstarter and Backerkit, as of 10 Mar 2017.

Most prolific literary character in gaming

Created by Irish writer Bram Stoker for his 1897 novel of the same name, the Transylvanian vampire Dracula has haunted at least 42 videogames. Many of these have been atmospheric adventures, including CRL's notorious 1986 text adventure *Dracula* and Microïds' point-and-clicker *Dracula: Resurrection* in 2000. However, the bulk of Drac's gaming appearances have been as a chief antagonist and sometimes protagonist in Konami's dark fantasy series *Castlevania* (above).

MINI-BYTES

The next *Silent Hill* game was to be a collaboration between developer legend Hideo Kojima and movie director Guillermo del Toro (below). But after Kojima parted ways with Konami, the publisher canned the game. "One of the most moronic things I've ever witnessed," said del Toro.

Most enemies killed in *Resident Evil 7: Biohazard* (Xbox One)

Without giving away any spoilers, Capcom's 2017 game introduces multiple new enemies to the franchise, including the highly grotesque Molded. As of 9 Mar 2017, "Anderson Breda" had killed 6,013 enemies on the Xbox One, according to TrueAchievements.

Fastest blindfolded completion of *Castlevania: SotN*

On 14 Jan 2016, USA's "romscout" completed Konami's gothic classic *Symphony of the Night* (1997) while blindfolded, in a time of 53 min 41 sec. The gamer repeated the feat, albeit with a slower time, at Summer Games Done Quick in Jul 2016, raising money for charity.

Having set a record in 2015 for **most game sequels released in a year** (three), Scott Cawthon's *Five Nights at Freddy's* is now being made into a movie. The indie horrors – equally revered and feared for their jump-scares – are centred on Freddy Fazbear's Pizza restaurant.

First Oscar winner to star in a videogame

US actor Christopher Walken, who won an Oscar for the 1978 movie *The Deer Hunter*, stars in Take-Two's *Ripper*. The 1996 detective adventure is created exclusively from live-action footage.

First virtual reality horror videogame

Pre-dating the latest VR technology by more than 20 years, Looking Glass' *System Shock* (1994) was the first horror game that could be experienced in VR. The space-horror title was compatible with Forte Technologies' VFX1 headset, launched in 1995. This head-mounted tech was able to display *System Shock* in side-by-side stereo 3D.

Most critically acclaimed horror videogame

Capcom's undying classic *Resident Evil 4* (2005) still thrills years later. The Spain-set horror had a GameRankings score of 95.85%, as of 11 Apr 2017.

The **worst-rated horror videogame** is *Amy* (above). The 2012 nastie has a score of just 25.81% from 26 reviews. In it, players must protect a young girl from zombies.

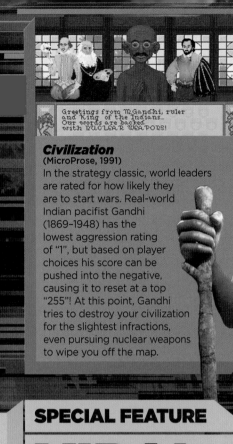

Civilization
(MicroProse, 1991)

In the strategy classic, world leaders are rated for how likely they are to start wars. Real-world Indian pacifist Gandhi (1869–1948) has the lowest aggression rating of "1", but based on player choices his score can be pushed into the negative, causing it to reset at a top "255"! At this point, Gandhi tries to destroy your civilization for the slightest infractions, even pursuing nuclear weapons to wipe you off the map.

Greetings from M.Gandhi, ruler and King of the Indians... Our words are backed with NUCLEAR WEAPONS!

The Witcher III: Wild Hunt
(CD Projekt RED, 2015)

In 2016, players of the hit RPG reported a stalker who followed them wherever they went. The over-zealous "fan" – a noblewoman NPC – developed such an affection for the game's hero Geralt that she would wait for him after hours of meditation, chase him while he was on horseback, and regularly spur him on with cries of "Long live the champion!" There was literally nothing players could do to deflect her clinginess. Eventually the developer patched the bug that caused this issue, but we'd like to think that when she was gone, Geralt may actually have missed her... Sort of.

SPECIAL FEATURE

VIRAL GLITCHES

Many game glitches are a source of frustration: they cause you to lose saves, be blocked from progressing further, or cost you precious items that took hours to locate. Sometimes, though, a glitch can be so bizarre that they're worth the trouble...

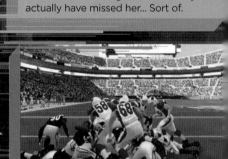

Madden NFL 16
(EA, 2015)

Being an American football pro typically requires having a firm grip, but a rare glitch in EA's gridiron sim gives every player buttery mitts! In a video published on YouTube on 13 Sep 2015, the Aimless Adventure Podcast showed this bug in action as players from the Arizona Cardinals and Carolina Panthers both failed miserably in their quest to gather a dropped ball. As one almighty dog-pile formed, the ball eventually rolled out of play after a comedic 9 min 20 sec – the **longest fumble in a *Madden* game**.

Red Dead Redemption
(Rockstar Games, 2010)

Owing to an error in loading models, original players of Rockstar's Wild West epic sometimes encountered animals with human bodies - or vice versa. As a result, it wasn't unknown for players to be threatened by a floating dog, or pursued by a cougar who was really a cowboy running on his knees. Rockstar eventually outed the bug via a patch.

The Elder Scrolls V: Skyrim
(Bethesda, 2011)

While glitches may be frustrating or funny to many gamers, for speed-runners they often assist in achieving faster completion times. One such time-saver in the popular RPG *Skyrim* is "horse-tilting" – and the flaw is every bit as bizarre as it sounds.

To horse-tilt in *Skyrim*, players must first save their game in third-person. Horses can then be tilted against a rock, just enough for their head to clip through the ground. If players dismount and reload their game, their movement speed increases. Gamers can then sprint – or even fly – through the RPG's world at a breakneck pace that would probably leave even Superman eating dirt.

The Sims 4
(EA, 2014)

This family-life sim is all about creating people to grow and live in a house of your design. Given that characters do eventually die, it's necessary for them to also have children, and these kids will take on the traits of the parents – at least *most* of the time. Every once in a while when a child is being created, something macabre happens. You'll encounter a baby with a weird mixture of adult and child parts. Or you'll just end up with a monstrous mess of pixels involving foot-long claws and eyes that pop menacingly out of sockets. Some players have coyly dubbed this eerie error the "demon baby glitch".

Heavy Rain
(Sony, 2010)

When players are nearing the end of a taut murder mystery, the last thing they probably need is some unintentional comedy to lighten the mood. But that's exactly what happened to a certain few in *Heavy Rain*. At a highly emotional point, gamers are prompted to call out to their lost son Shaun. However, a bug has been known to cause that cry to endure indefinitely. As a result, players can spend the game's nail-biting climax listening to their character yell "SHAUN!" over and over at the top of his aching lungs.

Assassin's Creed IV: Black Flag
(Ubisoft, 2013)

In Ubisoft's pirate adventure, it's not entirely unknown for players to find their ship, the *Jackdaw*, in some precarious predicaments – especially when glitches rear their disfigured head. Thanks to one bug, players may find the *Jackdaw* mysteriously sunk, sometimes with a watery hole to denote its spot in the ocean depths. Fortunately, for gamers hanging around, the vessel does eventually rise again – albeit with its entire crew levitating and screaming!

SCI-FI

Science-fiction has been a staple of gaming diets since *Space Invaders* stormed arcades in 1978. From repelling alien invasions to piloting gargantuan ships through uncharted territories, the genre expands the very realms of gaming.

Most subscribed female games broadcaster on YouTube

A "true geek" who loves to "make people smile", "iHasCupquake" – aka Tiffany Herrera from Los Angeles, USA – had 5,461,793 subscribers as of 29 Mar 2017. She also held the record for **most viewed female games broadcaster on YouTube**, with 2,132,895,223 views.

Her channel emphasises her gaming adventures – including *Minecraft* and *Overwatch*, whose tank hero D.Va she recreated for our photoshoot.

"To be recognized for years of hard work is an honour. I never imagined that any of this was possible. I'm just doing things I love to do."
Tiffany "iHasCupquake" Herrera on her GWR title

TRANSHUMAN GAMING

Transhumanism is the idea that humans can be enhanced beyond their physical and mental limitations through science. Games such as the *Deus Ex* series are packed with transhumanism, showcasing a not-too-distant future in which humans wear cyborg limbs and brain implants. Sounds sci-fi? Some of these developments aren't far-fetched: the most potent gaming tech is now converging with the real world. Take a look...

Real-life Jensen arm

In 2016, UK company Open Bionics fitted 24-year-old amputee Daniel Melville (UK, right) with a functional bionic arm that replicates the one worn by Adam Jensen (above) in Square Enix's cyberpunk RPGs *Deus Ex: Human Revolution* (2011) and *Mankind Divided* (2016). It's the **first working prosthetic based on a game**. Having worn the arm to several major gaming events, Daniel said: "I've shown people it's not a cosplay piece but something functional that I use in my real life. It's been life-changing."

Space Invaders by mind control

In Oct 2006, neurosurgeons and engineers at Washington University in St Louis, USA, devised a hands-free system enabling a teenager to play *Space Invaders* using only his mind. With a brain-wave reader known as an electrocorticographic (ECoG) attached to his brain, the teen amassed 5,000 points in the retro shooter – the **highest score in *Space Invaders* by brain-power only**. The technology was originally developed to diagnose epilepsy.

The brain implant *Guitar Hero*

In Apr 2016, a paralysed 24-year-old regained the ability to play *Guitar Hero* thanks to an experimental brain implant. This tiny device converted the man's thoughts into electronic signals, which were channelled to electrodes attached to his sleeve. These in turn stimulated his muscles. It was the first time that thought signals had ever been used to reanimate paralysed human muscles.

Q&A WITH OPEN BIONICS CO-FOUNDER SAMANTHA PAYNE

How did your *Deus Ex* arm happen?
It started with a Tweet, really. One of our first wearable arm prototypes was covered in Swarovski crystals and had fibre optics running up it that turned blue and flashed at night. When we posted a video of it online, it went viral. Our followers remarked that *Deus Ex* was finally becoming reality so they tagged the series' development team in our online posts, insisting we should both work together. The *Deus Ex* team took the bait and tweeted us. It went from there. Their Jensen arm looks insane.

How closely does your Adam Jensen arm mirror the one from the games?
Stylistically, it's an exact replica. But of course there are a few features that exist in the sci-fi universe that aren't in our real prosthetic. The arm in the game can punch through walls, it has a tether coil-like stun gun and it has a sword inside it – I don't know how that physically fits in!

How did you find Daniel?
Dan [see left] was one of our very first volunteers back when we started developing prosthetics in Nov 2014. Just by working with us, he was the first person to wear a 3D-printed, multi-grip bionic hand. We knew Dan was a huge gamer, so when we teamed up with *Deus Ex* we thought it would be really nice to build the Jensen arm especially for him, because by then he'd trialled some of our heavy, really ugly arm prototypes. Dan was over the moon.

All of your bionic arms are 3D-printed models. What's the basic tech?
The control system in the arms, and the way they operate, is the standard control system that you'll find in other bionics. However, the unique thing about our arms is that they're stylized – they come from the world of sci-fi, whether that's *Deus Ex*, Star Wars or Marvel. They're completely 3D-printed and we can make them very small for children. After Dan's arm, we built a smaller Jensen arm for a 10-year-old girl in the UK called Tilly.

The hands are multi-grip with movable fingers. Will the tech ever be powerful enough that amputees can play videogames with them?
It's not a question of power. The hand can hold a controller and it can press a button, but gamers need speed and flexibility. You only really get one movement from the thumb, which is open and close, so you don't have that much directional control over it. I don't know if there will ever be a hand agile enough to play a game in the future.

But that's the beauty of the future – we can't always predict it, right?
Absolutely! When the *Deus Ex* team first started designing *Human Revolution* in 2007, they didn't think bionic prosthetics would look or function that way until 2026 – but they've got one earlier!

Is game tech being used in the medical industry in other ways too?
Yes, grant money is up for grabs if you can gamify a health-care experience. Lots of people are working on using VR to treat patients without the need for pain medications. And in prosthetics, VR is being used to teach amputees how to use their device. There's lots going on!

Lazy eye begone

In Mar 2015, *Assassin's Creed* developer Ubisoft teamed up with Canada's McGill University to develop *Dig Rush*, a stereoscopic glasses puzzler designed to treat amblyopia ("lazy eye"). The game's use of colour trains weaker eyes to become stronger.

No pain, no VR game

While the VR craze has been revolutionizing gaming experiences, some companies have been using the same tech to improve health care. In Firsthand's *SnowWorld*, burn victims can manage their pain on a psychological level by venturing into an icy virtual world inhabited by penguins and snowmen. Firsthand later developed *COOL!* and *GLOW!*, two mind-training applications that incorporate biosensors to dynamically alter the player's experience based on their medical needs.

SCI-FI

OVERWATCH

A squad-shooter set in an unsettled future of renegade robots and outlandish heroes, *Overwatch* was the runaway smash of 2016. It's the fastest-selling game in Blizzard's history and has swiftly forged a massive eSports scene.

First *Overwatch* world champions

"South Korea utterly destroyed everyone in the *Overwatch* World Cup," ran Mashable's headline as South Korea were crowned inaugural world champs in Blizzard's newest eSport. The 16-nation tournament was staged at the 2016 BlizzCon in Anaheim, California, USA, on 29 Oct–5 Nov. South Korea beat Russia 4–0 in the final, having not lost a single map throughout the event. Sweden beat neighbours Finland to finish third.

"The game is, at its essence, about these heroes and the things that you're able to accomplish with them."
Jeff Kaplan of developer Blizzard Entertainment

Most popular *Overwatch* hero (Season 2)

According to the stats site Overbuff.com, the 61-year-old German adventurer Reinhardt (left) was picked by 11.39% of PC "Competitive" players during *Overwatch*'s second season, which ran from 6 Sep to 23 Nov 2016. A monstrous adversary, Reinhardt fulfils the Tank role and uses a Barrier Field to protect his team-mates while dealing out hurt with his mighty Rocket Hammer.

Most popular cross-platform console beta for a new franchise

Anticipation for *Overwatch* was huge, as evidenced when 9.7 million players participated in its public beta test just weeks before the game's release on 23 May 2016. This smashed the previous record of 6.4 million by Ubisoft's *The Division* (2016).

Longest kill-streak (Season 3)

PS4 player "saud2034" recorded a kill-streak of 59 during *Overwatch*'s third season, which ran from 30 Nov 2016 to 22 Feb 2017. The player's key heroes were D.Va and Zarya.

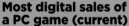
Most digital sales of a PC game (current)

Based on SuperData research, *Overwatch* was downloaded 11.2 million times by PC players in 2016 – that's more than three times the combined digital sales of *Battlefield 1* on Xbox One and PS4.

Blizzard's shooter was also the **most watched new game on Twitch in 2016**, according to the streaming platform.

Most critically acclaimed eighth-generation shooter

With its exuberant art style and goofy humour, *Overwatch* was a hit with critics. As of 16 Mar 2017, the PS4 version held a GameRankings score of 90.87% from 23 reviews. This put it ahead of *DOOM* (89.04%) and *Titanfall* (86.71%), both on Xbox One.

Most matches played by a pro *Overwatch* player (Season 2)

Overwatch's Competitive Play is divided into seasons that typically last two-to-three months. In Season 2, Anton "cooler" Singov (RUS) of the team ANOX competed in 1,584 matches, achieving a respectable 51.07% win rate.

Most "healing" in a competitive game of *Overwatch* (Season 1)

Overwatch isn't solely about eliminating the enemy. It's also about supporting your team-mates on the battlefield, boosting their abilities and healing their battered bodies. During the game's first season, Australian YouTuber "OnSolace" healed 55,451 points of damage in a single competitive PC match, according to the Master Overwatch leaderboards.

Highest win rate by a pro *Overwatch* player (Season 2)

Canada's Lane "Surefour" Roberts, of eSports outfit Cloud9, was the most victorious pro in Season 2. According to Overbuff.com's leaderboards, the hotshot was on the winning side in a fist-pumping 76.06% of his 188 matches.

Tallest videogame action figures

Created by Hollywood designer Steve Wang (TPE), *Overwatch* figures depicting the characters Genji (left), Pharah and Tracer each measure approximately 3.8 m (12 ft 5 in) high – 1.08 m (3 ft 6 in) taller than the world's **tallest man ever**, Robert Wadlow (USA). The figures were displayed in giant boxes at the game's launch, in France, South Korea and the USA.

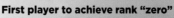

First player to achieve rank "zero"

On 24 Aug 2016, Dale "Bacontotem" Brown (USA) made headlines for deliberately achieving the lowest rank possible in *Overwatch*'s "Competitive" mode, playing with the archer Hanzo. Owing to the game's elaborate matchmaking, this took weeks of planning – and losing.

MINI-BYTES

Despite being an FPS, *Overwatch* has inspired fans to make unofficial dating sims based on the game. Amusing titles include *Re:Load – An Overwatch Dating Game* and, inevitably, *Loverwatch*.

STAR WARS

A long time ago, in a galaxy far, far away, Apple made the cheekily titled *Starwars* (1978). Over the next four decades, the *real* franchise has proved stronger than a Wookiee. With the force awake again, new games – and records – keep coming.

Most game adaptations of a movie scene

The battle of Hoth from *The Empire Strikes Back* (1980) has been fought in at least 22 videogames. It made its first appearance in the **first official *Star Wars* game**, 1982's *The Empire Strikes Back*, and featured most recently in 2015's *Battlefront* (EA, pictured).

It also holds the record for **most videogame re-enactments of a fictional battle**, beating the trench run from the first film. The battle – a snowy skirmish between the Rebels and the Empire – introduced the iconic AT-AT walkers.

$1m

DONATED
to five charities in Jun 2016 by current *Star Wars* licence holder EA. (That's £746,347.)

Most prolific game series based on a film licence

From 1982's *The Empire Strikes Back* to 2016's *LEGO® Star Wars: The Force Awakens*, George Lucas' franchise has spawned 138 videogames.

Of the more recent additions, two of the most high-profile were Bandai Namco's arcade rail shooter *Star Wars: Battle Pod* (2014) and EA's multiplayer shooter *Battlefront* (2015, left).

Tallest *Star Wars* cosplay costume

Created by Julian Checkley (UK) and his Order 66 Creatures and Effects studio, a fully mobile costume of *The Force Awakens'* Grummgar stands at 2.69 m (8 ft 9 in) tall. It took 100 days to build and was designed to replicate the official height of the character (a big-game hunter and mercenary).

Julian said: "It's *really* heavy. I can walk unassisted for a maximum of around 30 minutes before I die!"

Best-selling *Star Wars* game

LEGO Star Wars: The Complete Saga (2007) – which condenses *LEGO Star Wars: The Video Game* (2005) and *LEGO Star Wars II: The Original Trilogy* (2006) into a single game – had sold 15.29 million as of 23 Feb 2017.

The **best-selling *Star Wars* game (single platform)** is the PS4 version of *Star Wars: Battlefront* (EA, 2015), with 8.42 million sales. Adding *Battlefront*'s Xbox One and PC versions brings its total to 13.12 million.

Rarest *Star Wars* game

The only known prototype of *Ewok Adventure* (1983) was sold for $1,680 (£1,018) in 1997. The shoot-'em-up had been created for the Atari, but was cancelled when publishers Parker Brothers opted for *Death Star Battle*.

Designer Larry Gelberg told retro site Digital Press that Lucasfilm didn't allow killing Ewoks: "That's why, when they get shot out of the sky, they shake themselves off and go find another hang-glider. Pity. I would have liked to kill Ewoks."

Largest voice cast in an MMO

A total of 314 actors recorded dialogue for *Star Wars* MMO *The Old Republic*, launched on 20 Dec 2011. They included Jennifer Hale, also known as *Mass Effect*'s Commander Shepard.

Most arcade games based on a film licence

There have been eight official Star Wars arcade games: from Atari's 1983 original to *Star Wars: Battle Pod* in 2014.

An unlicensed Star Wars arcade game in 1979 was a bootleg of Taito's popular *Galaxy Wars*.

First game with digitized movie speech

Atari's 1983 *Star Wars* arcade game set a trend by featuring digitized excerpts from the original 1977 movie.

Students Flavio Tozzi, Dave Roberts and Mike Ohren (all UK) set the **highest group marathon score** on the game: 1,000,000,012 points. The trio played in shifts at Leeds University in West Yorkshire, UK, from 12 p.m. on 15 Jun 1985 to 2:46 p.m. on the 20th.

The **highest single-player marathon score** for the arcade game was achieved by Robert Mruczek (USA) in 1984. Playing for 49 hr straight on a single credit, he ended his epic two-day run with 300,007,894 points.

Most critically acclaimed *Star Wars* game

The Xbox version of 2003's RPG *Star Wars: Knights of the Old Republic* boasted a GameRankings score of 94.21%, as of 23 Feb 2017.

The runner-up was 2001's *Star Wars Rogue Leader: Rogue Squadron II*, on GameCube, with 90.04%. That game, however, holds the record for the **most critically acclaimed space-flight simulation**.

MINI-BYTES

LEGO Star Wars: The Force Awakens marked the game debut of Harrison "Han Solo" Ford. His likeness had featured in instalments of *Star Wars: Battlefront*, and his other film franchise spawned LEGO's *Indiana Jones* series, but neither featured the man himself.

Fastest completion of *Star Wars: Battlefront* survival mode without blasters (team of two)

The force was with brothers Liam and Jake Thompson, aka "TWiiNSANE" (UK), on 7 Apr 2016. Playing on *Battlefront*'s Rebel Depot map at Guinness World Records' headquarters in London, UK, they beat all 15 waves of the shooter's survival mode in 10 min 24 sec. To qualify for the record, the duo were forbidden to use their primary blaster weapons. Instead, they relied on power-up cards.

HALO

Since its debut as an Xbox launch title back in 2001, *Halo* has been the FPS series most Xboxers turn to. It follows a futuristic war, waged between humans and a sinister alien alliance.

Most Achievements in an Xbox title

Essentially four titles packaged into one, *Halo: The Master Chief Collection* (2014) crams in 600 Achievements for players to finish. Its challenges range from completing campaigns to listening to the Thirsty Grunt talk about his eating habits. However, the **most Achievements for a single game** is 408, held by the Microsoft fighter *Killer Instinct* (2013).

Most critically acclaimed shooter for any Xbox console

Released for the original Xbox console in 2001, Bungie's *Halo: Combat Evolved* was the game that introduced Master Chief – a cybernetically enhanced super-soldier (right) – to the gaming masses. As of 26 Apr 2017, its mighty GameRankings score of 95.54% still outranked any other Xbox shooter.

Most played Xbox game on TrueAchievements

Based on player accounts tracked by the Xbox site TrueAchievements, *Halo 3* (2007) is the most played game on any Xbox console. As of 17 Feb 2017, some 259,000 players had unlocked at least one Achievement in the game. Upon release, IGN hailed it the "most complete game on any console".

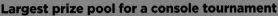

Most participants in an FPS relay

Commemorating the *Halo* legacy in style, 54 gamers took turns playing the first four *Halo* games for 47 hr in Madrid, Spain, on 17 Apr 2015. The event was organized by Xbox Spain as it ramped up the buzz for *Halo 5: Guardians*, which was released six months later.

Fastest completion of *Halo Wars*

Playing the Xbox One version on 14 Apr 2017, Canada's "AP777" finished Ensemble's real-time strategy spin-off in 1 hr 52 min 34 sec, as verified by Speedrun.com.

Largest prize pool for a console tournament

A resounding prize pool of $2.5 million (£1.72 million) was on the line at the 2016 *Halo* World Championship, held in Hollywood, USA, on 18–20 Mar 2016. The tournament's prize – unprecedented for a console game – was partially funded by microtransactions in *Halo 5: Guardians*.

At the contest, the US team Counter Logic Gaming (below) blasted their way to victory in *Halo 5*, pocketing a first prize of $1 million (£690,522).

Highest Xbox Live GamerScore

A GamerScore is based on the number of Achievements that a player has completed in specific titles (mostly on Xbox 360 and Xbox One). According to TrueAchievements, Raymond "Stallion83" Cox (USA) had racked up a formidable GamerScore of 1,519,370 as of 7 Apr 2017, retaining a record that he has held for over eight years. Stallion83's highest haul of 3,300 was achieved on *Halo: The Master Chief Collection*.

Most elusive in-game reward in the *Halo* series

For 2009's *Halo 3: ODST*, Bungie devised seven fiendish "Vidmaster" challenges, including one that meant earning seven EXP on the seventh day of any month. Successful gamers won Recon armour.

Longest *Halo* marathon

Playing in a shopping mall in Helsinki, Finland, on 27 Oct 2015, super-fan Paavo "Paavi" Niskala (FIN) played all five main *Halo* titles for 50 hr 4 min 17 sec. "I planned the marathon quite well ahead, so I had already figured out what I would eat and when I would have a break," he said.

MINI-BYTES

When they're not battling aliens, the Spartan soldiers of *Halo* can be found... dancing! At least that's the premise of a 2016 YouTube video by Impact Props (below). Filmed at the RTX gaming convention in Austin, Texas, USA, it sees cosplayers getting groovy to '80s act A-ha.

All sorts of ambitious things get made in LEGO® bricks. One such item is this replica of *Halo 5*'s SPNKr Rocket Launcher, built by YouTuber "Nick Brick". Nick, who specializes in recreating videogame weapons, used up some 6,000 toy bricks in his creation.

Best-selling sci-fi shooter series

Excluding its spin-off strategy series *Halo Wars*, Microsoft's *Halo* franchise had racked up global sales of 64.57 million as of 7 Apr 2017, according to VGChartz. The games' success exceeds other space-bound heavyweights including Star Wars (35.84 million – series shooters only), *DOOM* (11.78 million), *Killzone* (11.15 million) and *Half-Life* (10.72 million).

DESTINY

It's quite rare for a debuting videogame to sell in its droves, but that's exactly what *Destiny* did in 2014. The online shooter is now a major beast in Activision's canon.

First solo player to beat the "King's Fall" raid
On 3 Dec 2015, YouTuber "The Great Gatsby" (USA) single-handedly slayed *The Taken King*'s boss Oryx – a feat designed for teams of six. The gamer claimed that he had played *Destiny* for more than 1,000 hr and had spent over 50 hr tackling the raid solo.

First solo player to beat the "Wrath of the Machine" raid
Some four weeks after the raid's release, France's "ScaRdrow" beat the final boss, the Fallen Aksis, in the "Wrath of the Machine" (see below left) on 22 Oct 2016. The jubilant player wrote on his YouTube channel: "Hey guys, craziest challenge I've ever attempted. I still can't believe I got this."

Best-selling debut series for eighth-gen consoles
The current glut of consoles have enjoyed many debuting game series (those not based on an existing franchise), but none have sold better than Activision's *Destiny*. As of 5 Apr 2017, the Bungie-developed FPS had shifted 12.95 million units across PS4 and Xbox One (including expansions), according to VGChartz. The sci-fi behemoth outperformed Ubisoft's *The Division* (7.19 million) and Blizzard's *Overwatch* (4.52 million), although the latter was only released in May 2016.

First team to beat the "Wrath of the Machine" raid in *Destiny: Rise of Iron*
Following the raid going live on 23 Sep 2016, the six-man unit "Clan Redeem" took just over 2 hr to crack it. "Raids" are co-operative missions in *Destiny*, known for their fierce challenges. "Wrath of the Machine" was released for *Destiny*'s 2016 *Rise of Iron* expansion.

Longest videogame spaceship
As home to the Hive god Oryx, the *Dreadnaught* from the *Destiny* expansion *The Taken King* is absurdly huge. Maths-savvy fans have compared it to the rings of Saturn and the Churyumov–Gerasimenko comet, concluding that the fortress measures around 3,500 km (2,174 mi) in length. That's about 25 km (15.5 mi) more than the diameter of Earth's Moon!

Most followed *Destiny* Twitcher
Hailing from the USA, "KingGothalion" (see Pro-File) is both a renowned *Destiny* player and games broadcaster. As of 5 Apr 2017, the shooter fan had 688,852 followers to his Twitch channel.

On 19 Sep 2015, "KingGothalion" also led a six-player fireteam to the end of the "King's Fall" raid from *Destiny: The Taken King* – the **first team to conquer the raid** in the 2015 expansion.

Most lethal weapon class in *Destiny* PvP
Of the 8,757,806 players that DestinyTracker.com has been monitoring since Aug 2015, the Shotgun class was used in 4,732,886,431 PvP kills, as of 6 Apr 2017. It accounts for 13.68% of all PvP kills, ahead of the Super (12.64%) and Hand Cannon (11.72%).

Rarest ship in *Destiny*
Every item in *Destiny* is ranked from Common (1) to Exotic (5) in terms of rarity, with the latter being the rarest. As the only "Exotic" ship in the game, the *Manus Celer Dei* is the most elusive – and also the most mysterious. The ship has been discovered within the game's files but there is currently no known way to unlock it. *Manus Celer Dei* is Latin for "Swift Hands of God".

MINI-BYTES
In May 2016, *Minecraft* player "infered5" hit the gaming news for his ambitious efforts to rebuild *Destiny* inside Mojang's sandbox world. The ongoing project, documented at the fansite PlanetMinecraft, is being hosted on the player's TheCrucibleMC server.

Attracting plenty of media attention are the high-end *Destiny* action figures launched by ThreeA in 2015 that stand at a sizeable 1:6 scale. Gamers can choose from Warlocks, Titans and Hunters in various styles, including the Bungie Store edition Hunter (below).

Most sniper rifle kills in *Destiny*
US hot-shot "RealKraftyy", aka Jesse, had chalked up 109,161 kills from 30,153 games in *Destiny*'s PvP "Crucible" activity as of 6 Apr 2017. "You do not want to see Kraftyy on the opposing team," he wrote. "If you do, I apologize in advance." The player also runs a successful Twitch channel, focusing on *Destiny*, that has accrued more than 230,000 followers.

Most viewed fan film based on *Destiny*
Inspired by Bungie's FPS blockbuster, the fan-made music video "DESTINY EPIC RAP | Zarcort y Piter-G" had 14,017,163 views on YouTube as of 6 Apr 2017. In the short film, popular YouTuber "Zarcort" (real name Miguel Ángel Martos Bello) raps over *Destiny* footage in Spanish. "Zarcort" also holds a record for another FPS, *Battlefield* (see pp.136–37).

DOOM

Debuting in 1993, id Software's sci-fi shooter series has inspired legions of imitators while racking up combined sales of over 10 million units. *DOOM* is revered for its pioneering FPS action and its suspenseful, outer-space chills.

First Easter egg hidden in a videogame soundtrack
When run through a spectrogram (a tool for visualizing frequency waves in music), the track "Cyberdemon" from *DOOM* (2016) displays creepy symbols. The Easter egg is a cheeky parody of times when old films and rock albums were alleged to contain hidden messages.

Fastest completion of *DOOM³*
According to Speedrun.com, renowned FPS gamer "Corpseflesh" (DEU) finished *DOOM³* (2004) on PC in 59 min 56 sec on 20 Sep 2016. It was the first time anyone had broken the hour barrier in the eerie FPS.

Most critically acclaimed reboot of a shooter
The Xbox One version of *DOOM* (2016) had a GameRankings score of 89.04% as of 16 Mar 2017. "A great and faithful encapsulation of its predecessors' fast-paced shooting, trademark gore and infamous demons," said gaming site DarkZero.
    This put it ahead of fellow FPS reboots *Return to Castle Wolfenstein* (86.75%), *Shadow Warrior* (75.47%) and *DOOM³* (87.63%). The latter, despite its name, is a reboot

First person to beat the "impossible" Ultra-Nightmare in *DOOM*
Ultra-Nightmare is an incredibly tough mode in *DOOM*'s 2016 reboot that developers said would never be beaten. It combines the game's meanest difficulty with the added challenge of effectively only having one "life". However, on 14 May 2016, just one day after its release, Norway's "Zero Master" survived the FPS' hellish space domains on this terrifying setting. "It is absolutely insane that people are pulling this off... a day after the game was released," wrote one follower of "Zero Master"'s YouTube page.
    The **fastest completion of Ultra-Nightmare in *DOOM* (2016)** is 1 hr 5 min 25 sec, achieved by "BloodThunder" (USA) on 16 Oct 2016.

Fastest co-op completion of *Brutal DOOM*
Brutal DOOM, a gameplay mod created by "Sergeant_Mark_IV", amped up the horror in various titles from the series. On 20 Jul 2015, French duo "Nan0kub" and "Alaedar" finished the mod's extreme take on *The Ultimate DOOM* (itself a 1995 update of the original *DOOM*) in 14 min 46 sec, as ranked at Speedrun.com. They were playing on the "Wussy" difficulty.

First videogames inducted into the World Video Game Hall of Fame
On 5 Jun 2015, id Software's original 1993 version of *DOOM* was one of six games inducted into the inaugural World Video Game Hall of Fame at the National Museum of Play in Rochester, New York, USA. It was joined by fellow legends *Super Mario Bros.*, *PAC-Man*, *Tetris*, *Pong* and *World of Warcraft*

66

Heaviest 3D-printed cosplay prop

Created by UK studio MyMiniFactory on 23 Apr 2016, a 3D-printed model of *DOOM*'s BFG gun weighs 15 kg (33 lb). Constructed from 75 individual 3D-printed components, the prop measures 1.5 m x 0.54 m x 0.58 m (4 ft 11 in x 1 ft 9 in x 1 ft 11 in) – the **largest 3D-printed cosplay prop**. It is so large that it typically requires three people to hold it in a standard firing position.

Fastest completion of *DOOM* (2016)

On 18 Feb 2017, PC player "WhiteHound" (USA) finished the 2016 reboot in 38 min 2 sec (without loads), according to Speedrun.com.

Most acclaimed player-made "SnapMap" in *DOOM* (2016)

The 2016 reboot of *DOOM* introduced a level-editor feature called "SnapMap", enabling players to create their own maps. As of early 2017, *Harvest DOOM* by "Bears" had been named one of the best maps by six sites, including GamesRadar and *PC Gamer*. The map was inspired by Nintendo's farming RPG *Harvest Moon*.

First single-life Nightmare completion of *Final DOOM*'s "The Plutonia Experiment"

On 7 Jun 2015, "Zero Master" (NOR, see left) completed "The Plutonia Experiment" on "Nightmare" difficulty without losing a life – some 19 years after the game was released. The 32 levels of "The Plutonia Experiment" are revered as some of *DOOM*'s toughest challenges. Designed by brothers Dario and Milo Casali, they were issued by id Software as part of *Final DOOM* in 1996. *Final DOOM* was a fan-made sequel to *DOOM II*, but also enjoyed an official release.

Most viewed *DOOM* video

Bethesda's "*DOOM* - Fight Like Hell Cinematic Trailer" had 10,165,933 views on YouTube as of 16 Mar 2017. It had been published less than a year earlier.

Most eSports tournament victories in *DOOM³*

There have been four *DOOM³* tournaments – in 2004 and 2005 – and China's Yang "RocketBoy" Meng won two of them, finishing runner-up in another. According to e-Sportsearnings, the bulk of his winnings came from his win at the ACOM Fatal1ty Shootout in China on 15 Oct 2004. The player won $120,748 (£67,194) – the **largest prize pool in a *DOOM* tournament**.

First FPS for the visually impaired

Released for PC in 2001, GMA's *Shades of Doom* is a shooter with no visuals. It is instead played by listening to audio cues such as wind and footstep echoes. The game's chilling atmospherics were loosely inspired by *DOOM* and it was hailed for its technical innovation.

Longest-running FPS developer

Few studios are as synonymous with first-person shooters as id Software of Texas, USA. Between the release of the WWII-set zombie shooter *Wolfenstein 3D* in May 1992 and the reboot of its seminal horror series *DOOM*, released on Friday, 13 May 2016, the prolific studio had been firing out shooters for 24 years. Its other titles include the *Quake* series (1996–) and 2011's *RAGE*.

MINI-BYTES

When 2010's fan-made mod *Brutal DOOM* was released, it won praise from series creator John Romero. In a video for IGN, he said that had his team released *Brutal DOOM* rather than *DOOM* back in 1993, "It would have destroyed the games industry."

In May 2016, Australian chainsaw carver Rob Bast created an 8-ft (2.4-m) sculpture of a Revenant (both pictured above), one of *DOOM*'s skeletal minions, for the reboot's launch. The art piece was exhibited at the Australian Centre for the Moving Image in Federation Square, Melbourne.

Claymation animator Lee Hardcastle (UK) made a parody video of *DOOM* (below) to celebrate the launch of the game's reboot in May 2016. The comically OTT video features cats and "cute" clay monsters re-enacting scenes from the shooter. It had 1,383,681 views on YouTube as of 16 Mar 2017.

DOOM is one of the most parodied games. Its most unlikely references include a scene in the obscure PC title *Muppets Inside* (1996), in which The Swedish Chef battles a horde of killer vegetables.

POST-APOCALYPTIC ROUND-UP

Warning: the end of the world is nigh! Developers have often predicted how a post-apocalyptic planet will look. These visions range from dusty wastelands inhabited by radioactive mutants to gorgeous green lands overrun by robots...

Fastest completion of *Metro 2033*

Russia's "Loadzee" finished the post-nuclear FPS in 2 hr 56 min 8 sec on 16 Jul 2016. "Loadzee" also made the **fastest completion of *Metro: Last Light***: 2 hr 54 min 31 sec on 19 Jan 2017.

Fastest completion of *Mad Max* (2015)

"PenAgain" (UK) finished the movie tie-in *Mad Max* in 2 hr 33 min 21 sec. The record, on the PC version, was set on 28 Sep 2015.

Fastest completion of *Horizon Zero Dawn*

Released to weighty acclaim in 2017, Sony's action RPG sees players trying to survive a futuristic Earth in which robotic creatures hold dominance and humans have returned to primitive tribes. On 5 Apr 2017, Germany's "Schattentod" overcame its pretty but perilous lands in 2 hr 45 min 30 sec, as verified by Speedrun.com.

The **fastest glitchless completion** is 2 hr 55 min 18 sec, by US gamer "torpidsloth" on 29 Mar 2017.

Fastest "Easy" completion of *RAGE*

"Takyon" sped through Bethesda's 2011 FPS in 1 hr 48 min 8 sec, playing the PC version on 11 Jun 2013, as verified by Speedrun.com.

Most downloaded mod for *Mad Max*

As of 6 Apr 2017, the "Mad Max 4K CineMod" by "cluclap1" had been downloaded 4,992 times by PC gamers. The mod enhances the overall look of the gritty 2015 movie tie-in.

Fastest "pacifist" completion of *Fallout 4* (survival mode)

Playing on the hardest difficulty, US streamer "The Weirdist", aka Kyle Hinckley (left), finished Bethesda's RPG in 26 hr 35 min on 19 Jun 2016, without being credited with a single kill. As the name suggests, a pacifist run involves making as few kills as the game allows.

Most downloaded mod for *Fallout: New Vegas*

Gambit77's "Armorsmith Extended" offers PC players a wider range of options for modding, wearing and combining *New Vegas'* clothing and accessories. It had been downloaded 3,512,568 times from Nexus Mods as of 30 Mar 2017.

First *Fallout 4* completion without being hit

On 5 Jul 2016, New Zealand's "T Ronix" finished *Fallout 4* without taking a single strike, boosting his attributes with "chems" or teaming up with companions (human, mutant or otherwise). The run took just over 25 hr. "Mother of all *Fallout* challenges COMPLETED!" he wrote on Twitch.

Best-selling RPG for PS4

The PS4 version of *Fallout 4* had shifted 7.56 million units as of 29 Mar 2017, according to VGChartz. This made it the eighth best-selling game overall on the platform.

The post-nuclear sequel was also the **best-selling RPG on the Xbox One**, with 4.47 million sales. This made it the sixth best-selling Xbox One title overall.

Most names spoken by a robot in a videogame

Codsworth, *Fallout 4*'s robot butler, can fight alongside players and call them one of 1,259 pre-recorded names (as of 29 Mar 2017, in the English-speaking version). These include Morpheus, Neo and Trinity (*The Matrix*), Kal-El (Superman), Erik and Xavier (X-Men) and Katniss (*The Hunger Games*).

MINI-BYTES

No sooner had 2016's *Fallout 4: Contraptions Workshop* DLC arrived than gamers put it to use building elaborate Rube Goldberg-style machines. Others went down a simpler route: trapping characters in stocks (below) and firing teddy bears and paintballs at them.

Horizon Zero Dawn was inspired by TV nature shows. Guerrilla Games' Samrat Sharma told the UK's *Evening Standard*: "We drew inspiration from *Planet Earth* and documentaries... One of the biggest inspirations was meerkats... Meerkats are always on the look-out."

Longest wait for a videogame sequel

A total of 26 years separates the 2014 role-player *Wasteland 2* (below) from the 1988 original (inset). The sequel – set in 2102, some 100 years after a nuclear war – was developed by inXile Entertainment after a Kickstarter campaign. The original game inspired the *Fallout* series.

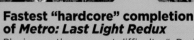

Fastest "hardcore" completion of *Metro: Last Light Redux*

Playing on the meanest difficulty, "aDark_Ranger" (USA) finished the remastered version of the 2013 horror FPS in 2 hr 53 min 10 sec on 28 Aug 2015. *M:LL* was developed by Ukraine's 4A Games and sees players (mostly) evading mutants in Moscow's underground networks.

SPACE SIMS ROUND-UP

"You just won't believe how vastly, hugely, mind-bogglingly big it is," said *The Hitchhiker's Guide to the Galaxy* about space. And everything about space sims is huge too, from the sums of money to the ships...

Most crowdfunded project

Launched as a crowdfunding campaign in Oct 2012, Cloud Imperium Games' *Star Citizen* had raised $146,421,823 (£117,167,000) from 1,778,767 "Star Citizens", as of 13 Apr 2017. Many of the pledges come from backers buying in-game spacecraft. Inevitably, it's also the **most crowdfunded videogame**.

Director Chris Roberts said that he'd originally hoped to make $4 million (£3.2 million), but interest in the space sim exploded. "I think this game will be up there with anything else the big publishers have done," he added.

"It's not even 'best damn space sim' anymore. It's 'best damn everything sim'."
Cloud Imperium's Chris Roberts on *Star Citizen*

Highest score on *EVE Valkyrie*

"TheLankyMan" held the top score in 2016's *EVE Valkyrie* as of 13 Apr 2017, with a total of 9,475,393 points. This was achieved despite fewer kills than the players ranked second and third. The multiplayer spaceship shooter game is an *EVE Online* virtual reality spin-off.

Fastest return trip to the Mun in *Kerbal Space Program*

Self-styled "astronogamer" Scott Manley (UK) designed a rocket that made a return trip from Kerbin (the space flight sim's main planet, loosely based on Earth) to the Mun (its moon) in 58 min 50 sec. The run – using version 0.9 of the game, was shown in a video published to YouTube on 25 Mar 2015.

Manley says he is "able to deliver astonishing scientific facts while... crashing digital simulations of spacecraft".

First open-world videogame

David Braben and Ian Bell's *Elite* (1984) introduced the now-common open-world mode. Players were free to roam the galaxy that formed the open world, trading in goods or contraband. The aim was to attain the rank of Elite; how the player got there was up to them.

ACORNSOFT
ELITE
for the Acorn Electron

10
MILLION
species found in *No Man's Sky* within days of its launch.

Largest space battle

On 10 Dec 2016, in *EVE Online*'s M-OEE8 system, up to 5,337 players battled for 6 hr over the player-made Keepstar Citadel. This had been under attack by the Pandemic Legion for months. At the battle's height, the Pandemic Legion outnumbered the monument's defending forces by more than 20 to one, according to developers CCP.

Most explorable planets

Hello Games' epic *No Man's Sky* (2016) has 18,446,744,073,709,551,616 (more than 18 quintillion) planets for players to land on and explore. Its giant universe is procedurally generated and every planet is unique. "Even if a planet is discovered every second," Hello's managing director Sean Murray told PlayStation.Blog, "it'll take 585 billion years to find them all!"

Largest accurate game galaxy

Although *No Man's Sky* (left) may, in theory, procedurally generate a larger fictional galaxy, *Elite: Dangerous* (2014) replicates our Milky Way with scientific accuracy. Makers Frontier Developments calculate that it generates an area measuring 4,918,906,760,000 cubic light years for players to explore.

Most money paid for a copy of *No Man's Sky*

In a video published on Dailymotion on 29 Jul 2016, mysterious Redditor "Daymeeuhn" was shown opening a boxed copy of *No Man's Sky* – two weeks ahead of its release. He had reportedly paid $1,250 (£948) for the "leaked" copy, having purchased it on eBay.

MINI-BYTES

No Man's Sky has paid tribute to rock star Lemmy of Motörhead, who died in Dec 2015. Among the resources to be collected in the game is a heavy metal element called Lemmium. Game writer Will Porter described it as "a little slice of anarchy, deep in simulated space".

Most downloaded mod for *Kerbal Space Program*

"MechJeb", for 2011's *Kerbal Space Program*, had been downloaded 1,785,386 times as of 13 Apr 2017. The mod, created in 2014, lets MechJeb windows be dragged anywhere on screen. Their positions are reused among all rockets.

Most skill points in *EVE Online*

Player "Stromgren" held 492,544,000 skill points as of 13 Apr 2017, according to eveboard.com. However, this total proved controversial. As the MMO site Massively Overpowered reported, players can buy "Skill Injectors" for their characters. Stromgren, they said, "used injectors to become *EVE*'s highest-skilled character literally overnight, adding over 100 million skill points that would normally take 4.3 years to train passively".

Longest-running convention for a single videogame

Since its 2004 debut, the EVE Fanfest in Iceland has attracted fans on an annual basis, missing only 2011. The biggest turnout was in 2013, when 4,000 gamers celebrated *EVE Online*'s 10th anniversary.

The event ends with a "party at the top of the world", featuring live music performances. The 2017 Fanfest took place on 6–8 Apr in Reykjavík.

SCI-FI

SCI-FI ROUND-UP

From planet-hopping platformers to the deepest RPGs, sci-fi has a stake in every area of the gaming universe. Alongside newbies such as *Raw Data*, veterans *Star Trek* and *Mass Effect* are as popular as ever.

Most prolific game voice actor
Debuting with the 1995 LucasArts adventure *The Dig*, Steve Blum (USA) had acted in 366 games as of 30 Mar 2017. This included an award-winning role in 2012's sci-fi RPG *Mass Effect 3* and voices in 2016's *Star Wars: The Old Republic – Knights of the Eternal Throne*.

Longest-running videogame franchise
Between Mike Mayfield's text-only adventure *Star Trek* (1971) and Cryptic's *Star Trek Online* (2016), Gene Roddenberry's franchise has spawned games for over four decades. Ubisoft's 2017 VR game *Bridge Crew* (featuring the USS *Aegis*, pictured) brings its run to an amazing 46 years. Above is original *Star Trek* icon William "Captain Kirk" Shatner, with *Guinness World Records* Editor-in-Chief Craig Glenday.

Most eSports tournaments for a videogame
StarCraft II: Wings of Liberty (2010) had been contested in 4,132 tournaments as of 30 Mar 2017. According to e-Sports Earnings, 1,630 players had collectively won $22,301,885 (£17,949,200), making it the fourth most lucrative game after *Dota 2*, *League of Legends* and *Counter-Strike: Global Offensive*.

StarCraft II's **largest prize pool** was $500,000 (£400,397), at 2016's World Championship Series Global Finals, in California, USA, on 27 Oct–5 Nov.

PRO-FILE:
YOUTUBER

ANGRYJOE (USA)
Subscribers: 2,766,333
Views: 655,126,773
Trivia: AngryJoe's most popular video is his review of 2014's sci-fi shooter *Destiny*.
(Info correct as of 30 Mar 2017)

Best-selling third-person shooter series

Microsoft's *Gears of War* series had sold 26.97 million units as of 30 Mar 2017, according to VGChartz.

The series began in 2006 and most recently gave us 2016's well-received *Gears of War 4*. However, with 6.75 million sales, 2008's *Gears of War 2* is the **best-selling third-person shooter videogame**.

Most critically acclaimed first-person shooter

Retro Studios' GameCube FPS *Metroid Prime* (2002) held a GameRankings score of 96.33% from 87 reviews, as of 27 Feb 2017.

Mass Effect 2 (2010) on X360 was the **most critically acclaimed RPG**, with 95.77% from 75 reviews.

Fastest completion of *Gears of War 4*

Describing himself as an old school gamer, the UK's "Swingflip" conquered *Gears of War 4*, in "casual" mode, in 3 hr 22 min 29 sec. This run, on 23 Dec 2016, was verified by Speedrun.com.

First videogame tournament

The Intergalactic *Spacewar!* Olympics was held on 19 Oct 1972 at Stanford University's Artificial Intelligence Laboratory in California, USA. Around 24 players are reported to have competed in the 1962 space combat game.

Longest end credits

The end credits of sci-fi platformer *Mighty No.9* (2016) roll for 3 hr 47 min 50 sec – an hour-and-a-half longer than *The Force Awakens* movie. The game was crowdfunded via Kickstarter, and its 67,226 backers are all listed in the credits.

First VR game to top the Steam chart

The sci-fi blaster *Raw Data* became virtual reality's first official "best-seller" when it topped Steam's chart during its "Early Access" period on 14 Jul 2016. Developed by Survios for the SteamVR-powered HTC Vive, the game features the "helper bot" Automo (left). On 15 Sep 2016, the developer told fastcompany.com that *Raw Data* was the first VR title to gross $1 million (£757,547) in a month and that at least 20% of HTC Vive owners had bought it.

Lowest completion rate for a PlayStation game

The PS4 version of MixedBag's retro-styled shooter *Futuridium EP Deluxe* (2014) is the toughest game unleashed on PlayStations, according to PSNProfiles. As of 30 Mar 2017, just 0.6% of 30,175 players had finished it – and no one had earned its gold "You are the best!" trophy, which requires a complete haul of 150 medals.

MINI-BYTES

Disruptor Beam's *Star Trek Timelines* (2016) includes a replica of a game from the franchise's *The Next Generation* TV series. The episode "The Game" revolves around an addictive videogame that turns the *Enterprise*'s crew into pawns. It appears in *Timelines'* iOS and Android versions as a very well-hidden Easter egg.

£250
MASS EFFECT
Price of the *Andromeda* collector's edition.

AUTOMO
DSA-1138

MERCHANDISE

The ever-rising popularity of merchandise has seen gaming burst out of the screen like never before. You can barely move in the aisles without bumping into plush toys, action figures, T-shirts, books, keyrings and posters related to your favourite games. But when you consider that *Angry Birds*-licensed merch made up 40 per cent of maker Rovio's $200 million (£155 million) revenue at its peak, it's easy to see why.

PAC-MAN

A big hit when he debuted in arcades in 1980, PAC-Man became the **first gaming character with merchandise**. By 5 Apr 1982, there were close to 200 products in the yellow-head's range, including jeans, pillowcases and toys. But that wasn't all...

TV
A television series was produced by Hanna-Barbera for the ABC network in the USA between 1982 and 1983.

Music
"PAC-Man Fever" was the **first hit single inspired by a videogame**. Written by the musical duo Buckner & Garcia, it reached No.9 in the *Billboard* Hot 100 in Mar 1982.

Board game
Players controlled one of four PAC-Man colours as they sought to gobble as many of the 60 on-board marbles as possible while avoiding the ghosts.

FROGGER

Konami's 1981 arcade smash *Frogger* became the **first videogame turned into a board game** when a table-top variation appeared in the same year. In the spin-off, players had to navigate three frogs to the opposite side of the board using the numbers shown on the six-sided dice. It was one of a number of videogame-inspired board games created by MB Games. Others included *PAC-Man* (see above), *Donkey Kong*, *Berzerk*, *Super Mario Bros.*, *The Legend of Zelda* and *Street Fighter II*.

MINECRAFT

Not just a record-breaking videogame (see pp.88–89), Mojang's sandbox legend has inspired an enormously successful spin-off book series, too. The series launched in 2013 with four handbooks and was followed up with the hexagonal reference guide *Blockopedia* in late 2014. By Feb 2016, the books' publisher Egmont announced that the ongoing series had shifted more than 2.5 million copies in the UK alone.

ANGRY BIRDS

Angry Birds has the **most merchandise licensees** with at least 400 across the world, including the toy maker Hasbro, LEGO® and party-goods maker Amscan. In Jun 2016, the games' developer Rovio Entertainment partnered with more than 20 book, comic, magazine and sticker publishers including Panini and Penguin.

On 11 Nov 2011, Rovio opened a shop in Helsinki, Finland, to sell official *Angry Birds* merchandise. The puzzlers were only the second gaming series to get their own dedicated retail outlet. The **first game franchise store** was Pokémon, whose original The Pokémon Center opened its doors in Tokyo, Japan, in 1998.

ANGRY BIRDS

XMAS CHEER

In 2014, UK company Numskull took advantage of enduring trends for ironic Christmas jumpers by launching official festive sweaters based on hit game franchises. The merchandise brand has since produced new designs and acquired new licences for each subsequent year. The 2017 range includes characters such as *Fallout*'s Vault Boy (right) and *Halo*'s Master Chief (far right), as well as encompassing such games as *The Elder Scrolls V: Skyrim* and *Candy Crush*. According to the company, the togs' annual sales have been on par with those of a videogame sitting in the top 10 chart.

SPACE INVADERS

Back in the 1980s, US food manufacturer Heinz (famous for soups and ketchup) produced a range of pasta shapes based on Taito's revolutionary 1978 shoot-'em-up *Space Invaders*. The tinned product was called Invaders.

TETRIS

Although it wasn't a licensed *Tetris* product, Marc Kerger's version of the classic puzzler, available to play on a T-shirt, was the **first playable videogame on an item of clothing**. The programmer-turned-fashion-designer used an Arduino Uno microcontroller board, 128 LEDs and two Adafruit Matrix controllers. The game was controlled by pressing soft buttons attached to the T-shirt. He showcased the garment in a video posted on YouTube on 15 Jun 2014.

LEGENDS

Some games define their own genres. Others simply transcend the very nature of gaming to become household names in their own right. From *Mario* to *Minecraft*, GWR salutes those that are fully deserving of "Legendary" status.

Highest score on *Donkey Kong*

For more than 35 years, diehard arcade fiends have battled to rule the scoreboard in Nintendo's 1981 classic – a war that was immortalized in the 2007 movie *The King of Kong*. On 5 May 2016, the USA's Wes Copeland (right, as Mario or "Jumpman", with his real-life girlfriend) achieved the astounding points haul of 1,218,000. It not only topped his earlier record, set on 19 Apr 2016, but also beat the scores of his long-time rival Robbie Lakeman (USA). Experts speculate that Copeland's performance could actually include every known point in the game.

"If I sat down and played every day for the next five years, I still don't think I'd be able to beat this score."

Wes Copeland on his record-breaking points tally

THE YEAR OF POKÉMON GO

It came. It conquered. GWR celebrates the 2016 mobile AR game that let you catch pocket monsters in real-world locations.

No game in history enjoyed a launch year quite like 2016's *Pokémon GO*. Both culturally and commercially, the augmented-reality game's impact sent shockwaves spiralling around the globe that could be felt everywhere, from Albania to Zambia.

Despite its staggered release throughout Jul 2016, the mobile title still smashed multiple records for downloads and revenue grossed in its first month (see pp.80–81). Meanwhile, it was impossible to read the news without seeing some story of a city rush for a rare critter, or players getting horribly lost while on their monster-hunting travels.

In tribute to Niantic's planet-conquering success, we look back on a selection of crazy highlights taken from the weeks following the game's Jul 2016 launch...

Kiwi quits job, embarks on full-time monster quest

Not long after the game's release, Tom Currie quit his bar-tending day job in Auckland, New Zealand, to hunt Pokémon full-time. By Sep 2016, Tom had reportedly travelled the entire length of his native homeland, clocking up 530 km (329 mi) in walking. He also caught two flights and was wined and dined by millionaire fans. "The most intensely full-on two months of my life," he told Stuff.co.nz.

Thousands flock to walk in Oz

When gamers organized the nation's first *Pokémon GO* walk in Sydney, Australia, on 10 Jul, more than 2,000 people showed up. Participants subsequently spent hours hunting and battling with creatures around the city's landmarks. One of the organizers said that his legs had seized up through too much walking.

Reporter rumbled

US State Department spokesman John Kirby (right) halted a political briefing to shame a reporter immersed in Niantic's hit. "You're playing the *Pokémon* thing right there aren't you?" the politician quipped during the July CNN broadcast. The reporter quickly hit back with "I'm just keeping an eye on it." Kirby had been discussing a global campaign to combat terrorism.

GO-ing underground

In Wiltshire, UK, four teens found themselves lost inside a cave 100 ft (30.4 m) underground while seeking digital creatures. The BBC reported that the "glum and embarrassed" quartet had to be rescued by the local fire brigade.

Pidgey hospital snare

Of the many strange *Pokémon GO* snaps, this one was a genuine viral smash. It showed US gamer Jonathan Theriot catching the avian beast Pidgey inside a hospital delivery room, while his wife lay on her bed. The shot, taken in July, accrued nearly 4 million views on Imgur. To round off the story, the mum gave birth to their daughter a few hours later. Thankfully, the couple named the baby Ireland rather than Pidgey!

Home is where the monsters lurk

In July, GamesRadar interviewed Boon Sheridan, whose converted church home in Massachusetts, USA (above), had been designated as a Pokémon gym by the game's location database (a gym is where *GO* players do battle). "Everyone was very respectful of the space," he insisted. "No one crossed the fence, opened the gate, crossed the boundary."

Lapras panic in Tokyo

When Lapras (right), a rare sea-creature Pokémon, was spotted in Tokyo's Odaiba waterfront district, Japan, in September, it sparked such huge crowds that cops had to exert control. Online videos of the incident showed hordes of gamers flocking across busy roads and causing major traffic jams, while police sirens wailed over the top.

Mayor closes bridge

Pokémon GO certainly has its fair share of influential fans. Soon after the game's release, the Mayor of Düsseldorf in Germany closed a city bridge because of the two "Pokéstops" that were located at either end. The Mayor's action enabled players to seek out free game items without being honked at by grumpy drivers.

Pikachu with extra cheese, please

In August, the Down N' Out burger joint in Sydney, Australia, celebrated the global critter pandemic by serving up some unique Pokémon burgers. "They seem rather sad, as if they have already accepted their inevitable demise," Kotaku observed of these culinary delights. The burgers (right) had taken chefs a whole month to design.

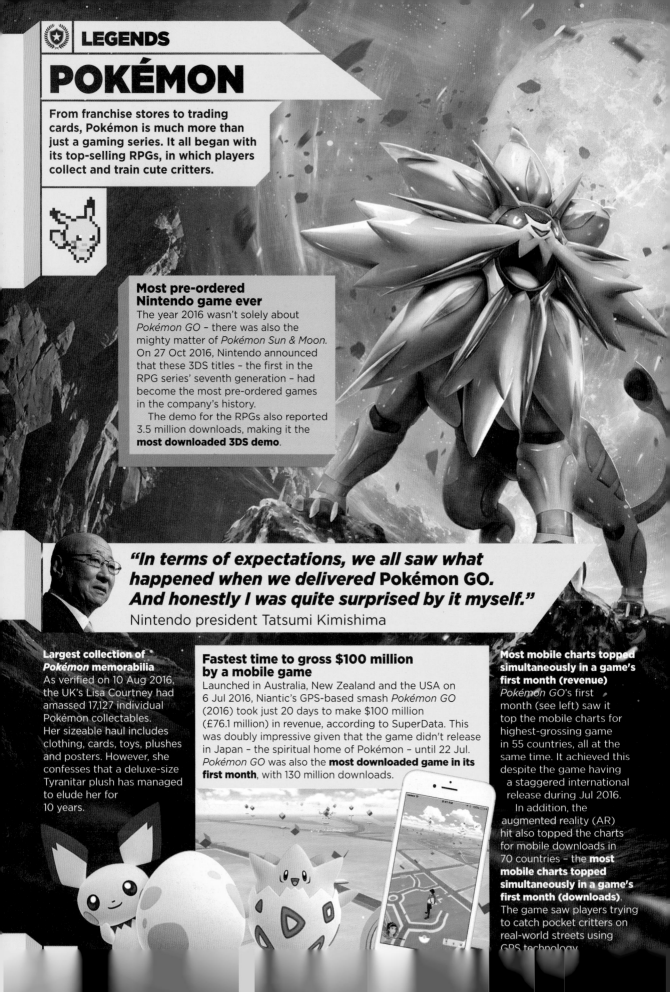

POKÉMON

From franchise stores to trading cards, Pokémon is much more than just a gaming series. It all began with its top-selling RPGs, in which players collect and train cute critters.

Most pre-ordered Nintendo game ever

The year 2016 wasn't solely about *Pokémon GO* – there was also the mighty matter of *Pokémon Sun & Moon*. On 27 Oct 2016, Nintendo announced that these 3DS titles – the first in the RPG series' seventh generation – had become the most pre-ordered games in the company's history.

The demo for the RPGs also reported 3.5 million downloads, making it the **most downloaded 3DS demo**.

> *"In terms of expectations, we all saw what happened when we delivered Pokémon GO. And honestly I was quite surprised by it myself."*
>
> Nintendo president Tatsumi Kimishima

Largest collection of *Pokémon* memorabilia

As verified on 10 Aug 2016, the UK's Lisa Courtney had amassed 17,127 individual Pokémon collectables. Her sizeable haul includes clothing, cards, toys, plushes and posters. However, she confesses that a deluxe-size Tyranitar plush has managed to elude her for 10 years.

Fastest time to gross $100 million by a mobile game

Launched in Australia, New Zealand and the USA on 6 Jul 2016, Niantic's GPS-based smash *Pokémon GO* (2016) took just 20 days to make $100 million (£76.1 million) in revenue, according to SuperData. This was doubly impressive given that the game didn't release in Japan – the spiritual home of Pokémon – until 22 Jul. *Pokémon GO* was also the **most downloaded game in its first month**, with 130 million downloads.

Most mobile charts topped simultaneously in a game's first month (revenue)

Pokémon GO's first month (see left) saw it top the mobile charts for highest-grossing game in 55 countries, all at the same time. It achieved this despite the game having a staggered international release during Jul 2016.

In addition, the augmented reality (AR) hit also topped the charts for mobile downloads in 70 countries – the **most mobile charts topped simultaneously in a game's first month (downloads)**. The game saw players trying to catch pocket critters on real-world streets using GPS technology.

First videogame franchise store
After being introduced to the world in 1996, the Pokémon franchise grew in popularity to such an extent that, in 1998, a dedicated store was opened in Tokyo, Japan. The Pokémon Center, similar to the Disney Store, sold merchandise that included limited-edition Game Boys and plush toys alongside backpacks and clothing.

First game series with its own science exhibition
The Pokémon Research Institute science exhibition opened in Tokyo, Japan, in Jul 2015, giving visitors the unique opportunity to "study" and "identify" different types of pocket monsters. These games were designed to help students hone skills in observing the real natural world.

Least popular Pokémon
When 562,386 trainers and fans were polled in the *Pokémon* General Election, held in Japan in May–Jun 2016, Simisear (above) was recognized as the least favourite of the then-720 critters. The red fire-monkey received the fewest votes.
Greninja (below) won 36,235 votes, making the bipedal frog-like creature the **most popular Pokémon**. He pipped Arceus, Mew and Pikachu to the gong.

Most viewed *Pokémon* channel on Twitch
A gaming social experiment, "TwitchPlaysPokémon" had 72,568,139 views as of 17 Mar 2017. The channel sees members tackling Pokémon games as a group, issuing commands through a chat room. To date, they had finished 24 games. The toughest was a bootleg version of *Pokémon Crystal*, which took them 230 days.

Most expensive Pokémon trading card (at auction)
On 18 Nov 2016, a mint-condition "Pikachu Illustrator" Trainer Promo Hologram trading card was sold at Heritage Auctions in California, USA, for $54,970 (£44,175). It was designed by the Pokémon artist Atsuko Nishida (JPN).

1998 P.M. JAPANESE PROMO
PIKACHU - HOLO
ILLUSTRATOR
MINT 9
26183731

ILLUSTRATOR
ポケモンイラストレーター

Best-selling RPG series
As of 17 Mar 2017, the Pokémon series had sold 264.22 million games worldwide, according to VGChartz.
The **best-selling Pokémon game** is its debut, *Pokémon Red & Blue* (originally *Red & Green* in Japan), released for the Game Boy in 1996. The RPG has sold 31.37 million units – over 8 million more than the 1998 sequel *Gold & Silver*.

MINI-BYTES
It took a year for players on Twitch's "TwitchPlaysPokémon" channel to catch all of *Pokémon Red*'s 151 creatures.

In a video interview with IGN, *Pokémon Sun & Moon* director Junichi Masuda named Psyduck as his all-time fave *Pokémon*. "I think that ducks are really cool, and I had Psyduck on my business card for a while, so I really like that design," he said.

Most viewed *Pokémon GO* fan video
"POKEMON GO SONG!!! by MISHA (FOR KIDS) [ORIGINAL]" by Misha/Mishovy šílenosti (aka Michal Florian, CZE) boasted 51,670,425 views on YouTube as of 17 Mar 2017. Despite becoming a viral sensation it clearly divided viewers, with 1,039,284 dislikes and 641,694 likes.

POKEMON
GO
SONG

Largest balloon costume
As verified on 27 Jan 2017, the UK's Tom Kent (left) created a Pikachu costume that measured 262 cm (8 ft 7 in) high and 159 cm (5 ft 2 in) wide. It was made from around 350 balloons. A magician by trade, Tom often creates huge air-filled suits for cosplay at comic conventions.

SUPER MARIO BROS.

Few heroes are as recognizable as Nintendo's poster-boy. First seen in 1981's *Donkey Kong* as "Jumpman", Mario went on to front a platform franchise that defined the genre – and set a whole new standard for games.

Largest Mario mural
Russian artists Art-Facade painted a 165-ft-tall (50.3-m) Super Mario mural on a Moscow building. The piece aimed to raise spirits and celebrate Mario's 30th anniversary in Sep 2015.

Most ubiquitous game character
Mario had appeared in 211 distinct titles as of 7 Apr 2017, excluding remakes and re-releases. In 2017, *Poochy & Yoshi's Woolly World* and *Mario Sports Superstars* added to his total, and the forthcoming *Super Mario Odyssey* (above) will extend his lead.

Games in which Mario has appeared have sold a total of 565.1 million copies, according to VGChartz, making him the overall **best-selling game character.**

Rarest *Super Mario* game
In 1991, Nintendo toured US colleges with *Nintendo Campus Challenge*, featuring mini-games of *Super Mario Bros. 3*, *Dr. Mario* and *Pin Bot*. After the tournament, all 1991 edition cartridges were destroyed save one. This was kept by a Nintendo employee and sold to US collector Rob Walters at a 2006 garage sale. In 2009, the game was resold on eBay for $20,100 (£12,350).

The **highest score on *Campus Challenge*** (using a reproduction) is 18,128,000, achieved by Paul J Tesi (USA) and verified by Twin Galaxies on 20 Dec 2016.

Most downloads for an iOS mobile game in one month
According to SuperData, Mario's **first mobile game**, *Super Mario Run*, was downloaded 90 million times in the month after its release on 15 Dec 2016 – despite some reports giving different figures. Forty million downloads were in the first four days.

2.8%

INCREASE
in Nintendo stocks' value after *Super Mario Run* was given a release date.

Most games completed simultaneously with a single controller

Using tools assistance so a controller could work off the same input for four games, "agwawaf" completed *Super Mario Bros.*, *Super Mario Bros. 3* and the US and Japanese versions of *Super Mario Bros. 2* simultaneously with a single controller. The run, using glitches and warps, lasted just 10 min 39.75 sec. A video of it was uploaded to YouTube on 4 Apr 2011.

Most expensive amiibo figure

A Princess Peach figure sold for $25,100 (£16,091) in an eBay auction on 9 Dec 2014. A manufacturing fault meant that the still-sealed princess's legs were missing, which secured her rarity value.

Largest joypad

As verified in Aug 2011, this functional NES pad is 366 cm x 159 cm x 51 cm (12 ft x 5 ft 2.5 in x 1 ft 8 in). Creators Ben Allen, Stephen van't Hof and Michel Verhulst, of the Netherlands' Delft University of Technology, used it to play *SMB*!

Largest collection of Super Mario memorabilia

Japanese collector Mitsugu Kikai has amassed a peachy pile of 5,441 items of Mario memorabilia. The Bowser-wowing stash was counted in Tokyo on 15 Jul 2010.

MINI-BYTES

After 20 years, speed-runners finally beat *Mario 64*'s underwater moat door in Sep 2016. The single-frame glitch allows Mario through the door, so that the game can be finished faster.

"Mario was what introduced millions of people to videogames and interactive entertainment, and I think that Mario will continue to serve that role."
Nintendo's Shigeru Miyamoto on the eve of *Super Mario Run*'s release

Fastest tool-assisted speed-run ever

At the SGDQ event in the USA on 9 Jul 2016, an NES R.O.B. robot (modified by "dwangoAC") used a glitch to finish *SMB3* in 2 sec. It leapt straight to the end screen, evading all action.

Most critically acclaimed videogame

Set in the not-so-dark recesses of space, the Wii's *Super Mario Galaxy* held a GameRankings score of 97.64% as of 28 Apr 2017. This rating is doubly impressive, having been aggregated from 78 reviews – an unusually large number. "Considerably better than *Super Mario Sunshine*," said Nintendo Life, which awarded the game 10 out of 10.

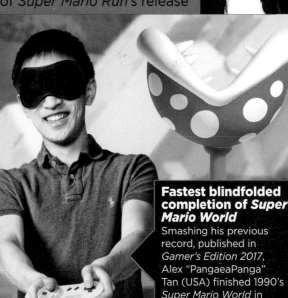

Fastest blindfolded completion of Super Mario World

Smashing his previous record, published in *Gamer's Edition 2017*, Alex "PangaeaPanga" Tan (USA) finished 1990's *Super Mario World* in 15 min 59 sec on 8 Aug 2016 while blindfolded.

"I actually died in the second level in the run," he said, "and almost wanted to start again!"

SUPER MARIO MAKER

Nintendo's 2015 title gives players tools to create their own Mario stages and share them with a sprawling player base. Some crazy creations have become legends in their own right.

First full remake of a Mario game in *SMM*

In late 2016, Dave Pickett (USA) reimagined Mario's 3D platform debut, *Super Mario 64* (1996), in 2D. The *Mario Maker* master explained how the feat was achieved in a video series, uploaded to his YouTube channel "BRICK 101". Tech site Digital Trends hailed the port as "simply perfect".

Most liked user-made *Super Mario Maker* stage

When *Mario Maker* users share their levels, others are invited to rate their designs by awarding stars. As of 3 Apr 2017, the user-built stage "Mission: Impossible" by US gamer "MKB" was the most popular. The course had amassed a total of 227,483 stars – or "likes" – from fellow players.

Most difficult level in *Super Mario Maker*

Snatching the title from another of his nightmarish creations, "P-Break", "Pit of Panga: U-Break" by "PangaeaPanga", aka Alex Tan (USA, right), had been completed by rival players a miserly 279 times from 4,088,347 tries, as of 3 Apr 2017. That's a completion rate of just 0.006824% and the lowest success score of any *Mario Maker* stage with at least 500,000 attempts to its name.

Largest *SMM* hackathon

"Hackathons" are sprint events in which developers get together to make apps and games. On 28–29 Jul 2015, Nintendo hosted a special *Mario Maker* "hackathon" at Facebook's HQ in California, USA. It saw more than 100 employees create *SMM* levels ahead of the game's launch.

PRO-FILE: YOUTUBER

ALEX "PANGAEAPANGA" TAN (USA)

Subscribers: 52,731

Views: 11,359,852

Trivia: Holds a *Super Mario World* blindfolded speed-run record (see p.83).

(Info correct as of 3 Apr 2017)

Most viewed *SMM* video

"Lets Play SUPER MARIO MAKER! Derpy Mushrooms + Real Life Undo Button? w/ AMIIBO Unboxing (FGTEEV)" by "FGTeeV" (USA), aka The Family Gaming Team, had been viewed 14,583,838 times as of 27 Mar 2017. Posted on 11 Sep 2015, the game's North American and European release date, the video sees the family guys unpacking the Wii U level-creator and giving it a play-test.

MINI-BYTES

Proving that he's a man of many talents (not just designing great games), Mario creator Shigeru Miyamoto (JPN) performed the *Super Mario Bros.* theme live on US TV with music group The Roots. A keen banjo player, Miyamoto played guitar for the *Tonight Show* broadcast, which aired in Dec 2016.

Most shared *Super Mario Level Maker* level

SMM enables users to share the courses they create via the Miiverse, Nintendo's social network for Wii U and 3DS. As of 27 Mar 2017, "Ugh... I Hate Underwater Levels!", created by the US gamer "λV☆YEAH!", had been shared 400 times via the Miiverse.

Most "world records" in *Super Mario Maker*

In *SMM*, "world records" refers to the number of fastest clear times that a gamer has achieved playing user-made levels. As of 4 Apr 2017, Japan's "タカ" (or "Hawk") held 17,746 of these titles.

Longest time trying to beat a *SMM* stage

To share a course in *SMM*, its creator must first beat it, to prove that it's possible. "ChompChompBraden", aka Braden Moor (USA), began making "Trials of Death" in Jan 2016 but – 660 hr of testing later – still hadn't cracked it as of 2 Apr 2017. His quest was being streamed on Twitch.

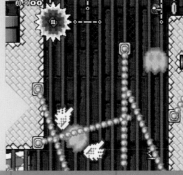

Most viewed fan film based on *Super Mario Maker*

As of 27 Mar 2017, "Mario Maker real life" by "THE rohail" had been viewed 20,449,016 times on YouTube. The spoof live-action video, partially inspired by the trailer, was actually made in Dec 2014 – many months before the game's release on 10 Sep 2015. Some YouTube users pointed out that the video doesn't really resemble the final game, prompting others to point out its production date.

7.2 million

COURSES created by *Super Mario Maker* players in the game's first eight months of release.

MARIO KART

Thrills and spills had long been racing-game hallmarks. But when *Super Mario Kart* roared off the starting grid in 1992, the genre took a wacky turn. Now it was thrills, fish, bottomless pits and bananas...

Fastest race time in "Animal Crossing" in *Mario Kart 8*

US gamer "SuperFX" finished the three "Animal Crossing" laps in 1 min 35.63 sec on 21 Nov 2016. The track – inspired by the game of the same name – was among new ones on DLC released in 2015.

Most critically acclaimed *Mario Kart* game

Mario Kart: Super Circuit (2001) for the GBA boasted a GameRankings score of 91.54%, from 39 reviews, as of 3 Apr 2017. *Mario Kart DS* (2005) ran it a close second.

The **most critically acclaimed kart-racer** overall is the Crash Bandicoot-fronted *Crash Team Racing* (Sony, 1999), with 91.78% from 32 reviews.

Most prolific developer of kart videogames

Nintendo developer Shigeru Miyamoto (JPN) had worked on eight *Super Mario Kart* titles as of 3 Apr 2017. This is one more than his colleague Hideki Konno, who was not involved in 2003's *Double Dash!!* Miyamoto's work on the series stretches from the 1992 debut *Super Mario Kart* to 2014's *Mario Kart 8*.

First kart-racer to include combat

Sega's *Power Drift* (1988) introduced go-karts to the racing genre. However, *Super Mario Kart*, four years later, was the first to incorporate combat in races. Weapons include banana skins.

Longest-running kart series

The original *Super Mario Kart* spearheaded a racing genre revolution when it screeched on to the SNES on 27 Aug 1992. As of the release of the Switch's *Mario Kart 8 Deluxe* on 28 Apr 2017, the shell-slinging series was still going strong 24 years 244 days later. Across that period, the series had produced 12 frenetic titles.

"My favourite videogame? Probably Mario Kart. [I] usually [play] as Toad. He's so cute!"

Scarlett Johansson reveals all to IGN

Longest *Mario Kart* (series) marathon

Australian gamers Josh Alexander, Harry Twyford, Matt Smith and James Hickman played the *Mario Kart* series (on the Nintendo 64, Wii and Wii U) for 35 hr 45 min on 4–5 Jul 2014.

They practised for the attempt – at Brauer College in Warrnambool, Victoria, Australia – for six months. One 10-hr training session made one of the four throw up and the others fall asleep!

Longest-running racing game tournament

While *TrackMania* and *Forza* have spawned competitive racing scenes, no tournament has run longer than the *Super Mario Kart* Championships. Staged in France annually, it had endured for 14 years as of the 2016 event, held in Strasbourg on 24–28 Aug. A total of 56 racers from nine nations vied for top spot in the Time Trial, Match Race, GP 150 cc and Battle Mode heats.

The **youngest competitor at the Championships** was Lucas Duarte-Leite (FRA) in 2010. Playing against gamers up to 28 years older, Lucas was 9 years 149 days old. Of the 33 entrants, he finished 26th.

MINI-BYTES

A 2017 commercial made it clear that Nintendo knows just where the Switch will be played. "Mario Kart 8 Deluxe - Play anytime, anywhere (Nintendo Switch)" opens with a gamer sitting on the toilet. "It's hard to fault Nintendo for being honest with us," remarked USgamer.

Thanks to Hot Wheels toys, US gamers can create *Mario Kart*-style races at home. Mattel issued 1:64-scale cars for Mario, Luigi, Yoshi, Princess Peach, Bowser and Toad in 2016.

Most *Super Mario Kart* Championships trophies

Victory at 2016's *Super Mario Kart* Championships brought the trophy tally of France's Florent Lecoanet to eight gold and three silver. Only in the first of his 12 appearances (2005) did he fail to finish first or second. Florent is pictured above, far right, with 2015's silver medallist Geoffrey Label and bronze medallist Julien Holmiere.

FFSMK PRESENTS THE 16th EDITION OF

SUPER MARIO KART CHAMPIONSHIPS 2017

From **15** to **19** AUGUST FOR THE 5TH TIME AT LA **SUZE** SUR **SARTHE**

Time Trial ⬡ Match Race ▲ Battle Mode 🔲 Grand Prix 150cc

MUST PRODUCED BY WWW.FFSMK.ORG

25 ANNIVERSARY

Fastest 32-track 200-cc completion of *Mario Kart 8*

When Nintendo added *Mario Kart*'s speediest vehicles, with 200-cc engines, to *MK8*, they created a hotbed of competitive gaming. On 22 Jan 2017, "MBisonFuté" (FRA) sped around all 32 of the game's original tracks (16 were added post-launch) in 1 hr 2 min 53 sec.

50cc
100cc
150cc
Mirror
200cc

CRAZY FAST! Braking is crucial.

OK

MINECRAFT

This sandbox sensation made household names of creator Markus "Notch" Persson and developer Mojang. It made icons of creepers, pigs and the mysterious Steve. And, as its trailer said, "It has no rules to follow..."

Largest Xbox 360 *Minecraft* city

Duncan Parcells (USA) began building Titan City in the Xbox 360 version's new Creative Mode in Oct 2012. Two years later, he posted the result to YouTube. Containing 4.5 million blocks, its details include skyscrapers and a public park.

Largest convention for a single videogame

A blockbusting 12,140 tickets were sold for Minefaire in Oaks, Pennsylvania, USA, on 15–16 Oct 2016.

Staged at the Greater Philadelphia Expo Center, the event hosted the **largest architecture lesson** on 15 Oct. An audience of 341 attended a presentation by Stephen Reid (UK) about historical architecture and building techniques, using a *Minecraft* reproduction of the ancient city of Pompeii.

At the event, the record for **tallest staircase built in *Minecraft* in one minute** (see opposite) was broken three times!

Most views for a dedicated *Minecraft* video channel

Launched on 14 Jul 2012, "DanTDM" (formerly known as "TheDiamondMinecart") by Daniel Middleton (UK, right) had 9,810,971,245 views as of 24 Apr 2017. This also represents the **most views for a YouTube channel dedicated to a single videogame**.

"*Minecraft* is special," Dan said. "Build, go on adventures, load other people's worlds... [It] does everything."

122 MILLION

copies of *Minecraft* sold, according to Mojang as of 27 Feb 2017.

First Game Boy game recreated in *Minecraft*

You can make most things in *Minecraft*, including fully functioning games designed for other systems. YouTuber "MrSquishy" (USA) spent a year-and-a-half building a playable version of the Game Boy's *Pokémon Red*. The intricate project – shown in "Pokemon Red in Vanilla Minecraft [1.11]" on YouTube – was finished on 11 Mar 2017 and used more than 375,000 Command Blocks.

Most downloaded *Minecraft* skin

Skins turn *Minecraft*'s Steve into anything from Iron Man to a penguin. The "Diamond Assassin (Diamond Axe Included!)" skin by "Dinothedinosaur97" gives him a hooded, ninja-style black-and-blue outfit. It had been downloaded a total of 173,450 times from Planetminecraft.com as of 24 Apr 2017.

Most wood collected in three minutes in *Minecraft* (console)

Enkil Fernando Ceron Alvarez (MEX) collected 99 blocks of wood in three minutes on 5 Sep 2015. His record was set at the Legends of Gaming Live event at Alexandra Palace, London, UK. Enkil was the fourth person to break the record at the event.

Most cobblestone collected in three minutes in *Minecraft: Pocket Edition*

At Legends of Gaming Live in London, UK, on 11 Sep 2016, Michael Conk (USA, left) and Riordan Parkes-Mahoney (UK, above) each collected 141 units of cobblestone in the mobile game. The cobblestone texture first appeared in *RubyDung*, an earlier title by Notch.

Tallest staircase built in *Minecraft* in one minute (tablet)

Lestat Wade (USA, right) built a 29-step staircase in 60 sec at Minefaire in Oaks, Pennsylvania, USA, on 15 Oct 2016. For the staircase to qualify for the record, it had to be possible for the player to walk up its steps without jumping.

Largest hand-made human body part in *Minecraft*

Minecraft might not seem the most obvious place to create realistic body parts, given that its blocks are cuboids. But that didn't stop YouTuber Dave Solheim (USA) building a giant human hand from 70,000 individually placed quartz blocks. Solheim referred to a blueprint to build the hand one layer at a time. "Minecraft Hand Flythrough", a look at the 80-hr project, was posted to YouTube on 19 Dec 2016.

Largest LEGO® *Minecraft* set

With 1,600 pieces (678 more than the second-placed "The Mine"), "The Village" was LEGO *Minecraft*'s largest set as of 24 Apr 2017. "The Village" refers to buildings in the Overworld that usually house villagers or zombies.

Largest *Minecraft* maze

No *Minecraft* maze is more daunting than the one built by YouTuber "Heat Born" (USA). The labyrinth measures 300 x 300 blocks, and is 10 blocks high. That's 90,000 blocks in total!

Longest marathon on a virtual reality game system

Georgie Barrat (UK, below), presenter of TV's *The Gadget Show*, played the VR *Minecraft* for 25 hr 24 min in London, UK, on 27 Jan 2017.

However, the **longest *Minecraft* marathon** is 35 hr 35 min 35 sec, achieved by Joseph Kelly (UK) in Cheltenham, Gloucestershire, UK, on 10–11 Oct 2015.

> *"I spent six hours rebuilding the house I grew up in. Hats off to the game – it's genuinely kept me entertained!"*
> Georgie Barrat on her VR marathon record

Largest live music concert in *Minecraft*

At Norway's Hamar Olympic Hall on 23 Mar 2016, British pop duo AlunaGeorge (Aluna Francis, left) headlined a show that was simultaneously recreated in *Minecraft*. The latter featured pre-selected players moving digital avatars in-game, in time to the music. In total, 1,200 spaces were available on the server for audience members and all were instantly taken.

PAC-MAN

Pop culture was changed forever by a cheerful yellow blob and his spooky foes. Munching pac-dots and bonus fruit is the basis for a franchise that's been going strong since 1980.

Longest-running dedicated videogame character

First called Puck Man (right), our hero hit Japanese arcades in May 1980 – over a year before Mario's debut. He had dodged ghosts and gobbled dots for 36 years 116 days when *PAC-Man Championship Edition 2* was released on 15 Sep 2016.

17 GAMES

added to Facebook Messenger in 2016, including *PAC-Man*.

First virtual reality (VR) *PAC-Man* game

For the first time in the history of the franchise, Virtuality's 1996 *PAC-Man VR* let gamers play from the perspective of the hero himself. It ran on an arcade machine, with a stereoscopic visor and joystick, and was networked to other VR machines to allow players to talk and compete for high scores within their 3D environments.

Largest life-size *PAC-Man* maze

Measured on 7 Jan 2015, the amazing maze above covered 580.86 m² (6,252 sq ft) – about the size of a basketball court. It was built in Los Angeles, California, USA, for Bud Light's advertising spot during Super Bowl XLIX. The construction included four power pellets and 256 dots. All were individually programmed to turn off when a player ran over them, as in the game.

Largest human PAC-Man

On 21 May 2015, in front of the Tokyo Tower in Minato, Japan, 351 yellow-clad participants came together to form the open-mouthed shape of the gaming icon.

The event was hosted by Sony to promote the movie *Pixels* and celebrate PAC-Man's 35th birthday. The shape was 10.5 m (34 ft 5 in) in diameter.

Largest re-enactment of *PAC-Man*

In *PAC-Manhattan* – created by New York University students in 2004 – people dressed as PAC-Man and the ghosts chased each other around Manhattan. Each was teamed with a controller who communicated the players' positions by phone. The playing field consisted of city blocks around Washington Square Park, with a total surface area of 171,029 m² (1,840,940 sq ft).

Smallest *PAC-Man* maze

On 11 Dec 2016, researchers from Stanford University in California, USA, created a *PAC-Man*-style maze measuring 500 x 900 micrometers (0.02 x 0.04 in). It used LEDs to guide single-cell microbes and was played using a "LudosScope" smartphone microscope.

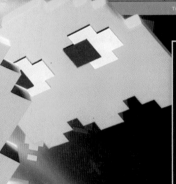

First animated TV series based on a videogame

In 1982, the year that the song "PAC-Man Fever" made No.9 in the USA, a *PAC-Man* cartoon by Hanna-Barbera hit the ABC network on 25 Sep. It ran for two series.

Thirty years later came the **first PAC-Man game based on a TV show**. *PAC-Man and the Ghostly Adventures* was released in 2013 to tie in with a TV series of the same name, which debuted in the USA on 15 Jun that year.

MINI-BYTES

At a *PAC-Man* 35th anniversary celebration, arcade legend Billy Mitchell (see below left) showed the game's creator a trick that makes the ghost-gobbler invincible. Check out "PAC-MAN 35th Anniversary: Billy Mitchell shows Toru Iwatani Lv. 255 Invincible Run" on YouTube.

Fastest perfect completion of *PAC-Man*

David Race (USA) first claimed the fast completion title in 2009 (see badge, right). He broke his own record on 22 May 2013 with a 3-hr 28-min 49-sec run, as verified by Twin Galaxies.

Race followed in the footsteps of Billy Mitchell (USA), who achieved the **first perfect completion of *PAC-Man*** – 3,333,360 points – on 3 Jul 1999.

"I was trying to come up with something to appeal to women and couples... The image of them eating cakes and desserts came to mind, so I used 'eating' as a keyword."

PAC-Man creator Toru Iwatani explains the inspiration for the game

Highest score on *PAC-Mania* (NES)

Terence O'Neill (USA) scored a massive 1,230,910 points on the 1987 NES version of *PAC-Mania*, as verified by Twin Galaxies on 18 May 2006. The score was almost double that of his nearest rival. Namco's *PAC-Mania* plays like the original game but with isometric views, new ghosts and a PAC-Man who can jump!

Most viewed video based on *PAC-Man*

In Apr 2009, French prankster Rémi Gaillard uploaded a video of himself in a PAC-Man costume being chased through a pool hall and supermarket by cohorts dressed as ghosts. As of 22 Mar 2017, it had racked up 62,802,967 views on YouTube.

First videogame for Android phones

PAC-Man was launched for Android phones on 23 Sep 2008. It cost $9.99 (£5.43) but was free to owners of the T-Mobile G1 Android handset. Players controlled PAC-Man by swiping the touchscreen, tilting the handset or using the trackball.

Most points on *Ms. PAC-Man* (turbo speed)

Sam W Miller (USA) earned 947,380 points on the arcade version of *Ms. PAC-Man*, in turbo speed mode, on 16 Nov 2013.

The 1981 game featured the **first playable female in a videogame**. Pacman.wikia says she is "PAC-Man's beautiful wife and the mother of Jr PAC-Man and Baby PAC-Man".

MINI-BYTES

Probably packing a higher calorie count than bonus fruit, PAC-Man doughnuts were available in Korean branches of Dunkin' Donuts in 2016. Kotaku hailed the fried delights as "strangely appropriate [because] PAC-Man's Japanese name is Pakkuman... from the phrase 'paku paku' – this means to open and close one's mouth".

These fabulous food items followed in the footsteps of Krispy Kreme's Pokémon doughnuts, made available in Korea earlier in 2016.

91

TETRIS

Alexey Pajitnov coded the first black-and-white *Tetris* on a Russian Elektronika 60 computer in 1984. Now in its fourth decade of dominance, the block-stacking, tile-matching puzzle has spawned hundreds of variants and imitations.

Largest videogame collection

Joel Hopkins owns a shelf-straining 17,446 games, as counted in Victoria, Australia, on 12 Jan 2016. These include one of the ultra-rare Japanese Mega Drive versions of *Tetris* (see below).

Born and raised in Melbourne, Australia, Joel is a long-time passionate player and collector. His interest began around the age of six, in the late 1970s, starting with the Atari and Commodore 64. Collecting became a passion when he was about 19.

His favourites include *Ghouls 'n Ghosts*, *Gradius*, *Castlevania: Symphony of the Night*, *Gran Turismo 3* and *Gears of War 3*.

Longest prison sentence for playing a videogame

On 10 Sep 2001, Faiz Chopdat (UK) played *Tetris* on his phone while on a flight home, thus "endangering the safety of an aircraft". The cabin crew warned him twice to turn it off. He was arrested on touching down in Manchester, UK, and sentenced to four months in prison in Sep 2002.

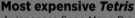

Most expensive *Tetris*

A Japanese Sega Mega Drive version of *Tetris* was offered for $1 million (£610,292) on eBay on 2 Aug 2011. It was posted by Spanish seller "shinsnk", who had bought it for €11,000 ($15,783; £9,633). One of fewer than 10 existing copies of the Mega Drive version, it was also signed by Alexey Pajitnov.

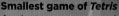

Smallest game of *Tetris*

A microscope was needed for "microTetris", played at the Physics of Complex Systems department at Vrije University in Amsterdam, the Netherlands, in Nov 2002. It used glass beads, each 1,000th of a millimetre across.

"The most striking reaction," said makers Joost van Mameren, Bram van den Broek and Theodoor Pielage, "was from the president of the Harvard Tetris Society, who has conferred the honorable title of Master in their Society to us".

Largest game of *Tetris*

A game of *Tetris* measuring 105.79 m² (1,138.7 sq ft) was played on 15 Sep 2010, on Channel 5 television's *The Gadget Show* in Birmingham, UK. It was created using 200 storage boxes, each with a bright light inside.

Largest official *Tetris* game cabinet

Debuting in Japanese arcades in Dec 2009, Sega's massive *Tetris Giant* measures 1.6 m wide, 1.7 m deep and 2.2 m tall (5 ft 2 in x 5 ft 6 in x 7 ft 2 in).

Most wins of the Classic *Tetris* World Championship

Jonas Neubauer (USA, above right) has won the annual Classic *Tetris* World Championship six times – most recently on 23 Oct 2016, when he beat Jeff Moore (above left). The only other winner of the event – in Portland, Oregon, USA – was Harry Hong, who beat Neubauer in 2014.

Most wins against the Master Tetribot in *Tetris Ultimate* in 24 hours

Serial record-breaker Isaiah TriForce Johnson (USA) registered 614 victories against *Tetris Ultimate*'s AI opponent Master Tetribot in a 24-hr live-stream on 7–8 Sep 2016. They played 1,217 games during this battle at the 6 Columbus hotel in New York, USA. TriForce described his foe in the two-player game as "the fastest and most difficult CPU *Tetris* opponent".

Most critically acclaimed *Tetris* game

Scoring an average of 87.1% from 59 reviews, *Tetris DS* for the Nintendo DS was the highest-rated *Tetris* title as of 21 Mar 2017, according to GameRankings. The 2006 title beat both *Tetris Axis* and *Tetris Splash*. "Gaming perfection reborn," enthused Pocket Gamer UK.

Tetris DS's 2.11 million sales as of 21 Mar 2017 make it the series' fourth highest seller. On top is the 1989 Game Boy version, whose 30.26 million sales earn it the title of **best-selling puzzle game**.

Isaiah TriForce Johnson (left) holds the **fastest time to achieve a perfect score on *Tetris DS***: 8 hr 10 min 22 sec on 19 Aug 2008, as verified by Twin Galaxies.

MINI-BYTES

Playing *Tetris* for about 1.5 hr a week for three months could make areas of the brain more efficient and thicken parts of the cerebral cortex. These were the conclusions of a 2015 video by PBS Digital's *BrainCraft*.

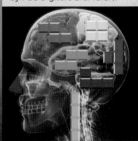

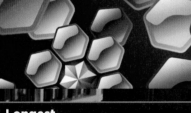

Most completed Xbox game achievement

The "Cluster Buster" in 2005's *Hexic HD* had been won by 259,383 gamers as of 21 Mar 2017, according to the Xbox site TrueAchievements. *Hexic HD* is a tile-matching puzzle designed by Alexey Pajitnov for the Xbox Live Arcade.

Longest-running puzzle videogame

Between Pajitnov's original puzzler on 6 Jun 1984 and Scientific's *Tetris Super Jackpot* on 14 Dec 2016, *Tetris* has endured for 32 years 191 days. There have now been 220 official *Tetris* titles across 65 platforms – the **most ported game**.

Largest architectural videogame display

Professor Frank Lee (USA) created a version of *Tetris* that was played on two façades of the 29-storey Cira Centre in Philadelphia, Pennsylvania, USA, on 5 Apr 2014. Made of LED lights, it measured 11,111.2 m² (119,600 sq ft).

CLASSICS ROUND-UP

From the cult heroes of yesteryear to timeless series such as *Sonic*, some games are built on classic gameplay. Whether it's the retro bat-and-balling of *Pong* or the flying fun of *Angry Birds*, these pages have it covered.

Largest fine art exhibition dedicated to one game character

The *Sonic the Hedgehog 25th Anniversary Collection* was displayed at Castle Fine Art in London, UK, on 1–5 Dec 2016. It was one of the first instances of original game-inspired art being commissioned from professionals and exhibited on a grand stage. Licensed by Sega and curated by Washington Green (whose George Yedinak is shown here with, on the left, *Gamer's* editor Stephen Daultrey), it featured 25 pieces by eight artists. Works included Robert Oxley's *Sonic* (above).

Highest-grossing animated movie based on a videogame

The Angry Birds Movie (USA/Finland) has grossed $349,334,510 (£281.6 million) at the worldwide box office, according to The-Numbers.com. This success makes it the second-highest-grossing film based on a game overall, behind only *Warcraft* (2016, see pp.42–43).

The pig-battling feather-fest premiered on 1 May 2016 and cost $73 million (£58.8 million) to make.

22k
RETWEETS
of the official Sonic verdict on *Mighty No.9*: "Better than nothing."

Most people playing a single game of *Pong*

Two-hundred-and-eighty-six people played *Pong* (1972) at the Royal Institution, London, UK, on 22 Jul 2016. The event, steered by Rob Sedgebeer and Steve McNeil of the live game show *WiFi Wars*, showcased tech that allows simultaneous control by hundreds of people.

Longest-running fan convention for a game character

In 2008, the UK-based Summer of Sonic, paying tribute to Sega's iconic hedgehog, became the first official convention for a single game character. The event has since been staged in 2009–2013 and 2016. The latter – hailed as the "biggest yet" – celebrated Sonic's 25th anniversary.

Highest score ever

On Atari's cancelled 1983 platformer *Garfield*, Tom Duncan scored 23,418, 862,404,272,676,864 (23 quintillion, 418 quadrillion, 862 trillion, 404 billion, 272 million, 676 thousand, 864), as verified by Twin Galaxies on 7 Jul 2008.

Highest score on *Bonk's Adventure*

Bonk's Adventure (1989) was the first in a cult series of 2D platformers, packed with cute but evil dino-creatures. As verified by Twin Galaxies on 22 Apr 2015, Canada's Ryan "starsoldier1" Genno scored a perfect 999,999 points. He celebrated by having the score tattooed on his arm beneath the series' baddie, King Drool.

Shortest development period for a film conversion

Derided as one of the worst games ever, the 1982 tie-in *E.T. the Extra-Terrestrial* was programmed in just five weeks. "By the time Atari and [film director] Steven Spielberg finished negotiations... there were only five weeks left to create the game and still make the Christmas market," coder Howard Scott Warshaw (USA) told *gamesTM*. Despite the mad rush, Atari's game still reportedly sold an initial 1.5 million copies, "mostly to grandmothers" according to one unnamed retailer.

Highest score on *Crossy Road*

To raise money for the Parkinson's UK charity and cement his role as "my son's hero", Ron Weston (UK) scored a record 862 on the iPad version of indie game *Crossy Road* in Jun 2016. He raised £1,310, smashing a £500 target. Two others promptly beat the record, only for Weston to reclaim it with a perfect score of 1,133, as verified by Twin Galaxies on 12 Jan 2017.

MINI-BYTES

Scheduled for release in 2018, a new Sonic movie will see Sega's mascot power on to the big screen in a mix of live action and animation. The film will be the blue blur's first since 1999's VHS/DVD release *Sonic the Hedgehog: The Movie*.

First colour game

As evidenced through research and restoration by ex-Microsoft man Ed Fries (USA) in 2016, the first colour arcade game was Atari's two-player maze challenge *Color Gotcha*. It was issued in Oct 1973, shortly before another colour arcade title, *Wimbledon*.

PUZZLES ROUND-UP

If you've burned out on collecting coins, battling Creepers and beating back the Empire, settle back with a puzzle game. From *INSIDE* to *Candy Crush*, a fantastic variety of games will hone your skills rather than your killing instincts.

Fastest 100% completion of *The Witness*

Quick thinking and memory helped US Twitcher "Jbzdarkid" navigate the mazes of *The Witness* (2016) in just 2 hr 29 min 34 sec. This record attempt at Jonathan Blow's acclaimed indie puzzler was performed on the PC version on 10 Apr 2017.

Emphasising speed rather than all-out problem-solving, gamer "taru" achieved the **fastest any% completion of *The Witness*:** 18 min 2 sec on 30 Mar 2017, as verified by Speedrun.com.

Fastest completion of *Unravel*

Austrian gamer Lukas "Boblerone" Popp – part of the speed-running trio "GamingDaddies" – finished ColdWood Interactive's *Unravel* (2016) in just 1 hr 26 min 17 sec. He spun his record on the PC version on 14 Mar 2016 – just a month after the game's release. The physics-based puzzler's hero is Yarny (below), who slowly unravels as he moves.

First watercolour game

Daedalic's puzzle-adventure *Candle* – released on Steam in 2016 – was drawn, animated and coloured exclusively with pen and watercolour paints. Developer Teku Studios said: "Many games are using digital tools, or a 'bones' system, to animate, but in *Candle* all the animations are made frame by frame with pen and paper, and then painted. Even the conversation blurbs of the characters are painted."

First multiplayer puzzle game for console VR

Keep Talking and Nobody Explodes launched with the PlayStation VR on 13 Oct 2016. Steel Crate's multiplayer puzzle game challenges one player to defuse a deadly suitcase in a VR environment, aided by team-mates who cannot see the bomb themselves. The VR version is a port of the 2015 PC original.

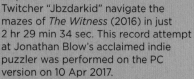

Most critically acclaimed iOS videogame

A big winner at the 2015 gaming BAFTAs, *Monument Valley* was also a hit with critics. As of 4 Apr 2017, the inventive puzzler had scored 90.05% from 20 reviews on GameRankings.

Fastest completion of *INSIDE*

On 2 Feb 2017, "lightdrew" (USA) finished Playdead's thought-provoking game (right) in 1 hr 7 min 55 sec. The indie has inspired lots of speed-runners. "Gotta love chain skip," said lightdrew.

Most critically acclaimed Xbox One game

Atmospheric puzzle-platformer *INSIDE* (2016) held a GameRankings score of 92.81%, from 55 reviews, as of 4 Apr 2017. Danish developers Playdead made 2010's creepy *Limbo*, and *INSIDE* – which puts a boy in an environment full of scientists and odd creatures – is equally eerie.

First BAFTA award for a puzzle game

The Nintendo DS mind-sharpener *Dr. Kawashima's Brain Training* won the Innovation category at the 2006 British Academy Video Games Awards.

At the 2017 ceremony on 6 Apr, the creepy *INSIDE* picked up four gongs – the **most BAFTA awards won by a puzzle game**.

Rarest Steam achievement in *Blocks That Matter*

The "Big Mama is proud of you" achievement for 2D indie puzzler *Blocks That Matter* requires players to complete 20 bonus levels. As of 4 Apr 2017, only 1.3% of gamers had made "Big Mama" proud.

The **rarest Steam achievement in *Quantum Conundrum***, of the puzzle-platformer's 25 non-DLC achievements, is "In less than 12 parsecs". Only 0.6% of PC players have unlocked it, by achieving goal times on all non-DLC maps.

MINI-BYTES

The puzzler *Snipperclips* was a popular launch title for the Switch – and the first puzzle game for the new console. It was originally designed in 2015 as *FriendShapes*: a flash game created by brothers Tom and Adam Vian (aka SFB Games) during a one-day jam.

Most games in a puzzle-adventure series

Eleven games have been made for Level-5's *Professor Layton* series. That includes sequels, spin-offs and crossovers for mobiles and Nintendo handhelds. A 12th title, *Lady Layton: The Millionaire Ariadone's Conspiracy*, releases in 2017. The series has also spawned mangas and novels.

Most played free-to-play game

Full of toffee, timebombs and tornadoes, *Candy Crush Saga* attracted an average 236 million monthly active users in 2016, according to SuperData.

In September, developer King unlocked a 2,000th level. This earned *Candy Crush* another record: **most levels in a match-3 puzzle game**.

GAMES WITHIN GAMES

Here's a fun fact: you don't even need special programs to make your own games any more. You can simply use existing games to build new ones.

From combining environment blocks in *DOOM*'s map-makers to the full-scale game design offered by *LittleBigPlanet* and *Minecraft*, anybody can make a game. And you don't need to worry about programming languages or making new art, either.

However, while most user-made levels have been entirely original, some of the most ambitious projects have seen existing games remade – and reinvented – inside other game engines. These works are often so impressive that they capture the imagination of the entire gaming world.

DOOM (1993)
Remade in: *DOOM* (2016)

Arguably the most interesting feature of Bethesda's *DOOM* reboot is "SnapMap", a tool that allows you to create maps without having to learn the intricacies of game design. Quite brilliantly, players have been using the toolset to build levels that featured in the original 1993 shooter.

The visuals in the variants might be different, but the familiar map layouts highlight beautifully that good game design is so often about creating a fun and engaging playing space – that's opposed to agonizing over whether the modern fashions are being implemented.

ORIGINAL

FINAL FANTASY VII (1997)
Remade in: *LittleBigPlanet 2* (2011)

Final Fantasy super-fan Jamie Colliver (UK) used *LittleBigPlanet 2*'s (Sony) level-creation tools to recreate Square Enix's 1997 RPG *FFVII* as a 3D platformer. The player's work included *FFVII*'s side-missions, cutscenes, soundtrack, boss fights and a version of the original battle system. Given that *FFVII* is one of the largest and most complicated Japanese RPGs ever made, the task took Jamie over two years to complete. He finally finished in Nov 2014. The remake's production was documented across 113 videos, uploaded to Jamie's YouTube channel "LittleBigPlanet Show".

ORIGINAL

THE LEGEND OF ZELDA: OCARINA OF TIME (1998)
Remade in: *Minecraft* (2011)

Given that *Ocarina of Time* is the **most critically acclaimed videogame**, any new variation on the N64 classic brings interest from far and wide. In 2014, "Project Hyrule", a group of *Zelda* aficionados, finished remaking the game's map within *Minecraft*. Seeing *Ocarina of Time*'s world through the context of *Minecraft*'s blocks highlights just how impressive its original artwork is and how well it stands up to being translated into a completely fresh aesthetic. If you play *Minecraft* and have any interest in *Zelda*, then you owe it to yourself to take a stroll through this map.

ORIGINAL

DONKEY KONG (1981)
Remade in: *Minecraft* (2011)

Before Mario there was Donkey Kong, the giant ape with a penchant for throwing barrels and wearing brightly coloured ties. You can now celebrate Nintendo's original mascot by replaying his 1981 arcade debut inside *Minecraft*, thanks to the 2013 creation of user "AxialMatt".

Just as in the classic game, the idea is to avoid obstacles being chucked at you by Kong and eventually make your way towards the Princess being kept prisoner at the top of a platform. *Minecraft*'s trademark blocky visuals work brilliantly alongside such classic gameplay.

ORIGINAL

DOOM (2016)
Remade in: *DOOM* (1993)

In an act of bizarre, time-bending cyclicality, an unnamed player remade some of 2016 *DOOM* within the pixels of its seminal 1993 original. The gamer used "Doom Builder" – a free level editor compatible with games based on the early *DOOM* engine – to transplant some of the reboot's enemies and weapons into the older system. On this occasion, getting the new elements to work in the original shooter did require some understanding of third-party programs. However, the results are an interesting combination of new meets retro.

ORIGINAL

SUPER MARIO LAND (1989)
Remade in: *Super Mario Maker* (2015)

"KHAce" is a YouTuber who possesses a real skill for building old games within the Wii U's *Super Mario Maker*. Arguably the most impressive of the offerings is *Super Mario Land*, a GameBoy outing released in 1989.

The first four worlds of the original are available in "KHAce"'s version, and all can be downloaded and played. However, *Super Mario Maker* doesn't include the green-tinged tile sets used in the Game Boy original, so the NES-era tiles have been used instead. Otherwise, it's a faithful reproduction of a classic title. "KHAce" has also recreated *Kirby's Dream Land* (1992) and *Mega Man 2* (1988).

ORIGINAL

DIABLO (1996)
Remade in: *Diablo III* (2012)

In early 2017, Blizzard developed and released a form of the original *Diablo* (1996) within 2012's *Diablo III*. By tracking down certain characters inside the game, you can transport yourself to a huge dungeon that mimics large swathes of the first game. The screen becomes pixelated, the player character walks rather than runs, character art is akin to that of 1996 *Diablo*, and you are restricted to only eight degrees of movement.

Sadly for fans, the area was available for just one month – as a celebration of the original's 20th anniversary.

ORIGINAL

PEACH'S CASTLE
(*SUPER MARIO 64* – 1996)
Remade in: *Halo 5: Guardians* (2015)

Yes, you read that correctly: Peach, the affable princess of Mario's desires, has had her castle from *Super Mario 64* rebuilt in Microsoft's *Halo 5*. However, as is more fitting to the latter, Goombas and mushrooms have been replaced with guns and futuristic armour.

The unlikely crossover was built by "Bearskopff" and made possible thanks to the shooter's Forge level-editing tools, which allow players to build their own maps to play online. Plenty of other *Halo 5* players have also turned to older games as inspiration for their levels.

ORIGINAL

SuperHeroes!

FICTIONAL SUPERHEROES HAVE BEEN ENTERTAINING COMIC FANS EVER SINCE THE LATE 1930s. IT WAS INEVITABLE THAT THEY WOULD ONE DAY BECOME MAJOR GAME CHARACTERS, TOO. SUPERMAN WAS THE FIRST TO MAKE THAT TRANSITION, WAY BACK IN 1978. SINCE THEN, HEAVYWEIGHT HEROES AND MEGALOMANIAC VILLAINS HAVE THRILLED GAMERS WITH THEIR CRAZY ABILITIES AND OUTLANDISH STORYLINES. NOW, AS SUPERHERO GAMING REACHES ITS 40TH ANNIVERSARY, GWR CELEBRATES WITH A CHAPTER DEDICATED TO THESE KINGPINS OF FICTION. IN THE WORDS OF MARVEL'S THE THING: IT'S CLOBBERIN' TIME...!

171,529

RANKING POINTS WON BY "SONICFOX" FROM INJUSTICE: GODS AMONG US TOURNAMENTS, AS TRACKED BY SHORYUKEN

MOST TOURNAMENT VICTORIES IN INJUSTICE: GODS AMONG US

Injustice: Gods Among Us (2013) is a DC Comics fighter from Warner Bros., developed by the studio behind the *Mortal Kombat* franchise. Often fighting as Batgirl, the USA's Dominique "SonicFox" McLean has won 13 major tournaments, according to the fighting-game site Shoryuken. For our shoot, a bat-clad "SonicFox" (right) squared up to his best pal Patrick Kelly, who was dressed up as the *Injustice* combatant Superman.

McLean is also the **highest-earning fighting games player**, according to e-Sportsearnings. As of 28 Apr 2017, the gamer had won $306,197 (£244,149) across 51 tournaments. Most of his prize money was achieved on 2015's *Mortal Kombat X*.

SUPERHEROES!

A BRIEF HISTORY OF SUPERHERO GAMES

WITH THE FIRST SUPERHERO GAME TURNING 40 YEARS OLD IN 2018, GWR LOOKS BACK AT FOUR DECADES OF PIXELATED, POLYGON-POWERED CRIME-FIGHTING. KAPOW! THWACK! WALLOP!

1978

SUPERMAN ON THE ATARI 2600 IS THE **FIRST SUPERHERO VIDEOGAME**. THE LANDMARK ACTIONER IS RELEASED TO TIE IN WITH THE MOVIE OF THE SAME NAME BUT FEATURES ITS OWN STORYLINE.

1982

PARKER BROTHERS' SPIDER-MAN WEB-SLINGS HIS WAY ON TO THE ATARI 2600 TO BECOME THE **FIRST MARVEL GAME**.

1986

> I WONDER WHERE BEVERLY AND PHILSIE HAVE GONE?

THE 8-BIT ACTION-ADVENTURE HOWARD THE DUCK IS THE **FIRST VIDEOGAME BASED ON A MARVEL FILM**. STRICTLY SPEAKING, THE EPONYMOUS WATERFOWL ISN'T A SUPERHERO BUT A MASTER OF "QUACK-FU".

1989

A SHAPE-SHIFTING DEVIL APPEARS AS A SPIDER-MAN AND BATMAN LIKENESS IN SEGA'S THE REVENGE OF SHINOBI. SEGA LATER SWAPS IN A REAL SPIDEY AFTER MARVEL GRANTS PERMISSION, MAKING IT THE **FIRST CROSSOVER VIDEOGAME**.

ZIPPING ON TO THE GAME BOY, THE FLASH IS THE FIRST DC HERO BESIDES SUPERMAN OR BATMAN TO GET A GAME. SUPERMAN AND BATMAN HAVE COLLECTIVELY STARRED IN 12 GAMES BY THIS POINT.

1991

MAGNETO AND WOLVERINE TAKE ON RYU AND CO. IN CAPCOM'S FIRST CROSSOVER FIGHTER X-MEN VS. STREET FIGHTER. THE TAG-TEAM BATTLER INSPIRES THE MARVEL VS. CAPCOM SERIES.

1994

SUNSOFT'S THE DEATH AND RETURN OF SUPERMAN IS THE **FIRST VIDEOGAME BASED ON A COMIC-BOOK STORYLINE**. MARVEL CHARACTERS FOLLOW SUIT, WITH SPIDER-MAN & VENOM: MAXIMUM CARNAGE RELEASED SOON AFTER.

1996

X-MEN: THE RAVAGES OF APOCALYPSE SEES MARVEL'S MUTANTS HEADLINE THE **FIRST LICENSED SUPERHERO FPS**. ZERO GRAVITY'S GAME IS A TOTAL CONVERSION MOD OF ID SOFTWARE'S QUAKE (1996).

1991

2000

SPIDEY CREATOR STAN LEE MAKES HIS GAMING DEBUT NARRATING NEVERSOFT'S SPIDER-MAN. THE GAME IS BUILT USING THE TONY HAWK'S PRO SKATER ENGINE, ENABLING WEBHEAD'S AGILITY TO SHINE THROUGH.

2002

MARVEL VS. CAPCOM 2 DEBUTS AT THE REBRANDED EVO FIGHTING TOURNAMENT. USA'S JUSTIN WONG WINS IT, PUMMELLING OPPONENTS USING SENTINEL, STORM AND CYCLOPS.

2003

CAPCOM INTRODUCES VIEWTIFUL JOE TO BEAT-'EM-UP FANS. THE SUPER-POWERED MOVIE GEEK SCORES 90%+ IN REVIEWS.

2004

MARVEL'S CATWOMAN GETS HER OWN FIGHTING ADVENTURE, COURTESY OF EA. IT'S BASED ON THE HALLE BERRY FILM OF THE SAME NAME.

WONDER WOMAN AND OTHER DC STALWARTS TAKE ON MK'S OTHERWORLDLY MISCREANTS IN MIDWAY'S CROSSOVER MORTAL KOMBAT VS DC UNIVERSE. ITS CONCEPT LOOSELY INSPIRES THE FIGHTER INJUSTICE: GODS AMONG US FIVE YEARS LATER.

2008

2009

NEW UK STUDIO ROCKSTEADY RELEASES BATMAN: ARKHAM ASYLUM, KICK-STARTING THE BEST-SELLING SUPERHERO GAME FRANCHISE. A VIRTUAL REALITY GAME IS ADDED IN 2016.

2012

STAN LEE CAMEOS AS A PLAYABLE CHARACTER IN MOVIE TIE-IN THE AMAZING SPIDER-MAN. HE'S EVEN GIVEN THE SAME WEB-SPINNING POWERS AS SPIDEY.

VIEWTIFUL JOE MASTERMIND HIDEKI KAMIYA OVERSEES DEVELOPMENT OF WONDERFUL 101 FOR WII U. THE AMBITIOUS SUPERHERO EPIC PUTS PLAYERS IN CONTROL OF A MASSIVE ARMY OF ATHLETIC DO-GOODERS.

2013

2014

A CULTURE FOR SUPERHERO MODS BOOMS WITH MINECRAFT AND GTA. A VIDEO OF SPIDEY GOING TOE-TO-TOE WITH THE HULK IN GTA IV GETS 45 MILLION VIEWS ON YOUTUBE.

2016

NECA LAUNCHES BLOCKY NINJA TURTLES ACTION FIGURES BASED ON THE 1989 COIN-OP TMNT: THE ARCADE GAME. THESE VERY LIMITED COLLECTABLES ARE SOLD AT SAN DIEGO COMIC-CON.

2017

TELLTALE DEVELOPS THE FIVE-PART ADVENTURE MARVEL'S GUARDIANS OF THE GALAXY: THE TELLTALE SERIES. THE STUDIO HAD PREVIOUSLY GIVEN BRUCE WAYNE (AKA BATMAN) ITS INTERACTIVE STORY-TELLING TREATMENT IN 2016.

SUPERHEROES!

SPIDER-MAN

CREATED BY STAN LEE IN 1962, SPIDEY WAS BITTEN BY A RADIOACTIVE SPIDER IN HIS TEENS, GIVING HIM A HOST OF ARACHNID-LIKE ABILITIES. HE CAN CRAWL UP WALLS, SPIN WEBS AND SWING ACROSS MANHATTAN'S EPIC SKYLINE WITH DIZZYING AGILITY. IT'S THESE AMAZING POWERS THAT HAVE MADE SPIDEY A TRUE GAMING HERO.

INFO

Real name: Peter Parker
Games: 37 (50+ inc. cameos)
Foes: Green Goblin, Venom
Abilities: Web-slinging, wall-crawling, sixth sense

THE 38TH **SPIDER-MAN GAME** WAS ANNOUNCED AT E3 2016. IT WILL BE DEVELOPED EXCLUSIVELY FOR THE PS4 BY THE RATCHET & CLANK STUDIO INSOMNIAC GAMES

Most Spider-Men and Spider-Women in a videogame

Taking place across the vast Marvel Multiverse, Gameloft's mobile title *Spider-Man Unlimited* had 134 playable Spider-Men and Spider-Women as of 23 Feb 2017. The game is an endless runner that revolves around the Green Goblin's bid to overthrow Spidey's "familiar" dimension with the help of a portal. New Spidey-people are continually added to the mix, which players can buy or gain by winning events.

MOST PROLIFIC VIDEOGAME SUPERHERO

When it comes to gaming adventures, no comic-book hero has been as busy busting virtual crime as Marvel's Spidey. To date, old web-head has headlined 37 of his own games, with a major 38th title in the works.

However, DC Comics' Batman is hot on Spider-Man's iconic red-and-blue heels. The Dark Knight has fronted 34 titles – making him the **most prolific superhero in DC games**.

In addition to Spidey's title roles, the web-crawler has cameoed in around 20 "non-solo" outings. His unlikeliest appearances include starring as DLC in Sony's 2008 smash *LittleBigPlanet* and as a boss in Sega's ninja actioner *The Revenge of Shinobi* (1989).

FIRST SPIDER-MAN VIDEOGAME

Spider-Man's gaming debut came in 1982, in *Spider-Man* on the Atari 2600. The game requires players to guide Spidey up the side of a skyscraper, avoiding the Green Goblin's bombs. It also has the distinction of being the **first official Marvel game**.

KINGPIN
The Amazing Spider-Man 2

Real name:	William Fisk
Occupation:	Businessman/ mob boss
Lives:	New York, USA
Attributes:	Strength, wealth, size
Adversaries:	Spider-Man, Daredevil

First Spider-Man arcade game

Spider-Man's debut in sweaty arcade halls came in 1991 by way of *Spider-Man: The Video Game*, a scrolling fighter with platform elements. Up to four players could join in the fun, selecting from Spidey, Black Cat, Hawkeye and Namor.

Most prolific Spider-Man voice actor

US actor Josh Keaton (inset) has voiced Spidey in five games, including 2010's *Spider-Man: Shattered Dimensions*. He has also played other characters in three Spider-Man movie-to-game adaptations, with the lead role in those outings falling to movie actor Tobey Maguire.

Fastest *Spider-Man* (2000) completion

Playing the "Easy" setting, the UK's "SamWhich" finished Neversoft's adventure in 27 min 40 sec. This was achieved on the PC on 22 Oct 2016, according to Speedrun.com.

The same player also secured the game's **fastest "Hard" completion**, in 34 min 44 sec on 15 Oct 2016. "Don't think I will be touching this," he wrote.

MOST WATCHED SPIDER-MAN GAMING VIDEO

The curious "Disney Cars Pixar Spiderman Nursery Rhymes & Lightning McQueen USA (Songs for Children with Action)" had been viewed 89,366,695 times on YouTube as of 17 Mar 2017. The video sees Spidey traversing *GTA IV* courtesy of a mod, while the nursery rhyme "Incy Wincy Spider" is sung over the top.

BEATEN IN 1 HR 29 MIN BY MATTMATT10111

FASTEST COMPLETION OF THE AMAZING SPIDER-MAN 2

UK speed-runner and "glitch-hunter" "Mattmatt10111" spun his way through Activision's 2014 movie tie-in in 1 hr 29 min 43 sec, as verified by Speedrun.com. The run was streamed on 6 Sep 2016.

The **fastest completion of *The Amazing Spider-Man* (2012)** was achieved by Dutch gamer "epicdudeguy" on 5 Dec 2016. The Twitcher recorded a time of 2 hr 3 min 52 sec.

First videogame to feature Stan Lee
Spider-Man creator Stan Lee appears as a voice artist in Activision's *Spider-Man*, released in 2000. Lee's narration promises players "more super-villains than you can shake a web at, and of course, non-stop web-slinging, wall-crawling action".

MOST CRITICALLY ACCLAIMED SPIDER-MAN GAME

The PlayStation version of Neversoft's *Spider-Man* (2000) has a GameRankings score of 86.53%, from 34 reviews. The story-driven beat-'em-up hit is loaded with a huge roster of Marvel characters including Venom and Mysterio. "Simply very fun," enthused GameSpot.

MINI-BYTES

Players completing everything in *Tony Hawk's Pro Skater 2* (2000) with a created boarder can unlock Spider-Man as a playable star. The extreme-sports classic was developed by Neversoft, who made the 2000 *Spider-Man* game (see left).

540 NO COMPLY + SPIDEY FLIP
15600 X2

BEST-SELLING SPIDER-MAN GAME

According to VGChartz, Activision's *Spider-Man: The Movie* (2002) had sold 8.4 million copies across all platforms as of 17 Mar 2017. The action-adventure, which is based on Sam Raimi's movie, is also the **best-selling game based on a Marvel character**. It has outsold its popular open-world sequel *Spider-Man 2* (7.7 million), the acclaimed RPG *X-Men Legends* (3.36 million) and *LEGO® Marvel's Avengers* (2.77 million).

First open-world game based on a Marvel character
Based on the movie of the same name, the Treyarch-developed *Spider-Man 2* features a full open-world environment. Released in Jun 2004, the non-linear action romp took inspiration from Rockstar's *Grand Theft Auto III*, released three years earlier. Our hero slings his way around a virtual Manhattan, picking up missions from thwarting robberies to delivering hot pizza.

700 ISSUES
of the *Amazing Spider-Man* comic, which ran from Mar 1963 to Dec 2012. The series was replaced by *The Superior Spider-Man*.

SUPERHEROES!

MARVEL ROUND-UP

THE MARVEL BRAND FIRST APPEARED IN COMICS IN 1961 AND SMASHED INTO GAMES WITH SPIDER-MAN IN 1982. SINCE THEN, MORE OF ITS HEROES HAVE HIT ARCADES AND CONSOLES, INCLUDING THE INDESTRUCTIBLE IRON MAN, THE MISFIT X-MEN AND THE CRUSHING HULK.

INFO

Famous faces: Spidey, the Fantastic Four, Deadpool, Marvel editor Stan Lee
Famous foes: Doctor Doom, Venom, Magneto, Loki

THE MIGHTY **WOLVERINE** HAS HAD FIVE SOLO GAMES, INCLUDING HIS 1991 DEBUT WOLVERINE ON THE NES

LARGEST COLLECTION OF X-MEN MEMORABILIA

Having begun his uncanny collection in 1989, Eric Jaskolka of Iowa, USA, now owns 15,400 items relating to Professor X and his mutant protégés.

The record haul, as of 28 Jun 2012, included trading cards, 6,300 comics, and multiple videogames. Most of the latter are cult retro favourites such as 1994's *Wolverine: Adamantium Rage*, 1995's *X-Men 2: Clone Wars*, 1996's *Mojo World* (all published by Sega) and 2000's *Mutant Wars* (Activision).

MOST PROLIFIC COMIC-BOOK TEAM IN VIDEOGAMES

From *The Uncanny X-Men* (1989) to *Days of Future Past* (2014), no comic-book crew has headlined more games than the X-Men. As of early 2017, they had starred in 27 of their own titles, plus five fronted by Wolverine. Only Batman and Spider-Man have more dedicated games.

Most playable comic-book characters in a licensed fighting game
Excluding variations such as Superior Iron Man, Kabam's mobile fighter *Marvel: Contest of Champions* (2014) features 81 playable characters from the Marvel Comics universe.

First comic-book tie-in for a game
The 1984 Marvel comic *Questprobe #1: featuring The Hulk* was a spin-off from Scott Adams' text adventure of the same name. Subsequent *Questprobe* games, based on Spider-Man and the Fantastic Four's Human Torch and the Thing, also had one-off comics.

IRON MAN

IRON MAN (2008)

Real name:	Anthony Edward "Tony" Stark
Occupation:	Weapons technologist
From:	Long Island, New York
Abilities:	Strength, Flight, weapons, gags
Adversaries:	Controller, Iron Monger

FASTEST COMPLETION OF CAPTAIN AMERICA AND THE AVENGERS (NES)

"Angel_Undead" finished 1991's *Captain America and The Avengers* – one of only six dedicated Captain America games – in 18 min 55 sec on 3 Feb 2017. "Not the run I was aiming for," admitted the Russian NES gamer, "but still pretty good."

MINI-BYTES

Several Marvel heroes have fallen victim not to villains, but to the curse of the cancelled game. Lost titles include *Spider-Man Classic* (the sequel to 2008's *Web of Shadows*) and 2002's *Daredevil: The Man Without Fear* (for which a YouTube film was made by DidYouKnowGaming? in 2016).

Just weeks after Disney cancelled its toys-to-life series *Disney Infinity* in May 2016, designs for a canned Doctor Strange figure were leaked. "[It] looks awesome," mourned the pop-culture site Nerdist, adding that the figure is now "lost forever on the astral plane".

First game set in the Marvel Cinematic Universe
Established with the 2008 movie *Iron Man*, the Marvel Cinematic Universe (MCU) was the studio's way of linking subsequent Marvel films through interweaving narratives. As such, Sega's third-person shooter tie-in *Iron Man* was the first game set in this consistent world. Robert Downey Jr reprised his lead role for the game, but that couldn't save it from savage reviews – GameSpot called it the "worst use of a great license".

FASTEST COMPLETION OF DEADPOOL

Activision's tongue-in-cheek beat-'em-up *Deadpool* (2013) earned a cult following among gamers. On 19 Mar 2016, PC player "Champloo" (USA) completed it, with loads, in 1 hr 12 min 6 sec, as verified by Speedrun.com.

Steve Blum's voicing of Wolverine in this and 14 other games secured him the record for **most videogame performances as a single superhero**, as of 22 Mar 2017.

MOST GAME PERFORMANCES AS THE HULK

US actor Fred Tatasciore (left) had, as of 22 Mar 2017, voiced the grumpy green giant in nine games, from 2005's *The Incredible Hulk: Ultimate Destruction* to 2015's *Disney Infinity 3.0*.

SuperHeroes!

BATMAN

WITH HIS PENCHANT FOR GADGETS AND HIS FLAWLESS FIGHTING SKILLS, GOTHAM'S DARK KNIGHT HAS MADE A CONSISTENTLY BRILLIANT GAME CHARACTER. HE WAS BORN ON THE PAGES OF DETECTIVE COMICS IN 1939, AND MADE HIS GAMING SPLASH ON HOME COMPUTERS IN 1986.

INFO

Real name: Bruce Wayne
Games: 34 (45+ including cameos)
Foes: Joker, Penguin
Abilities: Martial arts, detection, gadgetry

5 HOURS

Length of queues to play *Batman: Arkham VR* at Gamescom 2016.

MOST PLAYABLE ABILITIES IN A BATMOBILE

An indestructible beast in the eternal fight against crime, the Batmobile from 2015's *Arkham Knight* is loaded with 14 abilities and weapons, and 19 upgrades. The car's gadgets include an EMP, a 60-mm cannon and a forensic scanner.

> THE GRITTY **BATMAN: ARKHAM** SERIES IS PUBLISHED BY WARNER BROS. INTERACTIVE ENTERTAINMENT. SINCE 2009, IT'S YIELDED NINE TITLES

MOST GAME PERFORMANCES AS BATMAN

No actor is more synonymous with Batman's gruff tones than Kevin Conroy (inset). As of 13 Feb 2017, the US actor had voiced the DC Comics vigilante – plus his playboy alter-ego Bruce Wayne – in 13 game releases. This includes the *Batman: Arkham* series (above). A 14th game, *Injustice 2*, was due out in May 2017.

Conroy has also voiced the character 142 times across multiple animated series – the **most voice performances as Batman**. His credits include the 2016 adaptation of Alan Moore's cult 1988 graphic novel *Batman: The Killing Joke*.

First Batman videogame

The caped crusader's first appearance in pixels came courtesy of Ocean's isometric adventure *Batman* in 1986. Scored 93% by *Amstrad Action* magazine at the time, the game was remade as the DOS title *Watman* in 2000.

Least popular decision in *Batman: The Telltale Series*

In 2016, Telltale Games released an episodic graphic adventure in which players made decisions on behalf of Bruce Wayne. As of 21 Mar 2017, the least popular choice among PS4 players was staying silent while the butler Alfred indicted himself in past wrongdoings in *Episode 5: City of Light*. Just 2.1% of players let Alfred stew.

First Batman villain introduced in a videogame

A sinister martial artist who hails from Southeast Asia, Sin Tzu is the first official Batman villain to have debuted in a game rather than in a comic. The criminal provided the main rivalry in Ubisoft's 2003 beat-'em-up *Batman: Rise of Sin Tzu*. DC Comics celebrated the event with a novel and special-edition action figures.

MOST GAME PERFORMANCES AS THE JOKER

Disfigured crime lord The Joker has been the bane of superheroes, predominantly Batman, in around 25 games. As of 9 Feb 2017, legendary Star Wars actor Mark Hamill (USA) had voiced the cackling felon in 10 releases, including *Batman: Arkham VR* (2016).

MOST FUNCTIONAL GADGETS ON A COSPLAY SUIT

Designed and built in 2016 by special-FX master Julian Checkley (UK), a Batman cosplay suit based on the one worn in *Batman: Arkham Origins* (2013) features 23 fully functioning gadgets. These include a telescopic bat-sign projector (bottom pic), a gauntlet video screen, a Bluetooth bat-tracker, a grapnel gun and a gauntlet gas dispenser.

Most videogame adaptations of a superhero movie

Tim Burton's landmark 1989 *Batman* movie was adapted into six unique videogames published by three separate companies between 1989 and 1991. This included a side-scrolling beat-'em-up published by Atari for arcade halls. The most unusual adaptation, however, was a top-down *PAC-Man* clone released by Sunsoft for the PC Engine in 1990.

First open-world superhero game

Released in Jul 1998, Acclaim's PlayStation adventure *Batman & Robin* is considered to be the first superhero game with "full" sandbox mechanics. Players drive around an open-world Gotham City in 3D, solving puzzles and jumping out of their vehicle to beat up criminals. The game's key events occur in real time, meaning that they happen irrespective of whether the player has arrived on the scene.

Fastest completion of the *Red Hood* story in *Batman: Arkham Knight*

Described upon its release as "disgustingly short" by Destructoid, the *Red Hood* DLC for Rocksteady's *Batman: Arkham Knight* has provided plenty of competitive spoils for speed-runners. On 24 Jan 2016, *Arkham* series expert "Feanorus" (RUS) finished the mysterious antihero's story in 2 min 46 sec, as listed at Speedrun.com.

MINI-BYTES

While Batman famously protects the fictional Gotham City, the game *Gotham by Gaslight* would have seen him battling crime in 1880s Victorian England instead. The game was based on the 1989 graphic novel of the same name. Sadly, publisher THQ failed to secure the rights and it was cancelled.

CATWOMAN

BATMAN: THE TELLTALE SERIES

Real name:	Selina Kyle
Occupation:	Masked thief
Lives:	Gotham City
Attributes:	Acrobatics, Fighting, theft
Adversaries:	The Penguin

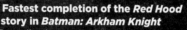

MOST CRITICALLY ACCLAIMED SUPERHERO GAME

Developed by Rocksteady (UK) in 2011, *Batman: Arkham City* on PS3 has scored a massive 95.94% on GameRankings, based on 33 reviews. The brooding brawler was the second release in Warner Bros.' ongoing *Arkham* series, which had sold 31.44 million copies as of 7 Feb 2017, according to VGChartz – the **best-selling superhero game series**.

MOST COUNTRIES FOR A VIDEOGAME ART EXHIBITION

To celebrate Batman's 75th anniversary in 2014, Warner Bros. Games and DC Entertainment created "Cape & Cowl" art exhibitions based on the game *Batman: Arkham Knight*. Seven countries – Mexico, Italy, Sweden, the UK, Germany, the USA and France – exhibited 114 unique art pieces from Jul 2014 to Jun 2015.

SUPERHEROES!

DC ROUND-UP

FOUNDED IN 1934 AS NATIONAL ALLIED PUBLICATIONS, DC COMICS LATER TOOK ITS NAME FROM ITS OWN "DETECTIVE COMICS" SERIES. THE STABLE'S HEROES HAVE GIVEN US MANY KEY MOMENTS, NOT ONLY PRODUCING THE FIRST SUPERHERO GAME BUT ALSO THE "BEST" AND "WORST" ONES!

INFO

Heroes: Superman, Supergirl, Green Lantern, The Flash, Wonder Woman, Batman
Felons: Lex Luthor, Harley Quinn, Darkseid, Brainiac

LONGEST-RUNNING GAME CHARACTER

Between the release of *Superman* on the Atari 2600 in Dec 1978 and the character's addition to *LEGO® Dimensions* on 15 Mar 2016 (below), the Man of Steel's gaming career has stretched for approximately 37 years 75 days – more than PAC-Man and Mario. That impressive run will be extended to more than 38 years when NetherRealm's fighter *Injustice 2* (main picture) thumps its way into stores for an anticipated mid-May 2017 release.

LOWEST-RATED SUPERHERO GAME

Scoring just 22.9% on GameRankings, Titus Software's *Superman: The New Superman Adventures* (1999) for the N64 has achieved cult status. GameSpy voted it "Worst Comic Book Game of All Time". Licence constraints, such as a request not to have Superman fighting real people, contributed to the game's plight.

MOST GAME PERFORMANCES OF A FEMALE SUPERHERO

Ahead of the release of *Injustice 2* in May 2017, Canada's Tara Strong (inset) had voiced the villainess Harley Quinn (aka Harleen Quinzel) in 10 game releases. Strong's performances can be heard in the *Batman: Arkham* series (right) and the 2015 MOBA *Infinite Crisis*, all published by Warner Bros. Interactive Entertainment.

THE INCOMING **INJUSTICE 2** MARKS TARA'S 11TH PERFORMANCE AS THE SINISTER PSYCHIATRIST HARLEY QUINN

MOST LICENSED COMIC CHARACTERS IN A GAME

Scribblenauts Unmasked: A DC Comics Adventure houses 1,718 heroes and villains from the DC universe, from Amazing Man to Zuggernaut.

In the puzzler – published by 5th Cell in 2013 – players jot down their favourite hero in Max's notebook, then summon them to solve puzzles and fight crime.

MINI-BYTES

Shoppers spent an astonishing $4.5 billion (£3.6 billion) buying DC Comics merchandise in 2016, including videogames. Popular collectables included the DC toys-to-life figures for *LEGO Dimensions*, which feature Aquaman and Wonder Woman.

THE FLASH

JUSTICE LEAGUE HEROES: THE FLASH

Real name:	Wally West
Occupation:	Crime-Fighter
From:	Keystone City
Abilities:	Super-speed, time travel
Adversaries:	Gorilla Grodd, Brainiac

First graphic novel with game characters

In 1983, DC Comics published a graphic novel based on Atari's seminal space combat sim *Star Raiders*. A shorter version of the comic was intended to be given away with Atari 2600 copies of the game.

Fastest completion of Justice League Heroes: The Flash

Released for the GBA as a companion to the console action-RPG *Justice League Heroes* in 2006, *JLH: The Flash* puts players into the speedy shoes of DC's nimblest hero as he bids to foil a robot invasion. On 27 Mar 2007, Mike Uyama (USA) blitzed through the actioner in 27 min 26 sec, as verified by Speed Demos Archive.

Fastest completion of Gotham City Impostors "Initiation" level

In this multiplayer FPS from 2012, opposing teams of vigilantes and villains face off in the Batman universe. On 28 Jan 2016, "MLGGaryIndiana" (USA) whizzed through the game's single-player training level in 4 min 57 sec, as verified by Speedrun.com.

FIRST VIDEOGAME MOVIE TIE-IN

Featuring its own original premise, *Superman* for the Atari 2600 was released in Dec 1978 to coincide with the major new *Superman* movie, starring Christopher Reeve in the title role.

The **first videogame adaptation of a movie** (where both film and game share plots) was *Raiders of the Lost Ark*, released in 1982.

Q&A JOHN DUNN

Programmer of Atari's *Superman* (1978) – the first licensed superhero game

How did *Superman* come about?
Warner had acquired Atari and wanted a game to tie in with its first *Superman* movie. Superman was my favourite comic-book hero from childhood so I volunteered. I created the story, the gameplay and the graphics. I even wrote the manual, which was unusual.

What were you most proud of?
That *Superman* pushed the graphics beyond being just a game machine to actually tell a story. The VCS [Atari 2600] graphics hardware was very primitive, essentially a souped-up *Pong* machine.

SUPERHEROES!

LEGO®

BEGINNING WITH *LEGO BATMAN: THE VIDEOGAME* IN 2008, THERE HAVE NOW BEEN SEVEN BLOCKY ADVENTURES FEATURING THE STARS OF MARVEL AND DC COMICS. THESE TITLES BOAST GIANT ROSTERS, ENABLING FANS TO PLAY AS EVERYONE FROM ANT-MAN TO ZATANNA.

INFO

Publisher: Warner Bros.
Developer: TT Games
Key series: *Batman, Marvel's Avengers, Marvel Super Heroes, LEGO Dimensions*

MOST MARVEL CHARACTERS IN A VIDEOGAME

Released in Jan 2016, TT Games' *LEGO Marvel's Avengers* doubles as a veritable who's who of Marvel stars. Excluding alternative costumed versions of the same character, the game (including DLC) boasts an epic 206 heroes, villains and sidekicks. Both the comics and the Marvel Cinematic Universe are covered, with the game's roster ranging from Thor and Hulk to the more obscure Fandral and Moon-Boy.

LARGEST COSPLAY COSTUME

A fully mobile Iron Man Hulkbuster suit, built by Thomas DePetrillo (USA, below), is 9 ft 6 in (2.89 m) tall. Tony Stark's own Hulkbuster features in the *LEGO Marvel's Avengers* game (above).

1031
LEGO PIECES
in the *Jokerland* construction-set toy, released in 2015.

Best-selling superhero game
According to VGChartz, *LEGO Batman: The Videogame* (2008) had sold 13.45 million units as of 17 Mar 2017. The title has outperformed *Batman: Arkham City* (11.1 million) and the 2002 tie-in *Spider-Man: The Movie* (8.4 million).

Most superhero movies condensed into a game
Excluding DLC, *LEGO Marvel's Avengers* spans the events of six Marvel films: *The Avengers, Avengers: Age of Ultron, Captain America, Captain America: The Winter Soldier, Iron Man 3* and *Thor: The Dark World*.

Most performances in a superhero game
Futurama and *Adventure Time* actor John DiMaggio (USA) voiced 15 characters, most of them super-villains, in *LEGO Marvel Super Heroes* (2013). Fictional faces powered by DiMaggio's throaty tones include Colossus, Galactus, Kingpin, Super-Skrull, Thanos, Ultimate Green Goblin and the tabloid mogul J Jonah Jameson.

Fastest completion of *LEGO Batman: The Videogame*
On 24 Jun 2016, *LEGO* speed-runner and Twitcher "Ozotuh" (UK) battled his way through *LEGO Batman: The Videogame* in 1 hr 27 min 2 sec, as verified by Speedrun.com.

Fastest completion of *LEGO Marvel Super Heroes*
Playing on the Xbox One on 21 Nov 2015, "Shadowsmith97" (USA) finished the 2013 adventure in 4 hr 40 min 4 sec.

FASTEST TIME TO BUILD THE BATMOBILE IN LEGO DIMENSIONS

On 4 Mar 2016, Leon Ip (UK) took just 1 min 13 sec to assemble the Batmobile toy for the 2015 toys-to-life hit *LEGO Dimensions*. The young gamer also recorded the **fastest time to assemble the starter pack characters in *LEGO Dimensions***, achieved in 32 sec on 9 Jan 2016.

MINI-BYTES

Following the success of the *LEGO Batman* toys, Warner Bros. released a movie spin-off in Jan 2017 – and it went down spectacularly well with critics. "Will Arnett has somehow become the greatest Batman of all time just by using his voice," cooed ABC Tucson in regards to the film's main star.

MOST PLATINUM TROPHIES

A Platinum trophy is the holy grail of any PlayStation game and can only be obtained by bagging every other trophy in the game. According to PSNProfiles, the USA's "Roughdawg4" had won 1,191 of these prizes as of 9 Mar 2017. His conquests range from *LEGO Marvel's Avengers* (below) and *Resident Evil 5* to *Barbie & Her Sisters: Puppy Rescue*.

12 DAYS
HOW LONG IT TOOK "ROUGHDAWG4" TO COLLECT ALL 35 TROPHIES IN LEGO MARVEL'S AVENGERS. HE COMPLETED THE GAME ON 17 JUN 2016.

ANT-MAN
LEGO Marvel's Avengers

Real name:	Scott Lang
Occupation:	Electronics whizz
From:	Florida, USA
Abilities:	Shrinking, speaking to insects
Adversaries:	Taskmaster, Yellowjacket

SuperHeroes!

MMORPGs

UNLESS YOU'RE BITTEN BY A MUTANT SPIDER. PLAYING MMO GAMES IS PROBABLY THE ONLY WAY YOU'LL GET TO REALIZE YOUR SUPERHERO FANTASIES. CREATE YOUR OWN MULTI-POWERED SAVIOUR – OR EVIL MASTERMIND – THEN DASH OFF INTO A VIRTUAL WORLD INHABITED BY HORDES OF OTHER HUMAN ROLE-PLAYERS.

INFO

Key titles: *City of Heroes* (2004), *City of Villains* (2005), *Champions Online* (2009), *DC Universe Online* (2011), *Marvel Heroes 2016* (2013)

Most "Perk Points" in *Champions Online*

In Cryptic Studios' costumed crime-battler, Perk Points are collected through accomplishments such as performing daredevil feats. As of 15 Mar 2017, the Champion "Silver Kitten", created by "Dardove" (USA), had accrued 35,585 Perk Points. A "Champion" is a player-made hero.

As of the same date, the Champion "Thundrax", created by Canadian player "Thundrax", had been active in the game for 1 year 136 days. That's the **longest play-time with the same Champion**.

MOST VOICE ACTORS IN A SUPERHERO GAME

Daybreak Game Company's *DC Universe Online* (2011) invites players to either fight or commit crime in a virtual comic-book world. The MMO's mighty list of DC Comics stars (who feature as non-player characters) was voiced by 122 actors.

Beyond English, the game was also performed in French, German, Italian and Spanish. It brings the entire cast to 500 actors – the **most voice actors for a superhero game (multiple languages)**.

> STAR WARS' **MARK HAMILL** VOICES THE JOKER IN *DC UNIVERSE ONLINE*. OTHER ACTORS INCLUDE WIL WHEATON AS ROBIN!

FIRST SUPERHERO MMORPG

Cryptic Studios set the massively multiplayer superhero craze rolling with *City of Heroes* on 4 Feb 2004. The now-defunct RPG enabled players to join forces as they battled baddies in the online city of Paragon. Successful quests led to players developing their heroes' superpowers.

MOST COMICS FOR AN MMO

City of Heroes inspired two volumes of spin-off comics between 2004 and 2007, with a total of 32 issues published. The second volume, published by Top Cow, featured tales penned by Mark Waid, who had previously written for DC Comics' *Superman* and *The Flash*, and Marvel's *Captain America* and *Fantastic Four*.

ROCKET RACCOON
MARVEL HEROES 2016

Real name:	Subject: 89P13
Occupation:	Space mercenary/officer
Lives:	In space/Halfworld
Abilities:	Weapons, claws, smell, speed
Adversaries:	Any intergalactic threats

First Marvel MMO game
Although Gazillion's *Marvel Heroes 2016* is the more well-known title, it's not the first MMO set in the Marvel universe. That prestige falls to the browser game *Marvel Super Hero Squad Online*, which was released as an open beta in Apr 2011 but shut down in Jan 2017. The game, also by Gazillion, was based on Hasbro's Super Hero Squad action figures, which depict characters in a stunted, cartoonish form.

Longest time playing
DC Universe Online
As of 8 Mar 2017, the US gamer Patrick, aka "pasufarin", had spent a grand total of 28,201 hr playing *DC Universe Online*, as verified by the MMO's publisher Daybreak Game Company. That amounts to 1,175 days – or more than three years – of super-heroic gameplay action.

MOST OFFICIAL SUPERHERO COSTUMES IN A VIDEOGAME

As of 14 Mar 2017, Gazillion had released 462 outfits for *Marvel Heroes 2016* (2013), each officially adapted from either a comic book or movie. Classy options include Deadpool as "The Kid", She-Hulk as a lawyer and a *noir* Punisher.

MINI-BYTES
The crowdfunded *Valiance Online* (below) by SilverHelm Studios is an indie superhero MMO intended to fill the void left by *City of Heroes*. The game, set towards the end of the 21st century, was poised to enter alpha testing in early 2017.

According to PCGamesN, there are seven "underrated" heroes that players should try in *Marvel Heroes 2016*: Squirrel Girl, Black Panther, Iron Fist, Taskmaster, Nova, Angela and Magik.

LONGEST-RUNNING SUPERHERO MMO (ACTIVE)

As of 14 Mar 2017, Cryptic Studios' *Champions Online* had been running for 7 years 194 days, since 1 Sep 2009. The game is based on the *Champions* table-top RPG, first published in 1981.

The developer's earlier *City of Heroes* ran for 8 years 300 days before closing on 30 Nov 2012: the **longest-running superhero MMO** ever.

12,728,131

CHAMPIONS (or "heroes") created by players in *Champions Online* since the game's 2009 launch, as of 1 Jan 2017.

SUPERHEROES!

FIGHTING GAMES

THE HULK HAS SUPER-STRENGTH AND SPIDER-MAN CAN WEB HIS FOES. BUT WHO WOULD WIN IN A PUNCH-UP? SUPERHERO FIGHTING GAMES PUT OUR CHAMPIONS TO THE ULTIMATE PHYSICAL TEST... AND PUT GAMERS UNDER PRESSURE TO MASTER SPEED, STRENGTH AND STRATEGY.

INFO

Heavyweights: *Injustice: Gods Among Us* (Warner Bros.), *Marvel vs. Capcom* (Capcom)
Hidden gem: *Avengers in Galactic Storm* (Data East)

Fastest completion of *X-Men vs. Street Fighter*
Algeria's "HassenZero" used the "strange" team of Ryu and Juggernaut to beat Capcom's first crossover superhero game. The record-breaking run, on 13 Oct 2016, was 8 min 3 sec, as verified by Speedrun.com.

"HassenZero" also holds the record for the **fastest completion of *Marvel vs. Capcom: Clash of Super Heroes***: 7 min 34 sec.

Least popular character in *Ultimate Marvel vs. Capcom 3*
Effectively a scary, oversized head, the supervillain MODOK is rarely seen in tournaments. According to EventHubs, just 101 pro players (out of 7,632) had used him as of 22 Mar 2017.

LONGEST-RUNNING CROSSOVER FIGHTING SERIES (THIRD PARTY)

Super Smash Bros. and *The King of Fighters* brought together characters from different franchises, but *Marvel vs. Capcom* united heroes from different third-party companies in a powerful franchise. The monumental match-up kicked off with *X-Men vs. Street Fighter* in Sep 1996 and is going strong more than 20 years later: *Marvel vs. Capcom: Infinite*, starring Iron Man (right) among others, will be unleashed in 2017.

Wolverine is the only Marvel character to appear in all of the first six titles in the series. Chun-Li and Ryu from *Street Fighter* also star in all six.

> NOT ONLY IS **CAPTAIN MARVEL** GETTING A MOVIE IN 2019, SHE'S ALSO STARRING IN *MARVEL VS. CAPCOM: INFINITE*!

LEAST POPULAR CHARACTER IN INJUSTICE: GODS AMONG US

Just 95 of 3,815 gamers had deployed Martian Manhunter for competitive bouts in the DC Comics fighter as of 22 Mar 2017, according to EventHubs. Lex Luthor is just ahead of him with 102.

WONDER WOMAN
Injustice 2

Human alias:	Diana Prince
Occupation:	Justice League warrior
From:	Themyscira
Abilities:	Strength, speed, lasso
Adversaries:	Cheetah, Circe, Ares

MOST TOURNAMENT RESULTS FOR AN INJUSTICE: GODS AMONG US CHARACTER

Batman uses his fists, feet and gadgets to winning effect in *Injustice*. According to Shoryuken, the dark knight had recorded 56 results in tracked game tournaments. (A "result" is typically a place in the final 32, 16 or eight, depending on the size of the tournament.) As of 22 Mar 2017, this placed him well ahead of Superman (44).

MOST EVO CHAMPIONSHIP SERIES TITLES WON

Established in 2002, the Evolution Championship Series (EVO) is an annual fighting game tournament held in the USA. Justin Wong (USA, right) has won eight EVO titles; for *Marvel vs. Capcom 2* in 2002–04, 2006, 2008 and 2010, *Street Fighter III: 3rd Strike* (2 vs. 2 teams, with Issei Suzuki) in 2009, and *Ultimate Marvel vs. Capcom 3* in 2014.

FIRST SUPERHERO FIGHTING GAME

The first one-on-one brawler to star licensed superheroes was *The Amazing Spider-Man and Captain America in Dr Doom's Revenge!*, released for home computers in 1989. Players controlled Cappy and Spidey against Rhino, Machete, Electro and, naturally, Doctor Doom.

MINI-BYTES

Injustice has featured only twice at EVO since the popular game's release in 2013. Phillip "KDZ" Atkinson (below) won its title in 2013, followed by Dominique "SonicFox" McLean (both USA) in 2014. Fans can look forward to players contesting its sequel, *Injustice 2*, at the 2017 EVO on 14–16 Jul.

Thirteen supervillains featured in *The Amazing Spider-Man and Captain America in Dr Doom's Revenge!* (Paragon/Empire, 1989), including cult comic stars Eduardo Lobo, Hobgoblin, Batroc the Leaper, Oddball and Grey Gargoyle. One of them, Rattan, was created exclusively for the game.

FEWEST TOURNAMENT RESULTS FOR AN INJUSTICE CHARACTER

The Joker had just two tournament results in *Injustice* as of 22 Mar 2017, according to the fighting-game site Shoryuken. Only "Grr" – ranked 45th in the world – used him successfully, at Summer Jam 8 in Aug 2014.

THE JOKER'S SPECIAL MOVES INVOLVE LAUGHING GAS AND EXPLODING TEETH!

MOST TOURNAMENT RESULTS FOR AN ULTIMATE MARVEL VS. CAPCOM 3 CHARACTER

UMVC3 players had achieved 1,241 results using Doctor Doom as of 22 Mar 2017, based on Shoryuken's statistics. The villain's highest-ranked user was world No.1 Christopher Gonzalez (USA, right).

SUPERHEROES!

ROUND-UP

HEROES COME IN ALL SHAPES, SIZES... AND SHELLS. AWAY FROM THE PAGES OF MARVEL AND DC COMICS, PLENTY OF OTHER HEROES HAVE BATTLED TO PROTECT THEIR WORLD FROM MISCREANTS AND EVIL MASTERMINDS. AND THEIR FIGHTS ARE OFTEN GREAT...

INFO

Battlegrounds: New York (Ninja Turtles), Earth during WWIII (The Wonderful Ones), Planet Popstar (Kirby), Movieland (Viewtiful Joe)

Fastest completion of The Wonderful 101 (normal)
On 19 Feb 2017, Dutch gamer "Ricy0sma" defeated the alien organization known as "The GEATHJERK Federation" in 4 hr 41 min 20 sec, as verified by Speedrun.com. "A small personal best but it's a nice one," he said.

MOST VOICE-ACTING APPEARANCES IN SUPERHERO VIDEOGAMES

Actor Fred Tatasciore (USA) had performed in 53 superhero releases as of 23 Mar 2017. He often voices heavyweight heroes and villains such as the Hulk, Bane, Rhino, Thing, Dr Doom and Doomsday. Fred's credits include *Teenage Mutant Ninja Turtles: Mutants in Manhattan*, *The Wonderful 101*, *Viewtiful Joe 2*, various Spider-Man, X-Men and Batman titles and, to come in 2017, *Injustice 2*.

HIGHEST SCORE ON TEENAGE MUTANT NINJA TURTLES: TURTLES IN TIME

Mike Waters (USA) used a single credit to earn 340 points on Konami's 1991 arcade favourite. The score, at the Galloping Ghost Arcade in Illinois, USA, on 3 Mar 2016, was verified by Twin Galaxies.

1991 Konami
Teenage Mutant Ninja Turtles: Turtles in Time

LARGEST SUPERHERO TEAM IN A VIDEOGAME

The ranks of Platinum's Wii U title *The Wonderful 101* (2013) far outnumber the Fantastic Four, X-Men, Teen Titans and Justice League. The game features 100 heroes, collectively known as The Wonderful Ones.

The "101" in the game's title has been speculated to refer to the 100 heroes, plus the person playing the game. (Additional characters are unlockable.)

The Wonderful Ones' leader is Wonder-Red, aka The Crimson Fist – by day a teacher called Will Wedgewood, by night a fighter with a giant fist. His associates include Wonder-Green, aka Jean-Sébastien Renault, and Wonder-Blue, aka Eliot Hooker.

GREEN'S UNITE GUN **CHRISTINE DAAÉ** IS NAMED AFTER THE HEROINE OF THE PHANTOM OF THE OPERA

WONDER PINK
The Wonderful 101

Real name:	Mariana Kretzulesco
Occupation:	Gymnast, student, superhero
From:	Transylvania, Romania
Attributes:	Unite Whip, Fashion sense
Adversaries:	The Guyzoch, Notoriyeah

First superhero created for a videogame

Melbourne House's *Redhawk*, released for the ZX Spectrum in 1986, featured a muscly superhero summoned by the magic word "Kwah!". Players typed their commands on the keyboard and saw the actions come to life in an animated comic strip.

Longest anime series based on a videogame character

Inspired by Nintendo's cutesy game franchise, *Kirby: Right Back at Ya!*, aka *Hoshi no Kirby,* ran for 100 episodes. Kirby – a pink, sphere-like creature – is a fantastical hero who inhales his enemies to steal their powers. The show ran from 2001 to 2003 in Japan and, in an edited form, the USA. Other prolific animes based on a game character included *Sonic X* (78 episodes) and *Viewtiful Joe* (51).

The **longest anime series based on a videogame**, however, is *Pokémon: The Series*. Launched in Japan on 1 Apr 1997 (and the USA in Sep 1998), this had hit its 20th season and 961st episode by 23 Mar 2017.

FASTEST COMPLETION OF VIEWTIFUL JOE

An eight-hour trek for the average player was slashed to 27 min 23 sec on 7 May 2014 by gamer "Tminator64" (USA). This was achieved by maintaining the hero's Viewtiful Effects Power for as long as possible. That enabled the time-manipulation for which the game was praised to kick in.

First user-generated content creator for an open-world console title

The PS3 game *inFAMOUS 2* (2011) – starring electricity-powered hero Cole MacGrath – features a user-generated content creator inspired by *LittleBigPlanet*. "[We] were like, 'That is a great idea,'" said Brian Fleming of developer Sucker Punch. "I wish we'd thought of that."

MOST CRITICALLY ACCLAIMED SUPERHERO RPG

In Irrational's 2002 cult hit *Freedom Force*, players control a band of heroes as they battle villains such as Nuclear Winter and Mr Mechanical. The game holds an 87.88% score on GameRankings, from 35 reviews, ahead of better-known RPGs such as *X-Men Legends* and *City of Heroes*.

MINI-BYTES

Deep Silver's *Saints Row IV* (2013) marked a change of direction for the huge-selling series. Once a gang-based romp in the mould of *GTA*, its fourth game was a loving spoof of the superhero genre. In it, players became a super-powered US president tasked with saving Earth from aliens!

Q&A | JOE MADUREIRA

Joe is a former Marvel comics writer/artist turned game developer. His comic series *Battle Chasers* is being turned into a game by Airship Syndicate.

How did you get into comic-writing?
I was an intern at Marvel. I was not good then, at all. But they saw promise. They gave me *Deadpool* and *Uncanny X-Men*.

Why did you move into games?
I was always a huge gamer. I've probably had every console ever. The excitement of the games industry was calling to me.

Any tips for getting into the industry?
Just draw, all the time – and love it!

CRONOS

Game: *God of War III* (2010)
Estimated height: 5,500 ft (1,676 m)
At more than a mile tall, this crag-faced monstrosity is the **largest land-based boss**. Our hero Kratos is a formidable presence at over 6 ft (1.82 m) tall – but, scooped up in one of Cronos' mega-mitts, he's reduced to the size of a flea. Kratos only defeats him when he falls inside Cronos' mouth and slashes his way free.

SPECIAL FEATURE

GIANT GAME ENEMIES

Whether they're monsters, super-villains or even real-world creatures, it's clear that gaming adversaries over the years have generally become bigger. Prepare to crane your necks way, *waaaay* back, as we pay tribute to some of the largest "hostiles" ever to stomp foot inside a videogame.

GOROG

Game: *Star Wars: The Force Unleashed II* (2010)
Estimated height: 30–40 ft (9–12 m)
Encountered inside a gladiatorial arena on the planet Tarko-se, this hunchbacked horror has teeth that poke out like crooked javelins, and skin that resembles a zombified rhino. When our hero asks the blind General Kota what the hell this thing is, the general retorts with one of gaming's mightiest understatements: "I have no idea. But it's *big!*"

RED EYE

Game: *Lost Planet 2* (2010)
Estimated length: 1,000 ft (304 m)
While resembling a spiky sandworm, Red Eye is in fact a member of a race of reptilian insects known as Akrid. Its prickly body is populated by dozens of circular red "eyes".

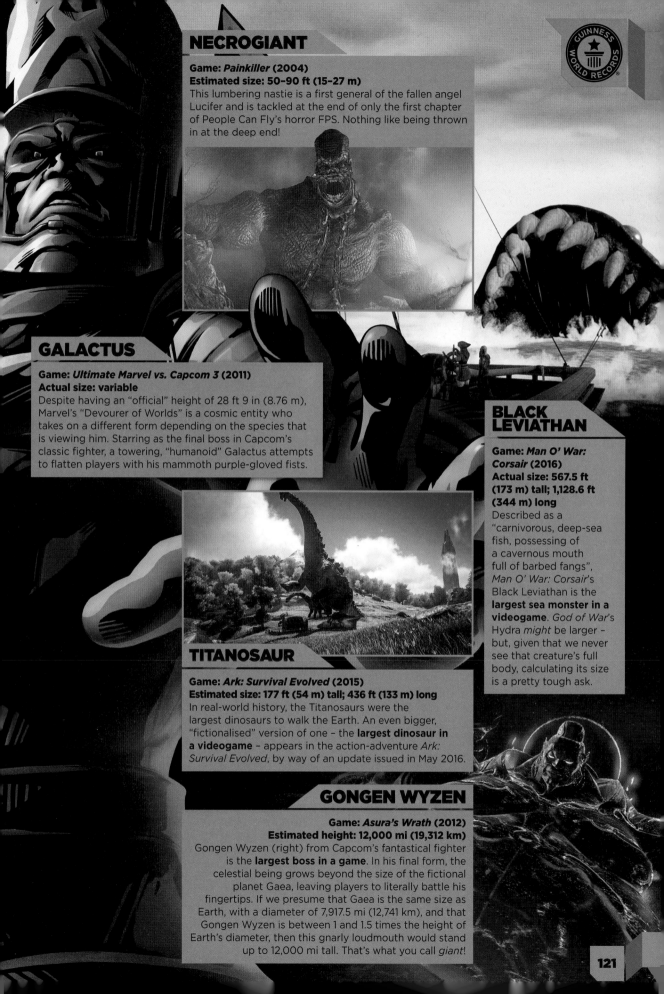

NECROGIANT

Game: *Painkiller* (2004)
Estimated size: 50–90 ft (15–27 m)
This lumbering nastie is a first general of the fallen angel Lucifer and is tackled at the end of only the first chapter of People Can Fly's horror FPS. Nothing like being thrown in at the deep end!

GALACTUS

Game: *Ultimate Marvel vs. Capcom 3* (2011)
Actual size: variable
Despite having an "official" height of 28 ft 9 in (8.76 m), Marvel's "Devourer of Worlds" is a cosmic entity who takes on a different form depending on the species that is viewing him. Starring as the final boss in Capcom's classic fighter, a towering, "humanoid" Galactus attempts to flatten players with his mammoth purple-gloved fists.

TITANOSAUR

Game: *Ark: Survival Evolved* (2015)
Estimated size: 177 ft (54 m) tall; 436 ft (133 m) long
In real-world history, the Titanosaurs were the largest dinosaurs to walk the Earth. An even bigger, "fictionalised" version of one – the **largest dinosaur in a videogame** – appears in the action-adventure *Ark: Survival Evolved*, by way of an update issued in May 2016.

BLACK LEVIATHAN

Game: *Man O' War: Corsair* (2016)
Actual size: 567.5 ft (173 m) tall; 1,128.6 ft (344 m) long
Described as a "carnivorous, deep-sea fish, possessing of a cavernous mouth full of barbed fangs", *Man O' War: Corsair*'s Black Leviathan is the **largest sea monster in a videogame**. *God of War*'s Hydra *might* be larger – but, given that we never see that creature's full body, calculating its size is a pretty tough ask.

GONGEN WYZEN

Game: *Asura's Wrath* (2012)
Estimated height: 12,000 mi (19,312 km)
Gongen Wyzen (right) from Capcom's fantastical fighter is the **largest boss in a game**. In his final form, the celestial being grows beyond the size of the fictional planet Gaea, leaving players to literally battle his fingertips. If we presume that Gaea is the same size as Earth, with a diameter of 7,917.5 mi (12,741 km), and that Gongen Wyzen is between 1 and 1.5 times the height of Earth's diameter, then this gnarly loudmouth would stand up to 12,000 mi tall. That's what you call *giant*!

REAL WORLD

Worlds apart from *Warcraft* and far, far away from Star Wars, planet Earth still has plenty of adventures to offer. From the heroics of *Tomb Raider* to the thrills 'n' spills of *GTA* and the fret-burning of *Guitar Hero*, it's all right here...

> **"Playing it is actually quite an exercise. It's a great alternative to running!"**
> Ilhan Ünal on his giant Game Boy

Largest Game Boy

Belgian Ilhan Ünal's giant version of the usually hand-held Game Boy console – measured in Antwerp on 13 Nov 2016 – is 1.01 m (3 ft 3.7 in) tall, 0.62 m (2 ft 0.4 in) wide and 0.2 m (7.8 in) deep.

The monster machine is fully functional, with everything running off a Raspberry Pi hidden in the oversized external connector socket. Tech student Ilhan said: "This world record proves how much I like doing what I do."

A month after GWR checked out Ilhan's colossal take on Nintendo's classic console, Netherlands' Jeroen Domburg was verified to have built the **smallest Game Boy** – a working scale model that is just 54 mm (2.12 in) long (see pp.14–15).

HISTORY OF THE WORLD THROUGH VIDEOGAMES

When creating their great works, programmers often turn to real life for inspiration. The following prove that games can be every bit as enlightening as they are enjoyable...

66 MILLION YEARS BCE +

Created with paleontologists, the crowdfunded *Saurian* (Urvogel Games, 2017) recreates the Hell Creek ecosystem of 66 million years ago. It features 19 species of dinosaur (six playable), and many of its details are based on fossil records.

1368–1644: THE GREAT WALL OF CHINA

With a main-line length of 3,460 km (2,150 mi), the Great Wall of China in northern China is the **longest wall**. Its history spans some 2,300 years, but much of it was built during the Ming Dynasty (1368–1644). Players can reconstruct it in Sierra's city-builder *Emperor: Rise of the Middle Kingdom*.

1346–1353: THE BLACK DEATH

During the medieval era, a plague killed 30–60% of Europe's population and some 75 million people worldwide – the **worst pandemic**. Green Man's 2016 MMO *The Black Death* tests players to survive these terrifying times.

1162–1227: GENGHIS KHAN

Genghis Khan founded the Mongol Empire, which became the **largest contiguous empire** following the conqueror's death in 1227. Koei's history sim *Genghis Khan* (1987) lets gamers play as Khan or a rival from Japan, Byzantium or England.

1476–1499: THE RENAISSANCE

The Renaissance period was kick-started in Italy, marking the cultural progression from medieval to the early modern age. For *Assassin's Creed II*, scholars advised Ubisoft on architecture and period garb. *The Wall Street Journal* described the 2009 stealth classic as being "as close as we've managed to get to real-time travel".

1564–1616: SHAKESPEARE

The English playwright William Shakespeare is the **best-selling playwright** of all time. In 2016, the University of California, USA, made *Play the Knave*, which enables players to design and perform scenes from his plays in virtual reality.

1650–1730: PIRATES

As merchant trade increased during the 17th and 18th centuries, so did the threat of sea pirates. Open-worlder *Sid Meier's Pirates!* (2004) is set across the Caribbean and features sailing, trading, robbery, land assaults and... dancing!

1156 BCE: ANCIENT EGYPT

R&P Electronic Media's transportative adventure *Egypt 1156 BC: Tomb of the Pharaoh* (1999) features historical locations from ancient Egypt, including the Festival Hall shrine of the Pharaoh Thutmose III.

218 BCE: HANNIBAL'S CROSSING OF THE ALPS

During the Second Punic War, the Carthaginian General Hannibal led his army across the Alps into Italy. His audacious campaign, involving war elephants, is referenced in the *Rome: Total War II* expansion *Hannibal at the Gates* and the 1992 PC strategy title *Hannibal* (above).

80 CE: ROMAN COLOSSEUM

In 80 CE, Roman emperor Titus opened an amphitheatre for hosting gladiatorial fights – the *original* death-matches – in front of 50,000 spectators. Koei's *Colosseum: Road to Freedom* (2005) throws players into the arena as they try to pay off debts – a motive of many volunteers.

793–1066 CE: VIKING INVASIONS

Paradox's multiplayer hack-and-slasher *War of the Vikings* (2014) provides a brutal look at the tussles between Anglo-Saxons (right) and invading Scandinavian warriors, which took place after the Romans withdrew from Britain. Up to 64 players can re-enact the bloody fighting.

363–476 CE: THE FALL OF ROME

Set 300 years after the end of *Rome: Total War* (2004), the *Barbarian Invasion* (2005) expansion tasked players with defending the tired and overstretched Roman Empire against Barbarian hordes.

More...

1666: THE GREAT FIRE OF LONDON

In 1666, a huge fire swept through England's capital, burning much of the city to the ground. The story is retold through a series of playable *Minecraft* maps, created by the Museum of London in 2016.

1775–1783: THE AMERICAN REVOLUTION

On 4 Jul 1776, the USA finally declared its independence from British rule, despite the fact that war would wage for another seven years. *Minecraft* players can recreate those events with the American Revolution Mod 1.7.10.

1803–1815: THE NAPOLEONIC WARS

Napoleon Bonaparte was a French political and military leader who pitted his empire against multiple European powers. This angsty period is covered in DLC for the action RPG *Mount & Blade: Warband* (Paradox/Koch, 2010).

Continued...

1848–1855:
GOLD RUSH

In 1848, someone found a pile of gold nuggets just sitting by the side of a river in California, USA. News spread fast and soon everyone wanted a piece of the action. Sierra's 1988 adventure *Gold Rush!* cast the player as a hopeful prospector looking for gold in California.

1853–1868:
THE END OF FEUDAL JAPAN

After centuries of technological and cultural isolation, Japan opened its ports to the outside world, setting in motion a chaotic chain of events that would see the end of the old Samurai order. The *Way of the Samurai* series (2002–2011) explores this turbulent period, where rifle-armed soldiers clashed with sword-swinging samurai.

1945–1959: FILM NOIR EXPLOSION

Post-war Hollywood saw a cultural thirst for menacing detective dramas, dubbed "film noir" by movie critics. These films were characterized by their moody lighting and ambiguous moral themes. Rockstar's 2011 adventure *L.A. Noire* plays like a noir flick in game form. It's set in 1947 Los Angeles, California, USA, and features crimes inspired by real-life cases, which writers had researched from old tabloids. The game even has the option of being played in black and white.

1939–1945:
WORLD WAR II

Co-created by film director Steven Spielberg in 1999, EA's *Medal of Honor* arguably kick-started the fascination for WWII videogames. The real-world conflict carries the terrible accolade of the **highest death toll from a war** – an estimated 56.4 million people were killed during its six years.

1963:
KENNEDY ASSASSINATION

John F Kennedy was the 35th president of the USA. Having begun his presidency on 20 Jan 1961, he was shot by the sniper Lee Harvey Oswald (or was he?) on 22 Nov 1963. It's re-enacted in the controversial "history sim" *JFK Reloaded* (2004).

1911: CLOSING OF THE AMERICAN FRONTIER

Described as *Grand Theft Auto* in the Wild West, Rockstar's *Red Dead Redemption* (2010) provides a gritty take on America's frontier during the early 20th century. Furthermore, it's the **best-selling Wild West videogame**.

1914–18: WORLD WAR I

Released in 2016, *Verdun* was the **first shooter to realistically depict a battle from the Great War**. The titular Battle of Verdun was fought between German and French forces in northern France for a gruelling 9 months 3 weeks 6 days.

1920–1933: PROHIBITION

2K's *Mafia* provides a gritty portrayal of organized crime in the USA. The series' 2002 debut is set during the latter stages of the prohibition era, when the US government had outlawed all alcohol trade. The game comes complete with Tommy guns, swanky spats and trend-setting trilbies.

1920s: HOLLYWOOD CINEMA BOOM

Hollywood's formative days were semi-captured in U.S. Gold's sim *Charlie Chaplin* (1988). Gamers played as the silent-movie clown as they vied – often in vain – to create funny scenes.

1978–79: THE IRANIAN REVOLUTION

iNK Stories' powerful adventure *1979 Revolution: Black Friday* (2016) is centred on a year-long revolt against the Iranian king. Its story is based on testimonies from both witnesses and freedom fighters.

1984–85: UK MINERS' STRIKE

In mid-1980s Britain, around 142,000 mine-workers staged a walkout, protesting against the closure of UK coal mines. Gremlin's 1984 platformer *Wanted! Monty Mole* satirized the industrial action. Players star as the hero mole as he collects coal for his family.

2011–PRESENT: NASA ROBOTIC SPACE PROBE

On 6 Aug 2012, NASA's Mars rover Curiosity landed on the "Red Planet" to investigate its potential for human habitability. NASA celebrated the mission's four-year anniversary in 2016 with a free mobile/desktop game entitled *Mars Rover*.

TOMB RAIDER

Created by Core Design in 1996, Lara Croft gave gaming its first truly powerful female lead. She's since become a cultural icon, a role model, a movie heroine and, of course, the star of a very successful game series.

Best-selling female game character

With lifetime sales of 40.88 million as of 22 Mar 2017, Square Enix's *Tomb Raider* has outsold every other franchise with a female lead. Its success has inspired novels, comics and movies. A major film reboot starring Alicia Vikander is scheduled for 2018.

The **best-selling *TR* game** is 1997's *Tomb Raider II,* with 7.53 million sales according to VGChartz. This puts it marginally ahead of the 1996 original, the 2013 reboot and 2015's *Rise of the Tomb Raider* (main picture).

> **"I meet a lot of girls that say that they really relate to Lara and they feel like her strength is inspirational."**
> Lara Croft voice actress Camilla Luddington

Largest collection of *TR* games

Tomb Raider may have only produced 11 main series games, but that hasn't stopped Spain's Alejandro Cambronero Albaladejo assembling 215 individual *TR* titles, as verified on 30 Jan 2017.

The rarest items among his regional variations and promos are a Japanese version of *TRIV: The Last Revelation* with exclusive stickers, and a US copy of the 2013 reboot, signed by Crystal Dynamics.

Most game performances as Lara Croft

The UK's Keeley Hawes has voiced *Tomb Raider*'s fearless adventuress in five games. These include *Tomb Raider: Underworld* (2008), *Lara Croft and the Guardian of Light* (2010) and *Lara Croft and the Temple of Osiris* (2014). Fellow UK actress Camilla Luddington has voiced Lara in two more recent adventures: *Rise of the Tomb Raider* (2015) and the 2013 series reboot.

Most official real-life stand-ins for a game character

Between 1996 and 2009, Lara Croft was officially represented by 10 women, hired by either the game's former publisher Eidos or its current developer Crystal Dynamics. Lara's official stand-ins include UK actress Rhona Mitra, UK model and gymnast Alison

Fastest completion of *Rise of the Tomb Raider*

German gamer "Leemyy" raced through the PC version of 2016's *Rise of the Tomb Raider* in 1 hr 52 sec on 28 Feb 2017.

Console speed-runs haven't been as fast, but, on 1 Apr 2016, France's "SamuraiBlue" achieved the **fastest completion (consoles)**: 1 hr 45 min 38 sec on the Xbox 360.

Most bosses killed in *Lara Croft and the Temple of Osiris* (Xbox One)

The four-player co-op game *Temple of Osiris* (2014) is the second multiplayer spin-off from the *Tomb Raider* series. According to TrueAchievements, "xx Lady LC xx" (UK) is the game's true protector of humanity. As of 22 Mar 2017, the gamer had slain 84 bosses.

The same adventure's most successful jewel-gatherer is "SterlingPanther". The player had collected the **most gems in *Temple of Osiris* (Xbox One)**, hoarding 125,395 of the treasures.

Largest gathering of people dressed as Lara Croft

At the Paris Games Week in France on 29 Oct 2016, a total of 270 fans dressed up as the action legend. One male participant cosplayed as a cel-shaded comic Lara, while most fans replicated her classic blue tank-top and shorts look (above). The gathering was organized by current *Tomb Raider* studio Crystal Dynamics.

Largest gallery of Lara Croft cosplay

As of 22 Mar 2017, the community site laracroftcosplay.com (aka tombraidercosplay.com) hosted 7,467 user photos. These were uploaded by 310 Lara Croft cosplayers from countries all over the world, including Russia, Italy, the USA and the UK.

PRO-FILE: TWITCHER

"JADEJOLIE" (UK)

Followers: 97,305

Views: 1,073,692

Trivia: Xbox once took the "Lara Croft of Twitch" to Siberia for a *TR* survival experience.

(Info correct as of 22 Mar 2017)

Largest collection of *TR* memorabilia

Rodrigo Martín Santos (ESP, right) owned 3,050 distinct Croft collectables, as verified on 26 Sep 2016. Recent additions include two life-size statues from Germany and an Arctic coat worn by Angelina Jolie in the 2001 film *Lara Croft: Tomb Raider*.

Rodrigo estimates that he has spent €300,000 (£259,563; $336,642) in 20 years of assembling the collection, now exhibited across two houses. Of his GWR title, Rodrigo said: "It has been an adventure that has changed my life. It has taken me across the world, talking about my passion."

MINI-BYTES

On 18 Dec 2016, as part of the series' 20th anniversary, the Royal Philharmonic Orchestra performed music from the first three *Tomb Raider* games at London's Hammersmith Apollo, UK. The classical-inspired scores were written by veteran UK composer Nathan McCree.

TOMB RAIDER

When the ground-breaking adventure series celebrated its 20th birthday in 2016, fans celebrated a legacy that stretches far beyond gaming. Lara Croft's star has now been felt in movies, music, comedy, fitness and more!

THE FACE
U2
spiritualized
milla
superpubs
this life
gillian anderson
melinda messenger
primal scream
SILICON CHICK
LARA CROFT
BIGGER THAN
FAMME WISER
THAN YODA

speakup
AUDIO CD
Interview ON CD
Angelina Jolie
Back in Force

computer and video games
TEKKEN 3
TOMB RAIDER 3
F-ZERO X
FASTEST RACE IN THE WORLD

MEAN MACHINES SEGA
MOVE OVER LINFORD
TOMBRAIDER

THE WITCHER 3
#5
The Game
RISE OF THE **TOMB RAIDER**
DE LA BOMBE SEXY À L'HÉROINE FRAGILE
PORTRAIT DE LA NOUVELLE LARA CROFT

What's Online
What THE MOST
BIG GUNS!
Pistol-packing Lara shoots to thrill...
PLUS: **Paaar!**
THE BEST OF THE NET
Inside: The very best the Web has to offer

NEXT GENERATION
Who's that girl?
And why are Mario, Sonic, and Crash so scared of her?
Apple wants you

GameStar
magyar nyelvű teljes játék: Knights & Merchants
Szexik és okosak
UT 2003
Battlefield 1942
AvP 2: Primal Hunt
Sudden Strike 2
Syberia
Steel of Hasta

WIZARD
TOMB RAIDER
POSTER MANIA!
FREE: DRAGON BALL Z CARD
PLUS: FALL TV PREVIEW PONTASED SEQUEL SUPERHERO TATTOOS

PlayStation 2
OFFICIAL magazine-UK
LARA CROFT **TOMB RAIDER**

"*We didn't realize how big* **Tomb Raider** *was going to become... Lara Croft made us all look very good at our jobs.*"

Ian Livingstone, of former publisher Eidos

Most magazine covers for a game character

Very few gaming characters have enjoyed the far-reaching impact of Lara Croft. Since making her game debut in 1996, the heroine has featured prominently on at least 1,230 magazine covers, as verified in Sep 2016. The total not only includes hundreds of gaming publications from across the world, but also magazines covering film, music, toys, technology, humour and general lifestyle. Such is the vastness of the *Tomb Raider* brand that Lara has been portrayed in multiple guises: through official videogame art, by real-life actresses and models, and in various cartoon artworks. If every one of Lara's cover mentions was included (not just those where she stars as a primary character), the total would be well over 1,400.

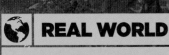
UNCHARTED

Starring the chiselled chops of fortune hunter Nathan Drake, Sony's action-adventure series combines epic tales with exotic locales. Many regard it as the PlayStation's finest treasure.

Most expensive videogame figure sold at auction

An anonymous fan paid $4,250 (£2,628) on eBay for a Nathan Drake vinyl figure on 31 Dec 2012. The piece was made by ESC-TOY for the release of *Uncharted 3: Drake's Deception* (2011) and was signed by the game's development team.

Largest petition against a videogame review

Released in May 2016, *Uncharted 4: A Thief's End* received near-universal critical praise – except in *The Washington Post*, who scored the game 4/10. As a result, 9,485 fans petitioned against the US paper's appraisal being listed by Metacritic's reviews database. It failed.

Fastest completion of *Uncharted 4: A Thief's End*

With their globe-trotting plots and Hollywood-style set-pieces, *Uncharted* games have provided a dramatic playground for speed-runners. On 11 Jan 2017, Mexico's "OmarZarco" finished the most recent main series blockbuster in 3 hr 44 min 56 sec, as verified by Speedrun.com. The gamer exhibited well-timed platforming, and employed various shortcuts and exploits.

The 2015 release of *Uncharted: The Nathan Drake Collection* saw the three earlier main games remastered for PS4. On 19 Mar 2017, the UK's "Hutchtee" achieved the **fastest completion of *Uncharted:***

Rarest PS3 special edition

There are only 200 copies of the "Fortune Hunter" edition of *Uncharted 2: Among Thieves* (2009) in existence. These were awarded to US competition winners and have occasionally been listed on eBay for as much as $7,721 (£6,233). The bundle includes the PS3 game, a guide book, an art book and a replica of the Phurba Dagger artefact. To further

Best-selling PS4 exclusive

Developed by US studio Naughty Dog, the *Uncharted* series has translated into pure gold for Sony since 2007. Its fourth main title, *Uncharted 4: A Thief's End* (2016), had sold 8.72 million copies as of 20 Mar 2017, according to VGChartz. It was the fourth best-selling PS4 title overall, behind multi-platform blockbusters *Call of Duty: Black Ops III* (14.77 million), *GTA V* (14.72 million) and *FIFA 17* (10.52 million). The PS4 exclusive sees Nate Drake hook up with his estranged sibling Sam as they hunt fabled pirate treasure.

Highest score per minute for "Bounty Hunter" mode in *Uncharted 4*

Uncharted 4's "Bounty Hunters" DLC includes a game mode challenging teams to reach a set score by collecting bounties from fallen players. As of 7 Dec 2016, "biokev56" topped the in-game leaderboards with a per-minute score of 720.

MINI-BYTES

An *Uncharted* film has been mooted from as far back as 2008, but it wasn't until Jan 2017 a synopsis was finally unveiled. Mirroring the premise of the first game, it sees Nathan Drake battling a rival to find a fabled city of gold. Shooting for the film was reportedly set to commence in spring 2017.

While Drake is the poster-boy of *Uncharted*, the forthcoming spin-off *The Lost Legacy* pits females Nadine Ross and Chloe Frazer (below) as its protagonists. Game Industry News lauded the incoming adventure as the "only game of 2017 tackling diversity".

Despite the poor score dished out by *The Washington Post* (see far left), *Uncharted 4: A Thief's End* was still Metacritic's highest-rated game in 2016. Nathan's quest for lost pirate treasure carried a score of 93, based on 113 critic reviews at the online reviews aggregator.

Most viewed live-action *Uncharted* fan film

With 648,982 views on YouTube as of 20 Mar 2017, "*Uncharted: Ambushed* (LIVE ACTION FAN FILM)" is the most popular fan-made film inspired by Sony's series. The Norwegian/Danish short was written and directed by Martin Sofiedal (NOR) and is based on the first scene from the 2007 debut *Uncharted: Drake's Fortune*. The short was filmed entirely in Oslo, Norway, over four days, and its post-production took more than a year.

Q&A WITH TROY BAKER

Troy stars as Nathan Drake's brother Sam in the record-breaking *Uncharted 4: A Thief's End*.

How familiar were you with the *Uncharted* series before taking on the role of Nathan's brother?
I vividly remember the first time I played *Uncharted*. I fell in love with [the characters] Nathan Drake, Elena and Sully, and the dynamic between them. When [game director Neil Druckmann] called me in for *Uncharted 4*, it was such a compliment. He wanted someone he could trust, who was a fan of the franchise, and could get along with [Nathan Drake actor] Nolan North.

Do you have a favourite scene from *Uncharted 4*?
One is the scene when the Drake brothers find this little tavern in Libertalia and sit down to have a conversation. What they say reveals so much about the characters. As for the most fun scene, the part where Sam is riding up next to Nathan with the gun truck chasing them is such a great Indiana Jones moment. And when they look at each other and say "Hop on!", it perfectly summarizes their relationship.

CALL OF DUTY

Conceived as a World War II shooter, Activision's *CoD* is arguably now the biggest blockbuster franchise on the planet. From historical warfare to space-bound skirmishes, the series enthrals millions of loyal fans.

Most videogame re-enactments of a real-life military campaign

WWII's Allied invasion of Western Europe, in Jun–Jul 1944, had featured in at least 53 games as of 30 Mar 2017, including *CoD 2* (2005, above). The campaign is commonly known as the Normandy Invasion or Operation Overlord.

Most played PlayStation game on PSNProfiles

Based on the 3 million (and counting) gamer accounts tracked by PSNProfiles, the PS3 blockbuster *CoD: Black Ops* (2010) is the most played game on any PlayStation console. As of 30 Mar 2017, it had an active player base of 1,017,616, putting it just ahead of Rockstar's *GTA V* (911,666).

Most watched game launch broadcast

On 5 Nov 2015, a total of 442,620 unique viewers watched the UK *CoD: Black Ops III* launch event live from Mayfair One, London. The party was streamed on the Twitch channel of "Syndicate" (UK, below right) and featured the pro soccer stars Héctor Bellerín (ESP) and Patrick Bamford (UK).

Highest-earning *Call of Duty: Black Ops III* player

CoD enjoys a fast-growing eSports scene, with gamers competing each year in its most recent release. The USA's Johnathan "John" Perez won $232,707 (£187,926) battling it out in 2015's *CoD: Black Ops III*, according to e-Sports Earnings. He was part of Team EnVyUs that won the *CoD* XP Championship in 2016.

> *"There just aren't many entertainment franchises on Earth that can generate the kind of passion that Call of Duty can..."*
>
> Activision CEO Eric Hirshberg

Most critically acclaimed *Call of Duty* game

Developed by Infinity Ward, 2007's *Call of Duty 4: Modern Warfare* on Xbox 360 has been the biggest hit with critics. As of 30 Mar 2017, it had scored 94.16% across 80 reviews on GameRankings, pipping its 2009 sequel *Modern Warfare 2* (93.57%) and the 2003 original *Call of Duty* (91.52%).

Longest marathon on a shooter

On 13–19 Nov 2012, *CoD* diehard Okan Kaya (AUS) displayed his total dedication to the series by playing *CoD: Black Ops II* (2012, right) for 135 hr 15 min 10 sec. Okan's feat had held the record for the **longest game marathon** overall, until he was gazumped by Carrie Swidecki's *Just Dance* session in 2016 (see pp.152–53).

Most followed Twitch channel

As of 22 Feb 2017, games broadcaster "Syndicate", aka Tom Cassell (UK, above left with GWR's Stephen Daultrey), had 2,458,351 followers on Twitch.

Tom is a huge *Call of Duty* advocate. Along with YouTuber Alastair "Ali-A" Aiken (UK), the duo recorded the **highest Team Deathmatch score using the knife and combat axe on *CoD: Black Ops III* (team of two)**. Their score of 148 was achieved in London, UK, on 4 Aug 2016.

Most subscribed *Call of Duty* YouTube channel

Having launched his YouTube channel back in 2006, the UK's "Ali-A", aka Alastair Aiken, is now a major figure among shooter fans. As of 30 Mar 2017, the broadcaster's dedicated *CoD* channel had recruited an army of 8,751,853 subscribers.

Ali-A's was also the **most watched *Call of Duty* channel**, totalling 2,213,900,401 views. Interestingly, Ali-A is now also a prolific *Pokémon GO* player, creating videos for his second channel, "MoreAliA".

Best-selling first-person shooter series

Since its 2003 debut, Activision's military juggernaut has topped charts all over the world. According to VGChartz, the series had shifted 263.61 million units across all platforms, as of 30 Mar 2017.

The series has been so chart-dominant that six of the 10 all-time FPS best-sellers are *CoD* games. The exceptions include EA's *Star Wars: Battlefront* and *Battlefield 3*. *CoD*'s 2011 instalment, *Modern Warfare 3*, is the **best-selling FPS**, with sales of 30.92 million alone.

Most disliked game trailer

Published on 2 May 2016, the "Official *Call of Duty®: Infinite Warfare* Reveal Trailer" endured a bizarre backlash from gamers. As of 21 Feb 2017, the video had been disliked 3,461,314 times on YouTube – a staggering 9% of its entire 37,208,216 views. While some gamers were unsure of the FPS' new outer space setting, journalists linked the fallout to the series' undying popularity, suggesting that success breeds contempt.

Most viewers for a *CoD* tournament

The 2016 *CoD* Championship on 1–4 Sep was watched online by some 20 million gaming fans.

MINI-BYTES

"PrestigeIsKey" was named the best *Call of Duty* YouTuber by RedBull.com readers in May 2016. The US broadcaster, aka Ryan B, fended off competition from the star-studded likes of "Ali-A" and "NoahJ456", claiming the accolade with 4,300 votes.

Fans of cult TV shows will be overjoyed that US actor David Hasselhoff (below) makes a somewhat surprise cameo in *Call of Duty: Infinite Warfare*. The *Knight Rider* legend appears as a theme park DJ in the game's first zombie map, *Zombies in Spaceland*.

Largest prize for a *CoD* tournament

Staged in Inglewood, California, USA, on 1–4 Sep, the 2016 *Call of Duty* Championship offered a prize pool of $2 million (£1.5 million) – doubling the cash bounty of its three previous tournaments. USA's Team EnVyUs, featuring "John" (above left), defeated Splyce 3–1 in the final to take home a first prize of $800,000 (£601,554).

BATTLEFIELD

Gritty and immersive, EA's (mostly) military series has set the standard for multiplayer shooters. Behind these games is Swedish studio EA DICE, whose Frostbite engine is one of the most revered in the biz.

First "Platinum" completion of *Battlefield I*

According to PSNProfiles, "Kymar17" (USA) was the first PlayStation gamer to achieve everything in *Battlefield 1*'s single-player campaigns, on 20 Oct 2016 – a day before the game's official release. *Battlefield 1* was hailed as a "history lesson" by Kotaku. Its five war stories include famous campaigns set in Gallipoli and the deserts of Arabia.

Most liked gaming video on YouTube

When EA published its "Official Reveal Trailer" for the World War I-set *Battlefield 1* on 6 May 2016, it sparked unprecedented celebrations for a gaming vid. In just four days, the trailer had an epic 1.9 million likes. By 17 Mar 2017, those likes totalled 2,116,622. The game's popularity was partly linked to the backlash suffered by its rival *Call of Duty: Infinite Warfare*.

The reveal is also the **most watched trailer for a shooter**, boasting 52,610,252 views.

Most times as "Most Valuable Player" in *Battlefield I* (XOne)

As of 17 Mar 2017, "FluMusic" (USA) had been awarded the tag of "best player" in 2,118 multiplayer skirmishes on the Xbox One. As the name suggests, Most Valuable Player refers to the combatant who has been the most effective on the battlefield.

Most popular beta for a shooter

A total of 13.2 million players participated in the public testing of *Battlefield 1*, which ran from 30 Aug to 8 Sep 2016. The figure smashed the previous record, held by Blizzard's *Overwatch* (9.7 million in May 2016). Publisher EA noted that the number of beta players was more than double the British and Ottoman soldiers that were deployed in the Middle East during World War I – the setting for the game.

Most successful country in *Battlefield 4* eSports tournaments

Players from France had collectively earned $42,107 (£33,601) competing in *Battlefield 4* as of 17 Mar 2017, according to e-Sportsearnings. The nation's outstanding performer was Florian Le Bihan, aka "DRUNKKZ3", who fought on the winning team in 40 competitions.

Most prolific first-person shooter (FPS) series

Between its 2002 debut *Battlefield 1942* and the release of *Battlefield 1* in Oct 2016, EA's *Battlefield* series has rolled out 30 titles, including expansion packs.

The **best-selling *Battlefield* game** is *Battlefield 3* (2011), with sales of 17.29 million as of 17 Mar 2017, according to VGChartz. Unlike the historical settings of the above titles, *BF3* envisages a fictional conflict in 2014.

Most viewed *Battlefield* fan video

Like its fierce military rival *Call of Duty*, EA's *Battlefield* has generated a fevered fan base on YouTube. The fan-made music video "BATTLEFIELD 4 RAP | Zarcort (Con Piter-G y Cyclo)" by Spain's ZarcortGame (below) had earned 24,541,758 views as of 17 Mar 2017. It features a rap dedicated to 2013's *Battlefield 4*, which the YouTuber performs alongside two musical compatriots.

Most times as "Most Valuable Player" in *Battlefield Hardline* (XOne)

As of 17 Mar 2017, gamer "FPS ImpactR6" had been awarded Most Valuable Player (MVP) in 3,115 multiplayer matches on Xbox One, according to TrueAchievements. In the crime shooter, players stage heists, rescue hostages and attempt assassinations.

The **most times as MVP in *Battlefield 4* (XOne)** was achieved by "UNLIMITED MIND", who was hailed as the "best player" in 6,798 multiplayer matches. *Battlefield 4* is set during a fictional world war in 2020.

Most digital sales of a PS4 game (current)

It may not have been released until mid-Oct 2016 but, according to SuperData, *Battlefield 1* still achieved more digital sales than any other console game in 2016. The acclaimed World War I shooter was downloaded approximately 2.3 million times for the PS4 by the end of the year.

The game also achieved the **most digital sales of an Xbox One game (current)**, selling 1.2 million copies.

PRO-FILE:
YOUTUBER

WESTIE (UK)

Subscribers: 338,006

Views: 59,218,709

Trivia: "World's Most Amazing *Battlefield*er since 2009", says his Facebook page.

(Info correct as of 17 Mar 2017)

842K

PIGEONS

sent in *Battlefield 1*'s new War Pigeons mode in the game's first week.

#XOesperar3

Most cash in *Battlefield Hardline* (Xbox One)

Released in 2015, the urban crime shooter *Battlefield Hardline* is the first in the series not to feature a military setting. As of 17 Mar 2017, "Bond 007" (UK) had made $145,215,008 of in-game cash on the Xbox One, according to TrueAchievements. Cash enables players to splash big on weapons, gadgets and vehicle upgrades.

longevity of *Counter-Strike*. Having evolved from a *Half-Life* mod, the (mostly) PC series pits two teams against each other in tactical skirmishes of urban combat.

First eSports tournament broadcast in virtual reality (multiple platforms)

The *Counter-Strike: Global Offensive* (*GO*) contest ESL One New York, at the USA's Barclays Center on 1–2 Oct 2016, was streamed live in virtual reality (VR). While eight *GO* teams fought for a share of a $250,000 (£192,571) pool, fans at home enjoyed panoramic views of the action, as if they were inside the game itself. The event was viewable online, on an app-enabled mobile device or – for the full experience – via a VR headset.

PRO-FILE: eSPORTS STAR

GABRIEL "FALLEN" TOLEDO (BRA)

Winnings: $445,884

Trivia: In 2012, the *CS: GO* pro founded the eSports organization Games Academy.

(Info from e-Sportsearnings, 8 Mar 2017)

Most eSports tournaments for a shooter

Despite the impact of console heavyweights *Call of Duty* and *Halo*, no shooter is as dominant in competitive gaming as the PC's *Counter-Strike: GO*. As of 7 Mar 2017, it had been the focus of 2,157 pro tournaments (alongside 573 involving the original *Counter-Strike*), according to e-Sportsearnings. It was the second most contested title overall after the sci-fi epic *StarCraft II: Wings of Liberty*.

> **"I never had any idols. I achieved everything myself."**
> *Counter-Strike* eSports legend Patrik "f0rest" Lindberg in 2007

Most prolific game mod franchise

Starting out as a humble *Half-Life* mod in 1999, *Counter-Strike* proved so popular that Valve turned it into a series. To date, it has spawned four main titles – *Counter-Strike*, *Condition Zero*, *Source* and the most popular, *Global Offensive* – plus *Counter-Strike Online*, the Japanese arcade game *Neo* and the spin-off *Nexon: Zombies*.

Most followed *Counter-Strike* channel on Twitch

"ESL_CSGO" had 1,895,225 fans on Twitch as of 8 Mar 2017. Run by the Germany-based eSports organization ESL, it live-streams *Global Offensive* tournament action.

As of the same date, it was the third most followed Twitch channel overall.

Twitch's **most followed individual *Counter-Strike* streamer** is "summit1g" – aka pro gamer Jaryd Lazar (USA) – who has 1,813,230 fans. The rifler is the fourth most followed Twitch broadcaster overall.

First gaming clan represented by an agent

In Jan 2005, *Counter-Strike* clan Ninjas in Pyjamas (left) began to be represented by sports agent Johan Strömberg. He remains active on their behalf.

The pyjama-clad ninjas' parent nation Sweden was the **highest-earning *Counter-Strike* country** as of 8 Mar 2017. Its total of $2,733,810 (£2,237,470), earned from events involving the games, was over a million ahead of second-placed Germany.

Most watched *Counter-Strike* machinima on YouTube

"Counter-Strike For Kids (Machinima)" – uploaded to YouTube on 23 Jul 2008 – had 18,197,925 views as of 8 Mar 2017.

The satirical video, by the US gaming channel Machinima, uses graphics from *Counter-Strike: Source* but was apparently intended to make its content more suitable for younger viewers.

MINI-BYTES

Following in the big footsteps of Shaquille O'Neal, who invested in the eSports organization NRG in 2016, Boston Celtics NBA star Jonas Jerebko (SWE, below) bought Renegades later that year. Once known for *League of Legends*, Renegades fields teams in *CS:GO* and *Call of Duty*. And prior to both Jerebko and O'Neal, the NBA's Rick Fox bought a team in Dec 2015, which he renamed Echo Fox.

Longest win streak in *Counter-Strike*

Swedish team Ninjas in Pyjamas have twice scored winning streaks lasting 23 matches in *Counter-Strike*, according to GosuGamers.

The first ran from 21 Sep 2012 to 12 Feb 2013, when they lost to Natus Vincere (UKR) in the group stage of the StarLadder StarSeries Season 5. The second began later that day when they beat Russian Roulette (DEU) in the same competition. The run ended on 7 Apr 2013, with defeat by Virtus.pro (RUS) in the play-offs.

First random drugs testing at an eSports tournament

ESL One looms large in the competitive *Counter-Strike: GO* calendar. And, as a sign of how serious eSports was becoming, its 2015 finals, in Cologne, Germany, on 22–23 Aug, introduced randomized drugs testing.

The initiative – in partnership with the World Anti-Doping Agency and Germany's Nationale Anti-Doping Agentur – brought eSports in line with other pro sports. All tested players at Cologne yielded negative results, but the procedure was to become a permanent part of all ESL One tournaments.

Highest-earning *Counter-Strike* player (series)

As of 7 Mar 2017, Filip "neo" Kubski (POL) had won $601,969 (£490,570) from 168 *Counter-Strike*, *Source* and *GO* events, according to esportsearnings.com. This toppled long-standing record holder Patrik "f0rest" Lindberg (SWE, $509,910; £415,547).

Longest pro match of *Counter-Strike*

An epic 88 rounds were fought between the UK-based *CS:GO* outfits Team XENEX and exceL eSports on 20 Apr 2015. The thrilling contest in the ESL UK Premiership included six overtimes and lasted 2 hr 43 min. Favourites XENEX beat exceL 46 rounds to 42, but the match lasted so long that every player recorded more than 75 kills.

Later in 2015, 27 million Twitchers watched ESL One Cologne on 22–23 Aug, making it the **most watched *Counter-Strike* tournament**. The audience for the German event peaked with 1.3 million concurrent viewers.

METAL GEAR

Metal Gear (1987) introduced hero Solid Snake and pioneered the stealth genre. The series broke new ground again with 1998's *Metal Gear Solid*, whose cinematic feel, tense gameplay and weighty narrative became the franchise's trademarks.

Longest cutscene in a game

Metal Gear Solid 4: Guns of the Patriots (2008) includes an epic 27-min cutscene. It appears within the **longest end sequence**, also from *MGS4*: 1 hr 9 min 4 sec of cutscenes are combined to wrap up the story.

"I put everything in the cut sequences," Hideo Kojima admitted in 2008, "which I kind of regret to some extent, because maybe there is a new approach which I should think about."

Best-selling stealth series

In the 30 years since the first *Metal Gear* game in 1987 (below), the series has inspired many imitators but continued to reign supreme on sales charts. Helped by its evolution into *Metal Gear Solid* in 1998, the franchise had sold a mighty 44.31 million units by 23 Mar 2017.

The individual **best-selling stealth videogame** is *Metal Gear Solid 2: Sons of Liberty*, with 6.05 million copies sold.

LIFE ▭ M·GUN 10
RANK ★

"Metal Gear Solid *was surprising. I just made what I wanted to play. I didn't expect it to perform that well."*
Hideo Kojima on his 1998 game

First stealth game to use motion capture

Metal Gear Solid 2: Sons of Liberty (2001) was the first game to use motion capture in the genre that the series had pioneered.

The acclaimed *MGS* sequel introduced other mechanics to the franchise. These included being able to peek around corners and using a first-person perspective to aim.

Most games in an HD collection

The *Metal Gear Solid HD Collection*, issued in 2011 for the PS3 and Xbox 360, features five titles: *Metal Gear*, *MG2: Solid Snake*, *MGS2: Sons of Liberty*, *MGS3: Snake Eater* and *MGS: Peace Walker*. All were remastered in high definition to take advantage of the consoles' power.

The collection omitted *Metal Gear Solid* itself, but illustrated the series' shifting gameplay and scenarios. *Metal Gear* is set in South Africa in 1995, whereas *Peace Walker* takes place in 1974 Costa Rica.

Longest marathon on a stealth game

Ben Reeves (USA) played the *Metal Gear Solid* series for an eyelid-nuking 48 hr, from 6–8 Aug 2011.

Most viewed *Metal Gear Solid* video on YouTube

GameNewsOfficial's "Metal Gear Solid 5 Red Band Trailer (E3 2013)" had 8,210,341 views as of 23 Mar 2017.

Longest time for an eSports debut by a game series

In Dec 2015 – 28 years and 18 games after *Metal Gear*'s 1987 debut – eSports organization ESL launched the *Metal Gear* Online Global Championship. Players competed in the online multiplayer section of 2015's *MGSV: The Phantom Pain*.

Most critically acclaimed stealth videogame

Metal Gear Solid 2: Sons of Liberty, on the PlayStation 2, held an average score of 95.09% on GameRankings, from a total of 68 reviews, as of 23 Mar 2017.

MINI-BYTES

In 2015, prosthetics designer Sophie de Oliveira Barata created a new limb for UK amputee James Young. The piece, subject of a BBC documentary, was based on *Metal Gear Solid V*. However, unlike the *Deus Ex* hand on pp.56-57, the arm was aesthetic rather than functional.

Longest cardboard box slide in *MGSV: The Phantom Pain*

Cardboard boxes and their many uses are a running joke in *Metal Gear*. In *MGSV*, on 31 Jan 2017, Tristen Geren (USA) slid in one for 1 min 42 sec, as verified by Twin Galaxies.

28 YEARS

Hideo Kojima worked on the *Metal Gear* series before parting ways with Konami in 2015.

Most disliked pachinko machine trailer on YouTube

As 2016 began, Hideo Kojima had left Konami. The publisher declared the franchise would continue without its creator. Kojima's loyal fans responded by voting down a trailer for a pachinko version of *MGS 3: Snake Eater* (pachinko is a mechanical game similar to pinball). As of 23 Mar 2017, it had 59,790 dislikes.

Longest solution to a boss battle

In a franchise famous for its bosses, *Metal Gear Solid 3: Snake Eater*'s veteran sniper "The End" (inset) is one of the most notorious. If the player saves the game during the battle, they can turn off the console and wait a full week – at which point the boss, born in the 1860s, will die of old age.

ESPIONAGE ROUND-UP

Fast cars, cool gadgets, sharp clothes – being a spy is a glamorous business. Then there's the thrill of infiltrating secret bases, beating up baddies and saving the world. But can you be as invincible in games as spies are in movies?

Most critically acclaimed movie spin-off

Not all movie-to-game licences flop. The Nintendo 64 gem *GoldenEye 007* (1997) – based on the 1995 James Bond film – has a GameRankings score of 94.7%. Developer Rare attributed its success to the studio having free rein rather than licensing restraints. The first-person shooter was ported to the Wii in 2010 (main picture).

Ten ZX Spectrum games were discovered in the N64 original in 2012 – the **longest time to find a hidden game**. Rare had used *GoldenEye* as a test platform for a software emulator, which was left in the final code.

Fastest completion of *Tom Clancy's Splinter Cell*

Playing in "hard" mode, "CotySA" finished the first *Splinter Cell* (2002) in 55 min 37 sec on 14 Apr 2014.

The **fastest completion of 2013's** *Blacklist* – the most recent *Splinter Cell* game (with series hero Sam Fisher, pictured right) – is 1 hr 11 min 41 sec, by "andyrockin123" (USA) on 9 Sep 2016.

Fastest completion of *007 Legends*

Celebrating the 50th birthday of the Bond film franchise, Activision's *007 Legends* (2012) features missions from *Goldfinger*, *On Her Majesty's Secret Service*, *Moonraker*, *Licence to Kill*, *Die Another Day* and *Skyfall*. On 31 May 2015, Canada's "ParallaxDG" conquered the Xbox 360 version in a shaken-not-stirred 2 hr 15 min 56 sec.

First James Bond videogame

Shaken But Not Stirred – a text-based adventure written by Richard Shepherd and published for the ZX Spectrum in 1982 – marked 007's videogame debut. The British MI6 agent – created by author Ian Fleming – has since starred in more than 30 games. This includes five based on Charlie Higson and Steve Cole's "Young Bond" books.

Longest time between a movie and game

EA's third-person shooter *007: From Russia with Love* debuted on 1 Nov 2005 – 42 years 22 days after the movie of the same name premiered on 10 Oct 1963.

The only game with voice work by Sean Connery (left) – the first big-screen Bond – it was also the first and last 007 title for the PSP.

Fastest completion of *Spy vs. Spy*

On 12 Feb 2016, Canada's "Remz" shaved 23 sec off a record that had stood for a decade. On the NES version of 1984's *Spy vs Spy*, they finished in 8 min 42 sec.

Developed by First Star Software, the game was based on a long-running comic strip about two rival sleuths, as featured in the satirical US magazine *Mad*.

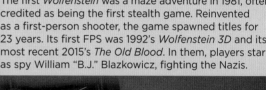

First in-universe queue for videogame entry

On its first day, 8 Mar 2016, *Tom Clancy's The Division* was so popular that thousands of players formed a line, in-game, to be peace-keeping agents in a disaster-stricken New York City.

This meant registering on a PC at a safe house, but the game was so realistic that only one player could gain access at a time. Gamers self-regulated admirably, but Ubisoft swiftly updated the code so that this step was no longer necessary.

Longest-running FPS series

The first *Wolfenstein* was a maze adventure in 1981, often credited as being the first stealth game. Reinvented as a first-person shooter, the game spawned titles for 23 years. Its first FPS was 1992's *Wolfenstein 3D* and its most recent 2015's *The Old Blood*. In them, players star as spy William "B.J." Blazkowicz, fighting the Nazis.

First game with opposing first- and third-person shooter gameplay

Tom Clancy's Splinter Cell: Pandora Tomorrow – released in 2004 for Xbox, PlayStation 2 and PC – introduced a multiplayer mode based on tactical combat. Called "Spies vs Mercs", the game of cat-and-mouse is played from a first-person perspective as a mercenary while the opposing spy is played from a third-person perspective.

This ingenious style was developed by Ubisoft Annecy, also responsible for the innovative multiplayer modes found in the *Assassin's Creed* series.

Fastest completion of *James Bond 007: Blood Stone*

Canada's "so_koneko" blasted through the PC version of 2010's third-person shooter in 1 hr 37 min 1 sec on 17 Jan 2015. "Pretty optimized route," the gamer mused. "Only a few mistakes."

Among the game's cast are actors Daniel Craig (right) and Judi Dench.

GRAND THEFT AUTO

Beginning life as a top-down actioner in 1997, *GTA* went on to revolutionize open-world gaming with 2001's *GTA III*. Even today, Rockstar's blackly comic series continues to give gamers a real sense of freedom.

Best-selling action-adventure game

Rockstar's *Grand Theft Auto V* (2013) had sold 59.89 million copies as of 29 Mar 2017, according to VGChartz.

GTA V's mighty tally helped boost the controversial franchise to global sales of 166.88 million units. This makes it the **best-selling action-adventure series**.

Most viewed trailer for an action-adventure game

Rockstar released a first trailer for *GTA V* on 2 Nov 2011, introducing fans to its Los Santos setting and bank-robber lead. The trailer had 47,095,960 views on YouTube as of 29 Mar 2017, retaining its record after five years.

Most played *Grand Theft Auto Online* playlist

Playlists are sets of jobs that multiple gamers can tackle simultaneously online. As of 29 Mar 2017, the most played was "Venture Off-Road", tackled 687,574 times. It features off-road races in hilly deserts, rural lands and mountains.

Most expensive vehicle in *Grand Theft Auto Online*

Extravagant vehicles are a sure sign of success in the crime sim's online arm. Launched on 10 Jun 2015 in the *Ill-Gotten Gains Part 1* DLC, the gold-painted Buckingham Luxor Deluxe private jet is a wallet-wilting GTA$10,000,000.

The game's **most expensive yacht** is the Aquarius Galaxy Super Yacht, released as part of the *Executives and Other Criminals* DLC in Dec 2015. This sets players back GTA$8,000,000.

Most liked custom job in *GTA Online* (PC)

GTA Online users can create "jobs", such as races and deathmatches, to be shared with fellow players. As of 29 Mar 2017, the PC race "Super Stunt Sky" by Brazil's "Guilherme_94" had been liked 306,000 times by fellow users. It provides an airborne track for up to 30 racers.

Most liked user photo in *Grand Theft Auto V*

Via the in-game app Snapmatic, *GTA V* and *GTA Online* players share photos taken on in-game phones. As of 29 Mar 2017, "Océano Pacífico", by Xbox 360 user "MILINKO81", had earned 26,583 likes. In an impeccable example of photo-bombing, the selfie captures a shark leaping from the waves.

MINI-BYTES

In 2015, *GTA V* players found an achievement that turns them into Bigfoot and brings forth a new beast (the furry fella in the gunsights, on the opposite page and below). Killing the beast – modelled on the 1985 film *Teen Wolf* – unlocks a feature in which players can create in-game movies.

Most subscribed non-English-language gaming channel on YouTube

El Salvador YouTuber Luis "Fernanfloo" Flores had 20,598,535 followers as of 29 Mar 2017. He broadcasts in his native Spanish, and his is the second most subscribed gaming channel overall. Fernanfloo's most popular (broadcasted) games include *GTA V*.

Most cash earned in *GTA Online* (Xbox One)

Brazilian gamer Raquel "RaquelRJ" Rangel had amassed $17,068,000,028,900 of in-game cash in the multiplayer section of *GTA V* as of 29 Mar 2017, according to TrueAchievements.

Most critically acclaimed open-world game

The PS3 *GTA IV* (left) held a GameRankings score of 97.04% as of 1 Mar 2017, just ahead of *GTA V*'s 97.01%.

However, *GTA V*'s PS4 version is the **most critically acclaimed game for an eighth-generation platform**, with 96.33%.

ASSASSINS ROUND-UP

For sneaky so-and-sos, fewer things are more exhilarating than stepping into the padded shoes of a virtual hitman. These games aren't about leaping into action, they're about strategy, patience, guile, craft... and being very, very quiet.

Most completed PlayStation game

Based on the accounts tracked by PSNProfiles, Ubisoft's stealthy PS3 thriller *Assassin's Creed II* (2009) is the most completed game on any PlayStation console. As of 1 Mar 2017, a total of 157,586 players (27.3% of its user-base) had led the assassin Ezio through a 15th- and 16th-century Italy, polishing off every mission in his wake.

The classic adventure also has the **most magazine covers for a game**: a total of 127 publications in 32 countries, in Apr 2009–Apr 2010.

First playable female in the *Assassin's Creed* series

Much was made of Evie Frye's starring role in 2015's *Assassin's Creed: Syndicate* (Ubisoft). However, Aveline de Grandpré pre-dates her as a playable character by around three years. Born of French and African origin in 18th-century New Orleans, USA, Aveline stars in the "side-story" game *Assassin's Creed III: Liberation*, released for PS Vita on 30 Oct 2012.

Most platforms supported by a stealth series

Since 2007, Ubisoft's *Assassin's Creed* games have been made for 16 different platforms, including webOS, iOS, Android and Facebook.

"I kidnap vegetarian kids and raise them on meat. I stole a baby from a candy store. I walk old ladies into traffic..." Actor Gary Busey explains why he should star as a target in *Hitman*

First *Hitman* target based on a real person

IO Interactive's series debuted in 2000, but it wasn't until 2016's entry *Hitman* that one of its targets was actually a *real* person. In the Italy episode "World of Tomorrow", 71-year-old Hollywood star Gary Busey (USA, below) appeared as an "Elusive Target", inviting players to bump him off for one week only. Busey had won a public vote-off to feature, beating his fellow US actor Gary Cole.

HITMAN
ELUSIVE TARGET #7

Italy
Sapienza

THE WILDCARD
THURSDAY 21ST JULY

Longest marathon on an action-adventure game

Belgian gamers Tony Desmet, Jesse Rebmann and Jeffrey Gamon acrobatically parkoured their way through *Assassin's Creed: Brotherhood* (2010) for 109 hr exactly, at the GUNKtv World Record Gaming Event in Antwerp, Belgium, on 18–22 Dec 2010.

Fastest completion of *Dishonored*

In Bethesda's 2012 classic, players star as the reluctant assassin Corvo Attano as they exact revenge on those who framed him for political murder. On 10 Sep 2016, German PC gamer "heny" flashed through the game in 33 min 28.744 sec, as verified by Speedrun.com.

Fastest completion of *Dishonored 2* as Emily Kaldwin

Despite taking most gamers 20 hr to savour its mystical story, Bethesda's 2016 sequel is often blazed through by speed-runners in under 30 min. On 11 Feb 2017, "bjurnie" (NLD) played as fallen empress Emily (right) to overcome tyrants, witches and clockwork soldiers in just 25 min 33 sec. He also achieved the **fastest completion with Corvo** (Emily's father): 26 min 44 sec on 15 Feb 2017.

Fastest time to assassinate an "Elusive Target" in *Hitman* (2016)

For its episodic game, IO Interactive introduced an "Elusive Target" feature in which gamers had a one-off opportunity to eliminate a special target in a limited time-frame (see Gary Busey, left). On 16 Sep, the player "LiGHTz OuTT 504" incredibly took just 19 sec to assassinate one Elusive Target, Nila "The Pharmacist" Torvik, on the game's Paris level. Nila is a deadly pharmaceuticals scientist who was linked to human experiments in the Third World. The player used an explosive rubber duck to dispatch the heinous fiend before casually escaping through a front gate.

Most signatures for an *Assassin's Creed: Syndicate* petition

In Oct 2015, a total of 2,271 disgruntled fans signed a Change.org petition, requesting that *AC: Syndicate* (2015) protagonist Jacob Frye (right) be able to toggle between a Victorian top hat and his society's iconic Assassin's hood. In response, GamesRadar ran with the headline: "Some people REALLY care about wearing the hood in *Assassin's Creed:*

Most challenges completed in *Hitman* (Xbox One)

In Square Enix's wryly humorous *Hitman* (2016), budding contract killers can undertake a variety of challenges, from being disguised as a catwalk model to decorating a cake for an obnoxious rock star. According to TrueAchievements, "Last Ride" had completed 33,704 challenges as of 1 Mar 2017.

SIM ROUND-UP

Mimicking the real world via simulation games became big news with 1989's city-building *SimCity*. Since then, few areas of life have escaped the genre's clutches, from wildlife to wild rides...

Most real-life roller-coasters rebuilt in a game

Real-life architect "Joey Designs" (USA) had accurately recreated 32 real-world roller-coasters in the 2016 simulation game *Planet Coaster*, as of 28 Mar 2017. These include Afterburn (below) at Carowinds amusement park in the USA. Designed to mimic "physics and the actual ride experience", the roller-coasters are available on Steam.

Largest ship in *World of Warships*

According to the historical consultants for Wargaming's MMO *World of Warships* (2015), the game's largest playable ship is the *Großer Kurfürst*. The German Tier X battle vessel is 300.5 m (985 ft 10 in) long. The craft is based on a class of battleships that were designed for the German Navy during World War II but never built.

Most Steam Awards won by a game

Euro Truck Simulator 2 (2012) and *Grand Theft Auto V* (2013) each won twice at the first Steam Awards in Dec 2016. The former (left) won the "I Thought This Game Was Cool Before It Won An Award" award ("Didn't have a huge marketing machine behind it, but you found it and loved it") and "Sit Back and Relax" (a game that provokes minimum stress).

Most videogame adaptations of a movie

Steven Spielberg's 1993 dinosaur classic *Jurassic Park* spawned 14 distinct games from 1993 to 2015. These include 2003's park-building sim *Jurassic Park: Operation Genesis*.

Most popular trophy in *Goat Simulator*

As of 29 Mar 2017, 86.68% of players on the PS3 version had earned the "What is its purpose?" award for smashing "Goathenge" – a stone circle in the town of Goatville. Designer Armin Ibrisagic told Indie Game Magazine that *Goat Simulator* "is a breakthrough in goat simulation... All you need is a computer screen to inject the lightwaves of digital goats through your eyes."

Highest PlayStation completion rate

All five trophies in the PS3 version of *Aabs Animals* (2013) had been collected by 99.25% of its 6,818 owners as of 28 Mar 2017. That's according to PSNProfiles, who track the kitten sim's owners.

PushSquare.com wrote: "If you're looking for any kind of gameplay [or] challenge... you had best look elsewhere."

First one-man dev team to win a BAFTA for a sim

Papers, Please, developed by Lucas Pope (USA), won the "Strategy & Simulation" category at the 2014 game awards. It casts the player as an official ensuring that only people with the correct paperwork enter a fictional eastern European country.

Most visited Nobel Prize game

The Nobel Prize site hosts educational games that simulate prize-winning achievements. Ranked first for visits is *Blood Typing Game*, which teaches players about blood transfusions.

MINI-BYTES

French *Planet Coaster* gamer Chuck Maurice uploaded his "Death Star Strike" to YouTube and Steam on 22 Jan 2017. The user-made ride imagines *Star Wars: A New Hope*'s iconic trench run as a roller-coaster.

First videogame released by a zoo

Created by staff at Minnesota Zoo, USA, and game developer Eduweb, *WolfQuest* is an educational wildlife sim that puts gamers in the role of a grey wolf in Yellowstone National Park. Made available for free in 2007, it was refined and released commercially in Nov 2015.

PRO-FILE: YOUTUBER

DAGGERWIN (UK)

Subscribers: 235,804

Views: 95,048,461

Trivia: The *Euro Truck* and *Farming Simulator* fan says his videos celebrate "slow-paced and realistic gameplay".

(Info correct as of 28 Mar 2017)

Best-selling PC game series

Since the release of *The Sims* (Maxis/EA) in 2000, the life-sim sandbox game and its descendants have grown into a global phenomenon. Their physical PC sales alone, as of 28 Mar 2017, totalled 36.72 million units, according to VGChartz. The game's designer was Will Wright (USA), who had helmed its predecessor, *SimCity*.

Longest-running train sim series

Debuting in Japan in 1996, Taito's *Densha de Go!* (*Go by Train!*) celebrated its 20th anniversary in 2016 with a four-screen arcade cabinet. In between, around 17 individual sims have been rolled out in Japan.

Largest charity game bundle

Indie site Itch.io's *The Good Bundle*, launched in Nov 2016, boasted 173 titles by 128 indie developers. Among them were ambient-musical exploration game *Proteus*, "interactive exploration simulator" *Gone Home* and "first-person destructive cat simulator" *Catlateral Damage*. Proceeds went to both the American Civil Liberties Union and Planned Parenthood.

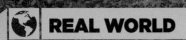
STRATEGY ROUND-UP

Strategy games commonly allow players to rewrite the history books, but occasionally the titles step into sci-fi and fantasy realms too. As the name suggests, they call for tactical thinking and no little patience...

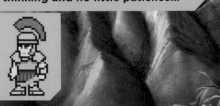

Most concurrent players on Steam for a strategy game

On its release in Oct 2016, *Sid Meier's Civilization VI* proved a hit. That month, the number of gamers undertaking its historical warfare at the same time peaked at 162,314. This topped genre heavyweights such as *Civilization V* and *Total War*'s *Rome II* and *Warhammer*.

Based on physical sales, *Civilization* is the **best-selling turn-based strategy series**. VGChartz reported 5.03 million sales as of 19 Apr 2017.

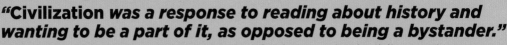

"Civilization was a response to reading about history and wanting to be a part of it, as opposed to being a bystander."

Developer Sid Meier on the inspiration for his empire-building series

22k

VOTES

from Xbox One players to make the Xbox 360 game *Sid Meier's Civilization Revolution* backwards compatible for their consoles.

Largest acquisition of a videogames studio

Chinese tech company Tencent Holdings announced on 21 Jun 2016 that it was buying 84.3% of Finland's Supercell – developers of the strategy hits *Clash Royale* and *Clash of Clans*. Tencent paid about $8.6 bn (£5.9 bn) for the deal – which Supercell's Ilkka Paananen said was partly inspired by Tencent president Martin Lau being a keen *Clash Royale* player: "It was almost impossible to get his focus back to the topics we had to discuss."

Fastest "short campaign" completion of *Rome: Total War*

Croatian PC player Antonio Peremin conquered 2004's *Rome: Total War* in just 3 min 9 sec on 7 Mar 2017, as verified by Speedrun.com. In that time, Antonio used a Greek faction to hold 15 provinces and outlast the rival Macedon and Thrace factions in 270 BC.

First zero-death "Impossible Ironman" completion of *XCOM*

On 11 Jan 2014, Finnish YouTuber Antti "Zemalf" Kokkonen completed the *XCOM* expansion *Enemy Within*, in "Impossible Ironman" mode, without a single character dying or country falling. The strategic, alien-battling run lasted 50 hr.

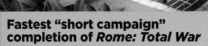

Highest-ranked *Offworld Trading Company* player

"blackmagic" was the highest-ranked player of *Offworld Trading Company* as of 18 Apr 2017. The gamer's enviable stats included a rating of 1,720 and a huge 139 wins. Set on Mars, Stardock's 2016 RTS focuses on victory through economics rather than fighting and killing.

Most critically acclaimed turn-based strategy videogame

A GameRankings score of 93.36%, from 59 reviews, put *Sid Meier's Civilization IV* (2005) ahead of *Galactic Civilizations II: Dark Avatar* (2007, 92.61%), as of 18 Apr 2017. Hooked Gamers wholeheartedly recommended *Civilization IV* "to any armchair strategist out there".

Highest revenue by a mobile videogame (current)

According to SuperData, Mixi's monster-collecting physics puzzler *Monster Strike* (2013) earned $1.5 bn (£1.21 bn) in 2016. It's a freemium game, generating money via microtransactions.

Most playable factions in a *Total War* game
The DLC for 2013's *Total War: Rome II* provides 117 different factions, of which 32 are playable.

Most downloaded mod for a strategy game
"Third Age – Total War" (a mod that turns *Medieval II: Total War – Kingdoms* into a map of Middle-earth) had been downloaded 5,783,258 times from moddb.com as of 19 Apr 2017. The mod, by "TW_King_Kong" (DEU), has a community rating of 9.7.

Longest professional game of *StarCraft II: Wings of Liberty*
On 13 Jan 2015, Wenlei "ZhuGeLiang" Dai (FIN) and Steffen "Lillekanin" Hovmand (DNK) fought in *StarCraft II* for 4 hr 10 min 1 sec of in-game time, or just under 3 hr in real time.

Most YouTube views for a videogame TV commercial
Starring "AngryNeeson52" (actor Liam Neeson), "Clash of Clans: Revenge (Official Super Bowl TV Commercial)" had earned 159,949,600 views on YouTube as of 19 Apr 2017. It was originally shown on 1 Feb 2015 during the half-time of Super Bowl XLIX.

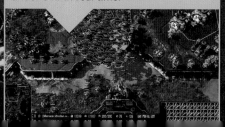

MUSIC ROUND-UP

Rhythm titles are a great thing. They can keep you fit, refine your reflexes and even bring your rock-star dreams to life – all without sticking you on a smelly tour bus in between games...

Most songs in games by a rock band

No act has dominated gaming more than US punks Green Day. As of 30 Mar 2017, their anthems had been used 57 times in 11 different titles (excluding downloadable songs). Forty-seven appear in 2010's *Green Day: Rock Band*, and they've starred in series such as *Shaun White Skateboarding*, *Tony Hawk*, *NHL*, *Need for Speed* and *Madden NFL*, plus the raunchy *BMX XXX*.

> **"I'm not a gamer. I've played the drums [in Rock Band] and I'm terrible."**
> Green Day frontman Billie Joe Armstrong on tackling his band's game

40%

SALES INCREASE
of Aerosmith records after the band released their *Guitar Hero* game (right) in 2008.

Longest videogame marathon

Carrie Swidecki (USA) played *Just Dance 2015* for 138 hr 34 sec on 11–17 Jul 2015. Having set dance records four years in a row, Carrie this time broke the overall gaming marathon record. She streamed the whole attempt (at Otto's Video Games & More! in Bakersfield, California, USA) on Twitch and raised $7,305 (£4,677) for ExtraLife4Kids.

Best-selling rhythm game series

Activision's *Guitar Hero* series had sold 62.12 million units as of 30 Mar 2017, according to VGChartz. That put it roughly 2 million ahead of its nearest rival, Ubisoft's *Just Dance*. Aerosmith's series debut was in 2006's *Guitar Hero II*, before they got their own game (above).

First videogame recognized as an official sport

On 9 Dec 2003, *Dance Dance Revolution* was acknowledged by Norway's government as an official sport. Just five years after its first game, the series was registered as "machine dancing".

Longest *SingStar* marathon

Julian Hill (UK) sang for 24 hr 21 min 25 sec on 13–14 Apr 2012, raising funds for London's Great Ormond Street Hospital.

Most triggers in a *Theatrhythm Final Fantasy: Curtain Call* track

"Advent: One-Winged Angel" – played in its "Ultimate" form – lasts 6 min 4 sec and has 776 trigger points to tap, slide and hold to the beat.

MINI-BYTES

"Through the Fire and Flames" is one of *Guitar Hero*'s trickiest tracks. The original's guitarists – DragonForce's Herman Li and Sam Totman (below) – tried it, as seen in the YouTube video "Can DragonForce play their own song in *Guitar Hero*?". The answer was a conclusive "No".

Fastest Coda Low% completion of *Crypt of the NecroDancer*

Coda is a fiendishly difficult mode of the rhythm-based dungeon-dweller *Crypt of the NecroDancer* (Brace Yourself Games, 2015). In Coda, everything runs at double speed and the fireball-shooting Death Metal boss is especially nasty. A Low% completion is the hardest type, restricting players from picking up any items. So such a run was perceived by gamers and developers as virtually impossible. Yet, on 21 Jul 2016, "SpootyBiscuit" managed it in 12 min 35 sec.

"I honestly thought that no one would ever beat it," programmer Ryan Clark told Kotaku. "He has defeated my game utterly, and I couldn't be happier about it."

Most songs in games by a metal band

Metal giants Iron Maiden (UK) had 51 tracks featured in 15 games (excluding DLC), as of 30 Mar 2017. This includes their own rail shooter *Ed Hunter* (1999) and RPG *Legacy of the Beast* (2016, below), *SSX*, *GTA*, *Madden*, *Tony Hawk*, *Rock Band* and *Guitar Hero*.

Most popular character in cosplay

Hatsune Miku is the star of Yamaha's *VOCALOID* voice synthesizer applications. As of 30 Mar 2017, there were 85,248 photo uploads tagged with her name at the cosplay community site WorldCosplay.net – more than double that of any other character. Hatsune has also headlined her own rhythm games for Sega since 2009.

153

ROOM ESCAPES

Whether it's dungeons or doctors' offices, jails or bedrooms, the ultimate goal is the same: escape!

The exits are locked. Your surroundings are strange. A series of puzzles stand between you and freedom, but it'll take creative thinking to make it all click.

If this scenario sounds familiar, it's likely you've fallen for escape games – a subgenre of puzzle games in which players are challenged to break out of an environment by deciphering clues and using objects.

Hundreds of these titles can be found on gaming sites and app stores. They have also inspired a flood of real-world "escape the room" venues. The first was dreamed up by Takao Kato (right) in Kyoto, Japan, in 2007. In 2012, Kato's friend Kazuya Iwata brought the concept to the USA. By 9 Mar 2017, around 2,760 escape rooms had opened in 97 countries.

Who knew getting trapped would become one of the best ways to spend a night out?

Q&A WITH TAKAO KATO

Takao Kato, of publisher SCRAP, is credited with being the father of real-life escape rooms. He opened the first Real Escape Game entertainment facility in Kyoto, Japan, in 2007, and has helped launch the concept around the world.

What inspired you to bring videogame escape rooms to the real world?
One day, we were discussing events for the magazine that we publish. I asked a girl who worked at SCRAP, "Have you found anything fun recently?" She said, "I played escape games online all night yesterday." I got an idea to make it a real-life event, and Real Escape Game came into the world.

What made you think the genre would be fun in real life?
I thought it would be something I could enjoy. I got bored with videogames and puzzle-solving games because they were too easy. I had been longing to play a more immersive game, so I was excited by the idea of Real Escape Game because it meant making my long-cherished dream finally come true.

What's your reaction to the worldwide popularity of physical escape rooms?
I am glad. It's as if I have many children and descendants all over the world! We have produced our game in Asia, made a company in the USA, and are making it in Europe too.

How do you see real-world escape rooms evolving?
It will get more immersive, and the trend probably will not stop. It may even become a next-generation movie. However, I think virtual reality (VR) and real-life escape may not meet. "True" reality is still stronger than virtual reality.

We will see more games that provide new experiences, like SCRAP games such as *Time Travel Lab*, where you play the time-travelling experience. The next escape rooms won't just be about solving puzzles: players will experience more stories or meta systems.

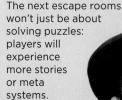

> ## "We want players to be baffled but willing to continue working the puzzles out..."
> Barry Meade of Fireproof Games

ESCAPE GAMES CHRONOLOGY

1980s–1990s
The ingredients of escape games begin to appear in text adventures such as *Behind Closed Doors* (Zenobi Software, 1988). Escaping confined environments becomes increasingly common.

2001
Mystery of Time and Space (Jan Albartus, 2001) transforms "escape the room" into a new genre. Compelling visuals and multiple locations enhance the point-and-clicker's appeal to gamers.

2002
The One Room Game Competition debuts in Italy, launching an annual interactive narrative competition that will run for years.

2004
Toshimitsu Takagi's *Crimson Room* kick-starts a series that brings mainstream attention to the subgenre. The concept inspires a wealth of "room escape", "escape the room" and "escape game" titles online.

2010s
Smartphones and portable gaming systems expose the genre to a wider audience. It matures via hits such as *Prison Break: Lockdown* (below) and the award-winning *The Room* and *Zero Escape*.

2014–16
Virtual reality (VR) takes the escape-game concept to another dimension. Titles for the Oculus Rift, Samsung Gear VR and other devices offer new ways to get a puzzle-gaming fix.

GRILLING FIREPROOF GAMES: 3 QUESTIONS

Fireproof Games' puzzle series *The Room* has been recognized by the BAFTA Games Awards and spawned best-sellers across multiple platforms. We picked the brain of Fireproof's co-founder and director Barry Meade.

How important is a narrative or story?
Narrative varies from title to title. The atmosphere is more important: the player must feel trapped, but enjoy the experience enough to feel it's a pleasant or exciting place in which to spend a few hours solving puzzles.

There are subtle ways to get narrative across besides straight-up dialogue and storytelling. We try to immerse our players, leaving only clues to pick up and read as they see fit.

How do you achieve the right balance of difficulty when designing puzzles?
Through plain enjoyment. We give tasks, but also a magical playground in which to solve them – one that they hopefully find captivating. We want players to be baffled but willing to continue working the puzzles out.

We help by making them "real". You don't have to employ preposterous abstract thinking. If players find a key, they need to find a keyhole, and if they turn the key in it, a mechanism will unlock. That helps not scare them off.

Will technology change the genre?
Puzzle games could marry exceptionally well to VR. The genre doesn't have lots of quick action, so it doesn't need to worry about navigation and nausea. And the extra immersion VR gives really complements a game like *The Room*.

If augmented reality becomes commercial, it could be a great canvas for our games. There's no contradiction with the tech, which is not the case for fast-moving or action-oriented games.

⚽ SPORTS

Whether true-to-life (*Football Manager*) or crazy (*Rocket League*), sport titles put gamers to the test. Strap yourself in for *Forza*, lace your boots for *Pro Evolution Soccer*, and don't let being under seven foot tall put you off *NBA Live*...

Most goals scored in a game of *Rocket League* (team of two)

Too young to drive but old enough to smash records, Shashipreetham Rao Ravella (India, right) and Jamal Gianni Ragno (UK, far right) struck 56 goals against an AI opponent on Psyonix's soccer-themed destruction derby.

The record-breaking match took place at Legends of Gaming Live in London, UK, on 10 Sep 2016. The pair hadn't known each other, but teamed up when they both hit the event's leaderboards. "It was pretty lucky that we met," remarked Jamal, "or we wouldn't have got the record!"

"Most of my schoolteachers said they dreamed of being in the GWR book when they were younger. So when they saw my certificate they were quite surprised!"

Shashipreetham Rao Ravella

XI WORLD CUP GAMING MOMENTS

The FIFA World Cup is one of the most prolific sporting events in gaming, having been playable (officially and unofficially) in more than 100 games since the 1980s. With the countdown to the 2018 FIFA World Cup in Russia underway, we celebrate 11 memorable moments from the beautiful game's ultimate showpiece...

1986

2 WORLD CUP CARNIVAL

Even its makers admit that the **first official World Cup (WC) game** was a disaster. After development issues, publisher U.S. Gold rehashed Artic's earlier, unlicensed *World Cup Football* and sold it with a wallchart. *Amstrad Action* scored it 0%.

1986

3 PETER SHILTON'S HANDBALL MARADONA!

Grandslam wryly renamed their goalkeeper sim after a 1986 World Cup goal in which Argentina's Diego Maradona punched the ball past English goalie Peter Shilton. Despite the reference, the game was set in England's domestic league.

1985

1 TEHKAN WORLD CUP

First known as *Tecmo Cup*, this fondly remembered 1985 arcade title from Tecmo slyly rode the excitement of the 1986 World Cup in Mexico for marketing purposes. It borrowed kit likenesses for several nations and utilized a trackball controller for super-speedy action.

1993

4 FIFA INTERNATIONAL SOCCER

EA's first *FIFA* game – kicking off the **best-selling sports series** – was released just ahead of the 1994 World Cup in the USA. It boasted a WC-style tournament mode, albeit with fictional player names owing to U.S. Gold holding the WC licence.

1998

5 INTERNATIONAL SUPERSTAR SOCCER '98

Before Konami's *ISS* evolved into *PES*, the franchise spawned a top WC game. *ISS '98*, released close to France '98, structured its gameplay around the event. Cover stars included Colombia's flamboyant Carlos Valderrama (above).

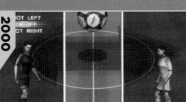

2000

6

MIA HAMM SOCCER 64

A redesign of *Michael Owen's WLS 2000* for the USA, this N64 title was the **first soccer videogame with female players**. It had a women's WC mode featuring 32 nations, plus sparse commentary from former forward Wendy Gebauer (USA).

2004

7

FIFA INTERACTIVE WORLD CUP

With FIFA's support, the eSports scene quickly developed its own World Cup. Launched in 2004, the annual FIWC sees gamers compete in EA's latest *FIFA* game. Mohamad Al-Bacha (DNK, above) was crowned 2016 champion.

2014

10

2014 FIFA WORLD CUP BRAZIL

EA's latest official iteration featured all 203 nations that took part in qualifying – the **most teams in a World Cup videogame**. It also included an EA Sports Talk Radio feature, with real-world pundits discussing the players' progress.

2010

8

2010 FIFA WORLD CUP SOUTH AFRICA

EA's slick *FIFA* spin-off is the **most critically acclaimed official WC game**, with a GameRankings score of 83.43%. Four years earlier, *FIFA 06: Road to FIFA World Cup* scored 62.55% – the **worst-rated WC game** based on at least 20 reviews.

2015

11

FOOTBALL MANAGER 2016

Sports Interactive's management games have been featuring the World Cup since the series' halcyon days. However, its 2016 game took an intriguing approach to the 2022 competition, which is set to take place in Qatar in winter. In the game, club protests over scheduling lead to it being moved to a new host nation for the summer.

2014

9

POKÉMON

Germany won the 2014 World Cup in Brazil, but Japan were the victors in gamers' eyes. The country's national side adopted Pikachu as its mascot, leading to a line of soccer merch including origami paper and doughnuts.

GUINNESS WORLD RECORDS®

SOCCER ROUND-UP

Few sports have translated as well to computer screens as the beautiful game itself. EA's *FIFA* is the **best-selling sports series**, with sales of more than 180 million, but other titles such as *PES* and *Football Manager* are also firm fan favourites.

Most voice actors in a soccer videogame

EA Sports' *FIFA 17* (2016) features a landmark cast of 22 voice actors as part of its RPG-style story quest "The Journey". In this mode – a first for the long-running series – players assume the role of fictional rising star Alex Hunter (right, with Wayne Rooney) as he forges a career in the English Premier League. The cast features pro soccer players such as England striker Harry Kane, who convincingly stars as himself.

> **"I went on YouTube, and you know you get the trending videos? There I was. There was my sweaty face. It's surreal."**
> Actor Tomiwa Edun on playing Alex Hunter in *FIFA 17*

Largest live attendance for an eSports tournament

Some 45,000 spectators watched the final of the *PES 2016* UEFA Euro 2016 virtual tournament in Paris, France, on 7 Jul 2016. The match was shown on a Supervision screen with a surface area of 432.54 m^2 (4,655 sq ft) – the **largest screen in a game tournament**. Spain's Alejandro Alguacil Segura (far left) proved victorious.

Most goals scored with the goalkeeper in *FIFA 17*

As verified by Twin Galaxies, Brazil's Fred Bugmann scored 21 goals with his team's goalie on 10 Feb 2017. Fred had strategically put Barcelona forward Lionel Messi in goal.

First one-man developer team to win a sports videogame BAFTA

Mobile RPG *New Star Soccer* (2012) beat *FIFA 13*, *F1 2012* and *Forza Horizon* to win the sports game BAFTA in 2013. The feat was all the more remarkable for the fact that the title was developed by one man – Simon Read (UK).

Longest single game of *Football Manager*

Before a liquid spillage cruelly destroyed his laptop, the UK's Darren Bland (above) had played the same game in *FM 2010* (SI Games) for 154 seasons. His in-game manager was 190 years old! As of 21 Dec 2016, France's Sébastien Griffet had managed OGC Nice in *FM 2009* for an astonishing 203 seasons, but technical issues in earlier versions of *FM* mean it's impossible to verify if the match-skipping "holiday" feature had been used.

Most followed *FIFA* Twitcher

As of 17 Mar 2017, soccer-mad gamer "Castro_1021" had 1,156,249 followers of his channel on Twitch – far more than any other broadcaster focusing on sports videogames. Hailing from Chicago, Illinois, USA, "Castro_1021" specializes in streaming EA's *FIFA* series, from building outrageous teams in the competitive online mode *FIFA* Ultimate Team to playing at events with real-life soccer pros such as Brazil's David Luiz.

Best-selling soccer videogame

With sales of 17.47 million across consoles, PC and hand-helds, according to VGChartz, the **best-selling soccer game (all platforms)** is *FIFA 15* (2014).

The PS4 *FIFA 17* (2016, right, with Chelsea's Eden Hazard) had sold 10.46 million by 17 Mar 2017, making it the **best-selling soccer game (single platform)**.

Fastest time to score a goal in *FIFA 17* on "Legendary" difficulty

Using Real Madrid's Welsh wing-wizard Gareth Bale, YouTuber "BennyCentral", aka Ben Perkin (UK), took just 10.59 sec to rustle the net on *FIFA*'s toughest setting on 30 Sep 2016. The record was set during a Facebook Live broadcast by the Dream Team at *The Sun* newspaper offices in London, UK. Ben said, "Gareth Bale is as good in the game as he is in real life."

PRO-FILE: YOUTUBER

HARRY "W2S" LEWIS (UK)

Subscribers: 9,814,002

Views: 2,467,246,710

Trivia: Part of the Ultimate Sidemen and known for his wild celebrations. His YouTube channel is the **most subscribed** and **most viewed dedicated FIFA channel**.

(Info correct as of 17 Mar 2017)

MINI-BYTES

FIFA 17 isn't the only soccer game with a story. The first part of Gremlin's *Roy of the Rovers* (1988) was an adventure game in which you had to rescue your kidnapped team-mates.

AMERICAN FOOTBALL

Its frantic blend of strategy and bone-crunching action make gridiron a true gaming champ. As John Madden once said, kids now learn this great sport by playing videogames...

Most common trophy in *Madden NFL 17*

According to PSNProfiles, the most common trophy for EA's latest football sim is "POW", which PS4 players earn by winning three tackle battles on offence. As of 2 Apr 2017, a massive 63.81% of gamers had achieved it.

The **most common trophy for the *Madden* series** is "Quick Off the Block" in the PS4 version of 2014's *Madden NFL 15*. A total of 85.19% of players had attained it by successfully performing the game's "off the line mechanic".

16

TEAMS

available in the first console version of *John Madden Football* in 1990.

Longest-running sports videogame series

Fronted by the legendary (now retired) US commentator and ex-coach John Madden (left), EA's *Madden NFL* series has endured for a quarterback-sacking 28 years. The series kicked off with *John Madden Football* (below) for the PC in 1988, and added *Madden NFL 17* to its ranks in Aug 2016.

Largest prize pool for an American football videogame tournament

Unveiled in Jun 2016, the four competitions that comprise the *Madden NFL* Championship Series carry a collective prize pot of $1 million (£796K). Champions also win rather dazzling belts.

First TV series based on a sports videogame

First airing on the US cable sports channel ESPN 2 on 6 Dec 2005, *Madden Nation* was a televised knock-out contest in which gamers competed in the latest *Madden* game, sometimes while paired up with real NFL pros. The show ran for four series, until 2008.

First videogame to feature real NFL players and teams
Although *Madden* kicked off in 1988, the series' debut didn't hold the official NFL licence. Instead, Atlus' *NFL*, released for the NES in 1989, was the first videogame to star real-life teams.

Most critically acclaimed American football videogame
Pipping a handful of *Madden* titles, Sega's Dreamcast classic *NFL 2K1* (2000) remains the highest-rated game of gridiron. It scores 94.5% on GameRankings, based on 21 critic reviews.

First Super Bowl correctly predicted by the Annual EA Super Bowl simulation
Simulating the match via *Madden NFL 15*, EA's game incredibly predicted the result of Super Bowl XLIX on 1 Feb 2015: a 28–24 win for the New England Patriots against rivals the Seattle Seahawks.

Best-selling American sports videogame series
EA's *Madden NFL* series had sold 127.93 million units as of 3 Apr 2017, according to VGChartz.
The single **best-selling American sports videogame** is 2006's *Madden NFL 07* (below), with sales of 10.02 million.

"Ladies sorry but... IT'S MADDEN *SEASON"*
Rapper Shad "Bow Wow" Moss tweets about his excitement for a new *Madden* game

Most used engine for sports videogames
As of 2 Apr 2017, EA's Ignite engine had powered 15 sports titles in the publisher's catalogue, including *Madden NFL 17*, *EA Sports UFC 2* and *NHL 17* (all 2016). According to EA, the engine's AI allows for in-game players who can "think, move and behave like real athletes".

Fastest completion of *NFL Street*
Debuting in 2004, EA's lauded but short-lived *NFL Street* series was an urbanized twist on gridiron, with a focus on freestyle tricks. On 2 Jun 2016, "RPGodfather" (USA) blitzed through the original's "NFL Challenge" campaign in 5 hr 40 min 1 sec.

BASKETBALL

There are lots of great elements in basketball games: sensational sim gameplay, massive soundtracks, real-life players. Best of all? You don't have to be crazy tall to play them...

First VR basketball videogame

NBA 2KVR was released in 2016 for the PlayStation VR, HTC Vive and Samsung Gear VR. Its collection of mini-games tests players' skills in a virtual-reality (VR) environment under the tutelage of Indiana Pacers star Paul George. In addition to this videogame, the 2016–17 season saw the *real* NBA embrace virtual reality in a big way. Select matches were filmed in VR.

Minnesota Timberwolves
21 kevin garnett
power forward

Most critically acclaimed basketball game

The PS2 version of 2003's *NBA Street Vol. 2* held a GameRankings score of 90.16%, based on 40 reviews, as of 4 Apr 2017. The fast-paced sim featured three-on-three match-ups and had a huge emphasis on flair and crazy tricks. It also included three versions of b-ball superstar Michael Jordan (see far right).

Longest-serving active basketball player in videogames

Kevin Garnett (USA, left) had starred in videogames for 21 years by the time he announced his retirement on 23 Sep 2016. The ex-Celtics and Timberwolves star debuted in *NBA Live 96* (1995) and was briefly playable in *NBA 2K17* (2016).

Rarest trophy in *NBA 2KVR*
As of 5 Apr 2017, just 0.93% of PlayStation gamers had achieved "Missin' Impossible" on the **first VR basketball game** (see above). Winning the trophy requires players to "complete Course 10 of Skills Challenge on All-Star difficulty, without a single miss, in SOLO mode". Just one player on PSNProfiles – "IkeDirty32" (USA) – had done it, on 9 Feb 2017.

Largest soundtrack for a basketball videogame

The slamming soundtrack of *NBA 2K16* (2015) featured 50 songs. DJs Khaled, Mustard and Premier chose 10 cuts each, ranging from the Ramones to Fergie. These were supplemented by two further playlists, which included the likes of LCD Soundsystem, Calvin Harris, Major Lazer and OneRepublic.

Earliest pre-release of a videogame

Fans who pre-ordered *NBA 2K17* were able to play the full game on 16 Sep 2016, four days ahead of its official release date. (*2K17* shares this record with 2017's *Halo Wars 2*). Cleveland Cavaliers star Kyrie Irving (below) is among the game's roster.

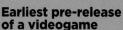

First basketball videogame

Basketball! was created for the Magnavox Odyssey and released in 1973 – the year after this first-generation console hit stores. Like many Magnavox titles, *Basketball!* required players to place a plastic overlay – in this case, depicting a basketball court – on their TV screen. This made the game's basic, blocky graphics seem more visually appealing.

The **first game with an NBA licence** didn't appear until 1980. *NBA Basketball* was released for Mattel's Intellivision, a second-generation console. MobyGames notes, "While officially licensed by the NBA, the game contains no team names or players."

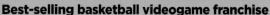

Best-selling basketball videogame franchise

Visual Concepts' *NBA 2K* series, which began in 1999, is the b-ball sales champ. As of 5 Apr 2017, it had sold a staggering 60.81 million copies, according to VGChartz.

The **best-selling basketball videogame** is *NBA 2K16*. Released in 2015, it had slam-dunked 8.23 million copies. The most recent, *NBA 2K17*, features Chicago Bulls star Jimmy Butler (left). *NBA 2K18*, scheduled for Sep 2017, will be the franchise's first for the Switch.

Most videogame cover appearances by a basketball star

Between 1992 and 2015, shooting guard legend Michael "MJ" Jordan (USA) had been on 10 game covers. His titles include the 1996 movie tie-in *Space Jam* (right) and a Japanese regional edition of *NBA Live 2002*. He also fronted a special edition of 2015's *NBA 2K16*, despite retiring in 2003.

> **"A lot of guys love to compete outside of being on the court, so we get to play virtual versions of ourselves... It's perfect in the summer."**
> *NBA 2K17* cover star Paul George of the Indiana Pacers

First HDR-compatible console game

The Xbox One S version of *NBA 2K17*, released in 2016, was the first game to offer true High Dynamic Range (HDR) support. HDR enhances colours and contrasts on screens and is seen as the next big step in display tech.

SPORTS ROUND-UP

By their very competitive nature, all sports can – and have – translated rather well into pixels. And we do mean *all*. You can play videogames for skateboarding, horse-racing and even (the fictional) ninja golf...

Best-selling extreme sports series

The USA's Tony Hawk (inset) is a legend both in gaming circles and in real-life skate parks. His skateboarding games for Activision (1999–2015) had shifted 54.9 million units as of 31 Mar 2017, according to VGChartz.

His 19 titles also give him the record for **most games endorsed by a pro athlete**.

Longest-running ice hockey series

Licensed from the USA's National Hockey League (NHL), EA's *NHL* franchise is second only to *Madden* as the longest-running sports series in gaming. The ice-cool sims debuted in Aug 1991 with *NHL Hockey* for the Sega Genesis and had skated out 26 main titles across 25 years, as of the release of *NHL 17* in Sep 2016.

The **most critically acclaimed ice hockey videogame** is EA's 2010–11 season iteration *NHL 11*. The sports sim has a GameRankings score of 89.5%. Destructoid hailed it "a supreme title".

> **"Tony Hawk is a 47-year-old millionaire who still dresses like he's 14. He is cool as hell and probably doing a 900 right now."**
>
> *VICE* magazine on skateboard legend Tony Hawk

GATORADE

Hortons®

IO TVs

Most critically acclaimed sports videogame

The PlayStation version of *Tony Hawk's Pro Skater 2* (Activision, 2000) boasts a GameRankings score of 94.75% based on 28 reviews. The masterclass in virtual skateboarding kick-started an explosion for extreme sports titles in the 2000s.

Ironically, the 2015 sequel *Tony Hawk's Pro Skater 5*, on the PS4, is the **worst-rated sports videogame**, scoring just 32.96%.

Highest score on *Tony Hawk's Pro Skater 2*: Hangar Level

The Hangar Level is one of the most popular stages for skate fans, and Matt Tholen (USA) recorded its highest score of 30,887,653, as verified on 25 Mar 2001 by Twin Galaxies.

The **best single combo on the Hangar Level** racked up a massive 8,009,394 points and was achieved by Hector T T Rodriguez (USA), as verified on 15 Apr 2006.

Longest-running horse-racing videogame series

Bolting out of the stalls in 1993, Koei's *Winning Post* series has been producing thoroughbred racing sims for approximately 24 years, as of the release of *Winning Post 8 2017* in Mar 2017. The games were released almost exclusively in Japan. In them, players are pitched as race-horse owners who are challenged with breeding winning steeds.

Longest-running baseball videogame series

Despite the USA being the spiritual home of baseball, Japan is home to the sport's longest-running gaming series. Following the release of *Jikkyō Powerful Pro Yakyū Heroes* in Dec 2016, Konami's *Jikkyō Powerful Pro Yakyū* (*Power Pro*) series had seen regular releases for 22 years. The first game, *Jikkyō Powerful Pro Yakyū*, was released in 1994 for the Super Famicom (SNES).

Most Xbox games completed
According to the player accounts tracked by TrueAchievements, Canada's "smrnov" had polished off 1,669 games with Xbox achievements as of 31 Mar 2017. The first game that he finished was the ice hockey sim *NHL 2K6* on Xbox 360, on 2 Jan 2006.

Rarest trophy in the *NHL* videogame series
As of 31 Mar 2017, only 0.12% of *NHL 12* PS3 players had won the "Raise Your Banner '12" trophy – awarded for getting all the other trophies.

Longest "word" used in a commercially released videogame title (English language)
The opening "word" in 2009 BASE-jumping simulation *AaaaaAAaaaAAAaaAAAAaA AAAA!!! – A Reckless Disregard for Gravity* (Dejobaan Games) features 28 characters.

6 MILLION FAN VOTES cast to select the cover star of EA's *NHL 2017*. The St Louis Blues' Vladimir Tarasenko won the public poll.

MINI-BYTES
Far from given up with games, Tony Hawk announced on Twitter that he was filming a documentary about his *Pro Skater* series, entitled *Pretending I'm a Superman*. The title was based on a song lyric by the punk band Goldfinger, who featured on the first game's soundtrack.

In 2016, the website A.V. Club flagged 14 videogames that it thought would make great Olympic events. The list included both *Speedball* and *Ninja Golf* – a 1990 oddity in which black-clad golfers have to fight their way to each hole!

Most ported sports videogame
The retro classics *California Games* (Epyx, 1987, below) and *Speedball 2: Brutal Deluxe* (Bitmap Brothers, 1990) have both been ported and remade for 16 different platforms. The former is a mix of summery events including BMX and surfing. Contrastingly, *Speedball 2* is a futuristic take on handball involving armour, power-ups and ice-cream vendors.

Best-selling golf videogame
EA's *Tiger Woods* series (now *Rory McIlroy*) might have ruled the courses in more recent years, but it was never able to dethrone *Golf* (1984). The plainly named NES game had sold 4.01 million units as of 1 Apr 2017, according to VGChartz.

The **most critically acclaimed golf videogame**, however, is *Tiger Woods PGA Tour 2003* on the GameCube, with a GameRankings score of 90.55%.

Fastest time to perform the entire Tricktionary in *OlliOlli*
Playing on a livestream in London, UK, on 27 Jul 2016, Samuel Brayley (UK) performed all 104 tricks in Roll7's skateboarding game in 2 min 48 sec.

He also achieved the **fastest time to perform the Tricktionary in *OlliOlli2: Welcome to Olliwood***: 1 min 47 sec. Samuel had spent a week devising a system in which he could memorize every trick in both titles.

ROCKET LEAGUE

Combining acrobatic vehicles with soccer-based gameplay, Psyonix's *Rocket League* became a talking point when it was unleashed in 2015. It quickly graduated from an indie game riffing on destruction derbies to an eSports favourite.

Fewest shots on goal in a *Rocket League* Championship Series game

A Season 2 league game between Europe's OhMyDog and Canada's Northern Gaming on 2 Oct 2016 featured a total of just three shots. Northern Gaming won 1–0 after 32 sec of overtime.

First cross-network game for Xbox One

A 2016 update made *Rocket League* the first game to enable "true" cross-network play between Xbox One and PC owners. Earlier titles such as *Killer Instinct* allowed cross-platform play on Microsoft servers, but *Rocket League*'s cross-compatibility works via Steam. A "step towards totally open multiplayer across all platforms," said GamesRadar.

Best-selling game on PlayStation Store (current)

In Jan 2017, Sony revealed that *Rocket League* was the most purchased title from the PlayStation Store in 2016 for both the USA and Europe. The game outsold the blockbusters *FIFA 17*, *Minecraft: PS4 Edition*, *Call of Duty: Infinite Warfare* and *Battlefield 1* to take the top spot in the year-end Top 20. At the UK store, it held a five-star score from 183,021 user ratings.

Most goals in a *Rocket League* Championship Series game by a single player

On 10 Jul 2016, Italian hotshot Francesco "Kuxir97" Cinquemani scored an incredible seven goals in a single game of the Season 1 online finals. His team FlipSid3 Tactics beat Supersonic Avengers 8–0 in the official competition, hosted by Twitch and developer Psyonix.

First *Rocket League* world champions

The *Rocket League* Championship Series (RLCS) is hosted twice a year. On 7 Aug 2016, the iBUYPOWER Cosmic team – Ted "0ver_Zer0" Keil (USA), Cameron "Kronovi" Bills (USA) and Brandon "Lachinio" Lachin (CAN) – beat FlipSid3 Tactics to become the first RLCS world champions.

Most assists in a *Rocket League* Championship Series game by a single player

Remco "remkoe" den Boer (NLD) and Mark "Markydooda" Exton (UK) each recorded five assists in single games in Season 1 of the RLCS: "remkoe" on 8 May 2016 and "Markydooda" on 3 Jul 2016.

Most watched *Rocket League* video

"PIE FACE CHALLENGE GAME w/ Let's Play ROCKET LEAGUE Part 3: BOTS! (FGTEEV Family Fun)" had 12,987,110 views on YouTube as of 6 Mar 2017. In it, the Family Gaming Team ("FGTeeV") combined *Rocket League* with the table-top game *Pie Face!* Players risked a face-load of whipped cream if they conceded a goal.

Longest single pro game of *Rocket League*

On 4 Dec 2016, in the Championship Series grand final in Amsterdam, Netherlands, Mockit Aces played FlipSid3 Tactics for 12 min 17 sec. This included the regulation 5 min of normal time and 7 min 17 sec of overtime. In the end, FlipSid3 Tactics triumphed by four matches to one.

Most goals scored in *Rocket League* using an instrument controller

New Zealand Twitcher and programmer Dylan "Rudeism" Beck claims to "play games wrong". On 5 Feb 2017, he used a *Guitar Hero* controller to score 88 goals against the AI in a single game.

MINI-BYTES

Rocket-powered cars playing soccer not crazy enough for you? Psyonix added a battle royale game mode called *Rocket League Rumble* in 2016. Players can collect power-ups such as the ability to freeze or punch the ball, or unleash a whirling tornado. Meanwhile, the Power Hitter, as the game's Wikia explains, "allows you to hit everything harder".

PRO-FILE: eSPORTS STAR

MARK "MARKYDOODA" EXTON (UK)

Winnings: $26,353

Trivia: Mark co-founded *Rocket League* squad Teamy Weamy, acquired by the US/European FlipSid3 Tactics.

(Info from e-Sportearnings, 3 Mar 2017)

Most critically acclaimed videogame for a fictitious sport

Before emerging as an eSports success, *Rocket League* was the highest-rated fictitious sport on GameRankings. As of 6 Mar 2017, its PlayStation 4 incarnation held a score of 87.16% from 31 reviews. "You don't need to be a fan of football or racing games," noted games™. "It'll appeal to anyone looking for a new thrill in gaming."

Most videogame BAFTAs won by a sports game

Rocket League won three awards at the 12th British Academy Games Awards. It beat *Destiny: The Taken King*, *Lovers in a Dangerous Spacetime* and *Splatoon* in the Multiplayer category; *Disney Infinity 3.0*, *FIFA 16* and *Guitar Hero: Live* in Family; and *Football Manager 2016*, *DiRT RALLY* and *FIFA 16* in Sport.

Rocket League was the night's joint biggest winner, with fellow indie games *Her Story* and *Everybody's Gone to the Rapture* also scooping three awards each. The event took place at London's Tobacco Dock, UK, on 7 Apr 2016.

FORZA

Often described as Microsoft's answer to Sony's *Gran Turismo*, the *Forza* series means that Xboxers aren't left breathing fumes on the starting grid when it comes to racing sims. Drive those beautiful machines hard...

Fastest time to complete the Race for the Record challenge in *Forza Motorsport 6* (team of two)
Austin Cindric (USA) and Alex Arnou (FRA) completed all three races of *Motorsport 6*'s Race for the Record in 1 hr 42 min 6 sec.

The duo raced on 12 Dec 2015 at the Petersen Automotive Museum in Los Angeles, California, USA.

Fastest *Forza Horizon 3* car
Forza Horizon 3's fastest stock (unmodified) car, as confirmed by developer Playground Games, is the 2012 Hennessey Venom GT. It can speed along at 273 mph (439 km/h).

The 2011 Bugatti Veyron Super Sport is second (268 mph; 431 km/h); third is the 2015 Koenigsegg One:1 (266 mph; 428 km/h).

Worst-rated *Forza* game
Forza Motorsport 5 (2013) was criticized for omitting much of *Forza 4*'s more popular content. However, its GameRankings score as of 2 Mar 2017 was a creditable 79.49%, from 46 reviews.

Most critically acclaimed racing game for an eighth-generation console

The Xbox One's classy *Forza Horizon 3* (2016) takes pole position with a GameRankings score of 92.14%, based on 56 reviews, as of 2 Mar 2017. It was the ninth most critically acclaimed racer overall.

The game is set in a sprawling open-world version of Australia, with locales based on the Outback and Surfers Paradise. AusGamers.com duly rated it 10/10: "A strong contender for Cobber of the Year, mate."

Most completed Xbox One game

According to the Xbox site TrueAchievements, *Forza Horizon 2 Presents Fast & Furious* had been completed by 56,298 players as of 15 Feb 2017 – a massive 57.6% of its tracked player-base. The standalone expansion was released to tie in with the *Furious 7* movie in Mar 2015. Players acquire desirable vehicles from the film by winning races.

Best-selling Xbox driving sim series

Forza has sales to back up the hype: 25.69 million across all Microsoft consoles as of 2 Mar 2017, according to VGChartz. The biggest seller is *Forza Motorsport 3* (2009), which has shifted 5.49 million units.

However, *Forza Motorsport 5* (2013), with 2.28 million, is the **best-selling racing game on Xbox One**. The slick racer squeals in ahead of *Forza Horizon 3* (2.12 million).

MINI-BYTES

Forza Horizon 3's stunning skyscapes are (mostly) the work of Mother Nature. The game's developers filmed the sky with a 4K camera, creative director Ralph Fulton told Kotaku. "That created over 1TB per day of data for an entire summer, to create an authentic Australian sky."

Most drivable surfaces in a videogame

Forza Motorsport 6 (2015) features 148 individual driving surfaces. Each one's friction is affected by weather variables.

Tied in to that are the game's sophisticated rain effects and 3D puddles. Each surface has its own unique porosity, meaning that rainwater settles on them differently. The resulting puddles offer their own values for friction, drag and elasticity.

Most cars in an eighth-generation platform racing game

Forza Motorsport 6 racers are spoiled for choice with a selection of 460 cars – twice as many as *Motorsport 5*.

This is far fewer than 7th-gen rival *Gran Turismo 6* – which, with 1,237, has the **most cars in a racing game**. But *Forza 6*'s mix of old and new vehicles – from the 1939 Maserati 8CTF to the 2017 Ford GT – is still impressive.

Longest marathon on a racing game

Cara Scott (UK), Andrea Lorenzo Facchinetti (ITA), Johannes Knapp (DEU), Hélène Cressot (FRA) and Jesús Sicilian Sánchez (ESP) all played *Forza 6* using a Ford GT on the Le Mans circuit for 48 hr 29 min 21 sec. The event was organized by Ford in Cologne, Germany, on 16–18 Aug 2016.

First electric vehicle in a *Forza* videogame

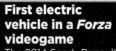

The 2014 Spark-Renault SRT_01E Formula E was added to *Forza Motorsport 5* via DLC. In real life, the car was the first to be approved for Formula E racing by the Fédération Internationale de l'Automobile (FIA), the sport's governing body.

RACING ROUND-UP

With gaming tech improving all the time, the only thing missing from the modern glut of racers is the wind messing up your hair. From the majestic realism of *Gran Turismo* to the nitro-burning joy of *Need for Speed*, sit back, strap in, enjoy...

Longest exclusivity deal between a game publisher and car manufacturer

In 2000, the German car manufacturer Porsche signed a deal with Electronic Arts, ensuring that its cars could only feature in EA games. Key to that, of course, was EA's big-selling *Need for Speed* series (below). That contract ended in 2016, after 17 years.

Best-selling driving sim series

Created by pro racing driver and game designer Kazunori Yamauchi (JPN), Sony's *Gran Turismo* series has sold 71.81 million units since its 1997 debut according to VGChartz, as of 4 Apr 2017.

The incoming *GT Sport* (2017, shown right) sees the series extend its record as the **longest-running PlayStation franchise**: currently 17 years 281 days, as of *GT6*'s Track Path Editor app landing on 30 Sep 2015.

First dedicated team-based racer

Inspired by retro racers and multiplayer online battle arena games, Gamious' top-down *Team Racing League* sees players racing online in groups of three. Its gameplay is unique in that players win – and lose – as one. The game was set to enter Steam Early Access in May 2017.

Most trophies in a videogame

According to PSNProfiles, the popular PS4 racer *DRIVECLUB* (Sony, 2014) has 128 possible trophies for virtual petrol-heads to collect, placing it ahead of *Rise of the Tomb Raider* and *Zen Pinball 2* (both 125) and the MMO *DC Universe Online* (123), as of 21 Mar 2017.

Most critically acclaimed racing videogame

As testament to the game's impact two decades ago, the original *Gran Turismo* (1997) for the PlayStation is still the highest-rated racer. As of 4 Apr 2017, Sony's sim had a GameRankings score of 94.95%. It sat ahead of key entries from rival series *Burnout*, *Forza* and *Project Gotham Racing*.

Most licensed bikes in a videogame

As of 5 Apr 2017, Milestone's *Ride 2* (2016) featured 232 real-world motorcycles, with more to be released as DLC. According to the developer, each of the game's models boasts a level of precision that's on par with the vehicles in *Gran Turismo*. The roster includes bikes from BMW, Ducati, Kawasaki, Suzuki, Triumph and Yamaha.

Most crowdfunded racing videogame

Slightly Mad Studios' *Project CARS* (2015) secured €2,255,535 (£1,901,150; $2,890,760) from public backers in Apr 2013, with the developer also adding to the total. In all, some 80,000 fans bought a creative "stake" in the sim's making – the **most "stakeholders" involved in a racer**.

Most videogame cars built in the real world

For *Gran Turismo*'s 15th anniversary, several car manufacturers designed exclusive concept cars to feature in the games. As of 4 Apr 2017, a total of 20 cars had been created, but three makers had also turned their designs into working, one-off models: the Mercedes AMG Vision Gran Turismo (VGT) (top right; in-game, bottom), the Volkswagen GTI Roadster VGT and the Bugatti VGT.

Greatest light-intensity range in a racing sim

Developed to make use of the High Dynamic Range (HDR) capabilities of the PS4 and PS4 Pro, *Gran Turismo Sport* (2017) supports up to 10,000 nits – the unit in which light intensity is measured. This far exceeds current picture expectations; the Ultra HD Premium standard for television sets is *only* 1,000 nits.

First racing videogame soundtrack CD

Psygnosis' futuristic racer *wipE'out"* was released on 29 Sep 1995, alongside a soundtrack CD. The album featured electronica acts such as The Prodigy – all selected as a means to encourage super-fast driving.

Most prolific racing videogame series

With 25 titles dating back to 1994, EA's *Need for Speed* series has had more games of its name released than any other racing franchise. A new free-to-play MMO, *Need for Speed: Edge*, is in development at EA's Korean studio Spearhead.

NFS games had sold 101.52 million units as of 4 Apr 2017, according to VGChartz. It's the **best-selling street racer series** and second only to *Mario Kart* (110.69 million) as the **best-selling racing series** overall.

Longest-standing videogame record

On 1 Sep 1982, Todd Rogers (USA) set a time of 5.51 sec on Activision's *Dragster* (1980), as verified by Twin Galaxies. That early GWR gaming record remained unbeaten for 34 years 215 days, as of 4 Apr 2017.

Longest-running publisher of arcade racing games

Out Run developer Sega has been making arcade-style racers for a period of 36 years. In 1976, the company launched *Road Race* and *Moto-Cross* (later rebranded as *Fonz*, left) into arcade halls. Its most recent racer, *Sonic & All-Stars Racing Transformed* (right), took its kart-fuelled fun on to consoles in Nov 2012.

SCALEBOUND

This Xbox One exclusive was hyped as one of 2017's most anticipated games; the co-op action RPG featured giant, loathsome monsters aplenty and a massive dragon companion. PlatinumGames director Hideki Kamiya even described it as "the biggest game of my career". So when Microsoft announced the game's cancellation in Jan 2017, it was a shock. Eurogamer blamed its demise on "issues with the game's engine" and "overdue deadlines".

THE DARK KNIGHT

EA's Batman game was to coincide with Christopher Nolan's *The Dark Knight* movie in 2008. But when its studio Pandemic missed its design goals, the game was pushed back to tie in with the film's DVD release. When that deadline was also blown, the game was ditched altogether. It cost EA some $100 million (£65 million) in lost revenue – the **costliest missed deadline for a videogame**.

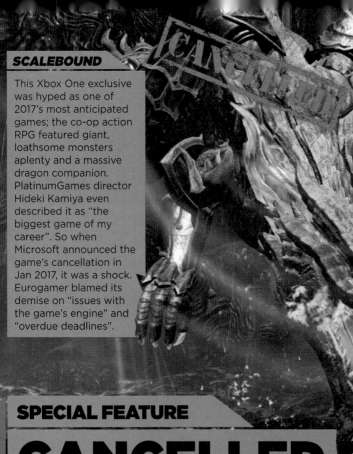

SPECIAL FEATURE

CANCELLED GAMES

Developers can pour months into bringing their works to life, but not every title sees the light of day. In some cases, games were not only potentially lucrative, but finished, too. GWR braves a walk through the sorrowful wasteland of the hits that never were...

STAR WARS: REPUBLIC COMMANDO 2

Having ended on a cliffhanger, fans were readily clamouring for a sequel to the 2005 FPS *Republic Commando*. However, turmoil at LucasArts sank that hope. Programmer Brett Douville told Cinelinx that one idea for the game-that-never-was had been to send gamers hunting Jedi as they execute "Order 66".

STAR WARS 1313

Star Wars games have been around since near the industry's inception. The franchise's ongoing saga and explosive space action have led to it becoming the **most prolific game series based on a film property**, but not every project in development saw the light of day. *Star Wars 1313* has acquired near-mythological status. It was conceived as a gritty Boba Fett game, and intended as a spiritual successor to the 2002 actioner *Star Wars: Bounty Hunter*. Formally announced in 2012, the game was cancelled less than a year later in the aftermath of Disney's acquisition of Lucasfilm. Fans remain hopeful that the title might one day be resurrected.

BEAVIS & BUTT-HEAD ARCADE

MTV's animated slackers had their first game in 1994. When the duo hit the big screen in 1996, Atari wanted an arcade follow-up. Operating from 3DO console hardware, the ensuing beat-'em-up failed to impress test audiences and it was dumped. However, in 2016 one of only 12 prototypes was restored by the Galloping Ghost Arcade in Brookfield, Illinois, USA.

ALIENS: CRUCIBLE

In 2006, Obsidian announced that it was developing an RPG set in the *Aliens* universe. But despite the game's reputed near-complete state, publisher Sega canned it in 2009. Several years later, it was speculated that the plug was pulled because fans wouldn't care for an RPG, so Sega put its resources into the 2013 FPS *Aliens: Colonial Marines*. Disappointingly for fans, that game emerged to poor reviews.

STAR FOX 2

Featuring Fox McCloud's band of space mercenaries, *Star Fox 2* was set to expand on the 1993 rail-shooter's premise. This time players would pick battles, adding a layer of strategy and exploration that the first game lacked. The space actioner was poised to release on the SNES in 1995, but Nintendo pulled the plug, reportedly fearful that sales would be affected by the impending launch of the N64. Instead, the publisher rebooted the original *Star Fox* in 3D for its new console.

THE LORD OF THE RINGS: THE WHITE COUNCIL

Amid multiple spin-offs from movies, *The White Council*, an open-world game, allowed players to cross Middle-earth, choosing to be good or evil. Announced in 2006, the RPG promised adventures based on the films and novels. It was put on "indefinite hold" in 2007, reportedly owing to management problems at EA.

STARCRAFT: GHOST

Perhaps the most notorious game to get the axe is *StarCraft: Ghost*. While technically a spin-off (rather than a sequel) to Blizzard's real-time strategies, it was a chance for fans to get a closer look at its beloved universe, this time in the guise of a stealth adventure. Sadly, *Ghost* was placed on "indefinite hold" in 2006, before being scrapped in 2014. Until then it had briefly held the title of **most delayed stealth game**.

175

FIGHTING

Ever since the first brawlers stormed 1980s arcade halls, fighting games have transformed gamers into ferocious martial artists. From *Street Fighter*'s crazy combos to *WWE*'s technical tussling, the genre remains a force in modern gaming.

Most played MMO (current)

According to SuperData, Neople's enduring *Dungeon Fighter Online* (2005) was the most played Massively Multiplayer Online (MMO) game in 2016. It attracted an average of 25.1 million players per month. The game mixes RPG character-building with side-scrolling brawling, paying homage to classic beat-'em-ups such as *Final Fight* (Capcom, 1989). It's especially popular in its native Asia, leading to a spin-off anime series and an English-language version. The game was relaunched globally in 2015.

STREET FIGHTER

Celebrating its 30th anniversary in 2017, *Street Fighter* created the blueprint for modern fighting games. It's averaged over a million sales a year and turned martial arts heroes Ryu and Ken into icons.

Most prolific fighting-game series

Excluding compilations and cross-platform ports, there had been 53 individual games in Capcom's *Street Fighter* series, as of 15 Mar 2017. This includes the main series, which debuted in 1987, spin-offs such as *Street Fighter EX,* crossovers including *Marvel vs. Capcom,* and some non-genre spin-offs, including card battle games and even a life simulation based on the 1994 anime *Street Fighter II: The Animated Movie.*

Largest collection of *Street Fighter* memorabilia

Canada's Clarence Lim owns 2,723 individual *Street Fighter* items, as counted in Ontario on 29 Jun 2014. "I'm honoured," he said of his record. "When I was a lad, my father would flip through the *Guinness World Records* books with me."

Least popular character in *Ultra Street Fighter IV*

Fighting-game site EventHubs lists Rufus as the least used character in competitive *Ultra Street Fighter IV* bouts. The dive-kicking American had a score of 361, based on his use in a primary, secondary or tertiary role. Just 181 of 13,994 players had called upon the fighter as of 22 Mar 2017.

Most tournament results for a *Street Fighter V* character

Playing as Chun-Li, competitive *SFV* players had achieved "top-placed" finishes in 433 tournaments as of 22 Mar 2017, according to fighting site Shoryuken. This puts the whirlwind-kicking queen (above right) far ahead of others from the latest game, including Ryu and Ken.

Highest-ranked *Ultra Street Fighter IV* player

With 217,891 points as of 22 Mar 2017, Japan's Daigo "The Beast" Umehara (right) is *Ultra Street Fighter IV*'s highest-ranked player overall, according to Shoryuken. The scoring system is based on a player's top 12 tournaments throughout his career.

First videogame based on a movie based on a videogame

Unveiled in arcades in Jun 1995, *Street Fighter: The Movie* was a one-on-one fighting game based on the 1994 movie version of Capcom's series. Looper.com included the effort in a list of "Worst Video Game Rip-Offs Ever", noting its debt to *SF*'s rival *Mortal Kombat*. A home-console version appeared in Japan.

Largest eSports fighting game tournament

The Evolution Championship Series (EVO) has only grown since its 2002 debut. EVO 2016 – in Las Vegas, Nevada, USA, on 15–17 Jul – attracted 10,024 individuals, fighting in nine games. The *Street Fighter V* tournament was the most subscribed, with 5,107 competitors – making it also the **largest Street Fighter tournament**.

25 YEARS

How long the developer took to identify the characters on *Street Fighter II*'s title screen. (It's Max and Scott.)

> ## "Until I get the check, [Mom's] not going to believe me."
> Du "NuckleDu" Dang on winning $230,000 at the 2016 Capcom Cup

MINI-BYTES

Created by design studio Soda Pop Miniatures, *Way of the Fighter* is a crowdfunded card-and-dice game inspired by *Street Fighter* and other 2D fighters. It narrowly failed on Kickstarter in 2016, but was successfully revived – and, as of 15 Feb 2017, had 1,385 backers pledging $91,905 (£73,514). It was scheduled for Aug 2017.

Jean-Claude Van Damme starred in the 1994 *Street Fighter* movie... despite being the inspiration for Johnny Cage in *Mortal Kombat*, which got its own adaptation the next year.

PRO-FILE: eSPORTS STAR

LEE "INFILTRATION" SEON-WOO (KOR)

Winnings: $184,046

Trivia: Lee has won four EVO titles competing in *SF* games. However, he couldn't drive when he won a car at a tournament in 2012.

(Source: esportsearnings.com, 22 Mar 2017)

Largest prize pool for a fighting-game tournament

The final of the 2016 Capcom Cup – held on 2–3 Dec in Anaheim, California, USA – concluded a season-long hunt for *Street Fighter V*'s 32 finest players. A prize pool of at least $350,000 (£277,000) was split among the top eight. In an all-American final, Du "NuckleDu" Dang defeated Ricki Ortiz, taking home around $230,000 (£182,000) – the **highest first prize for a fighting-game tournament**.

Most Capcom Pro Tour ranking points (cumulative)

From 2014 to 2016, South Korea's Lee "Infiltration" Seon-woo (above left) won 3,388 points by fighting in *Street Fighter* tournaments, as recognized by Capcom. He was tipped for glory at the 2016 Capcom Cup but

Most consecutive opponents on *Street Fighter V*

In 10 hr 36 min of play, UK fighting-game master Ryan Hart conquered 260 foes at *SFV*'s launch in Manchester, UK, on 16 Feb 2016. "I'm very proud of my record," he told redbull.com. "[It's] an acknowledgement of my

Longest marathon on a fighting game

A *Street Fighter X Tekken* bout lasting exactly 48 hr secured Anthony "AJ" Lysiak (USA) the fighting game record. The marathon was staged at the Game Emporium in Garrettsville, Ohio, USA, on 4–6 May 2012.

Most critically acclaimed *Street Fighter* videogame

Street Fighter IV (2009) on PS3 held a 93.64% rating on GameRankings as of 22 Mar 2017. It pipped 2010's *Super*

TEKKEN

Bold characters, muscle-twinging moves and a strangely compelling story that refuses to end... These are just several traits that have made Bandai Namco's 3D series the real deal. Dare you enter the King of Iron Fist event?

Greatest weight loss by a videogame character

In the console release of *Tekken 6* (2009), martial arts prodigy Robert "Bob" Richards becomes so absorbed with his celebrity status that his weight reduces from 155 kg (341 lb) to just 70 kg (154 kg) – a loss of 85 kg (187 lb). This more agile version of Bob became a DLC character called "Slim Bob" in *Tekken Tag Tournament 2*.

Longest-running videogame storyline

While fighting games aren't typically renowned for their storylines, *Tekken*'s ongoing saga of a global martial arts tournament – and the troubled Mishima family – has endured for 20 years 99 days. That's without any reboots or extended gaps. The smash debut released on 9 Dec 1994, while *Tekken 7*, (pictured with Heihachi Mishima, near right) pummelled its way into arcade halls on 18 Mar 2015. Bandai Namco had described its story as "dark".

Such a life-span also makes these big-time brawlers the **longest-running 3D fighting game series**.

Most female characters in a 3D fighting series

Since its debut, *Tekken* has created 23 playable female characters, from series favourite Nina Williams (left) to *Tekken 7* debutante Katarina Alves.

Koei Tecmo's *Dead or Alive* has also featured 23 females, seven of which are guests from other franchises.

Most moves for a *Tekken* character

The masked Mexican wrestler King II is armed with a ferocious 186 moves in *Tekken 7*. It beats the fighter's own previous record of 176, which he held for *Tekken Tag Tournament 2*.

Shortest *Tekken* character

At 155 cm (5 ft 1 in) tall, the cloned dinosaur Alex from *Tekken 2* (1995) is the shortest character to star in the series. Gon from *Tekken 3* (1997) – another dino – is likely shorter, but he's a one-time guest character who was never given an official height by Bandai Namco.

Best-selling fighting game series (minus crossovers)

A heavyweight in the arena and in the charts, *Tekken* games had sold 33.91 million units as of 2 May 2017, according to VGChartz. This excludes its own unlikely crossover, *Street Fighter X Tekken*, and comes ahead of *Tekken 7*'s home-version release in Jun 2017.

Highest-earning *Tekken* player

According to e-Sportsearnings, Daichi "Nobi" Nakayama (JPN) had won $55,658 (£44,963) by playing *Tekken 6* and *7*, as of 2 May 2017. His triumph at Japan's King of Iron Fist Tournament on 12 Dec 2015 earned him the bulk of a ¥5,000,000 (£27,112; $41,126) pot – the **largest *Tekken* tournament prize pool**.

First guest videogame character in *Tekken*

Strutting in from rival series *Street Fighter* (Capcom), Akuma (main picture, far right) is the first game character to guest in a *Tekken* title. The flame-haired terror is playable in *Tekken 7*, complete with his iconic fireballs and dragon punches.

The **first guest character in *Tekken*** overall is Gon from 1997's *Tekken 3*. This little dinosaur owes its origins to a manga series created in 1991.

First swordsman in a 3D fighting game

Yoshimitsu made his debut in the original *Tekken* on 9 Dec 1994, introducing swordplay to the 3D genre.

MINI-BYTES

Wang Jinrei (below left) and Ganryu (right) are the least popular characters in *Tekken* – according to series producer Katsuhiro Harada. He told VentureBeat: "Ganryu's pretty strong, but in both player usage and overall popularity, he's at the very bottom."

Largest *Pokkén Tournament* tournament

A total of 1,180 *Pokkén Tournament* players engaged in a critter-themed rumble at the 2016 EVO in Las Vegas, USA, on 15–17 Jul. Bandai Namco's *Pokkén Tournament* (2015) is a crossover fighter that combines *Tekken* mechanics with Pokémon creatures, such as the four-armed Machamp (right).

Most viewed fan film based on *Tekken*

As of 2 May 2017, "Real Life Tekken Fight | Hwoarang Vs Bruce" by "GingerNinjaTrickster" had been viewed 11,544,321 times on YouTube. The choreographed live-action film sees two martial artists replicating moves from the fighting series. One user comment read: "I hope Hwoarang washed his feet."

SUPER SMASH BROS.

Nintendo's now-legendary series challenges players to send their opponents flying from a host of crazy stages. It features a huge stable of unlikely fighting talent, from Link and Luigi to Pikachu and PAC-Man.

Longest winning streak of tournaments in *Super Smash Bros. for Wii U*

Chile's Gonzalo "ZeRo" Barrios won an incredible 56 consecutive tournaments from Nov 2014 to 18 Oct 2015.

Along the way, the competitive ace emerged triumphant from a pool of 1,926 entrants at EVO 2015 in Las Vegas, USA, on 17–19 Jul, with a "perfect" performance – the **largest fighting-game tournament won without dropping a round**. ZeRo breezed unbeaten through 10 "best-of-three" sets and a scintillating "best-of-five" grand final.

Most viewed combo video on YouTube

Hailed by Kotaku as the "most notorious *Super Smash Bros.* combo in history", the "Wombo Combo" became a viral hit when it was recorded during a pro *Melee* match in 2008. The attack saw the players "Tang" and "SilentSpectre" juggle an opponent in a two-versus-two match. As of 10 Mar 2017, the video had 12,314,758 views. A documentary was even made about its legacy in 2016.

Longest home run in *Super Smash Bros. Melee*

Melee features a mini-game in which players pummel a sandbag for 10 sec, then hit it up a baseball field. In "Falcon HRC 7288.0/2221.3 [WR]" – a YouTube video posted on 8 Nov 2016 – Mike "HRC typo" Bassett (USA) played as *F-Zero*'s Captain Falcon (left). He punched the battered bag a massive 2,221.3 m (7,287 ft 8.6 in) upfield.

Strongest recorded hit in *Super Smash Bros. 4* without use of items

Austria's "Beefy Smash Doods" pulled off a huge strike in *Super Smash Bros. for Wii U* that inflicted 158% of damage. It lasted just 8 sec and saw a tree being swatted with a baseball bat. "Smash 4 Wii U – The Strongest Hit", posted to the team's YouTube channel on 3 Sep 2015, shows the move.

Most played character in *Super Smash Bros. Melee*

The fabulous Fox McCloud had been chosen by tournament players 14,388 times as of 14 Mar 2017, according to smashboards. com. He's been a series regular since the N64's original *Super Smash Bros.*

The **most played in *Super Smash Bros. for Wii U*** is our old pal Mario – chosen 4,218 times as of the same date.

Most eSports tournament results for a single player

As of 10 Mar 2017, *Melee* supremo Jason "Mew2King" Zimmerman (left) had registered "high-placed" finishes in 513 pro eSports tournaments, winning 297 of them, according to e-Sportsearnings. He competes in all games across the *Super Smash Bros.* series, including the mod *Project M*.

Most popular *Super Smash Bros.* YouTube channel

"ZeRo" (see opposite) hosts a YouTube channel that, as of 14 Mar 2017, had 198,553 subscribers. "Mew2King Getting Falcon Punched 3 Times In 5 Minutes" is his most popular video by far.

100k

SIGNATURES on petition for *Melee* player "Leffen" – denied a US visa because the game is "not... a legitimate sport".

Largest *Super Smash Bros.* tournament

A total of 2,662 *Super Smash Bros. for Wii U* gamers competed at the EVO Championship Series on 15–17 Jul 2016. The event, staged across two venues in Las Vegas, Nevada, USA, was the biggest of its kind.

It was won by Canadian Elliot "Ally" Carroza-Oyarce, who has been hailed as *SSB*'s best Mario player.

Most popular character in *Super Smash Bros. Brawl*

The honourable Meta Knight had been used by tournament players 1,147 times as of 10 Mar 2017, according to smashboards.com. Traditionally from Nintendo's *Kirby* series, Meta Knight is a masked space-knight who captains a giant battleship. In 2011, it was reported that he was actually being banned from many pro *Brawl* tournaments for being too powerful.

FIGHTING ROUND-UP

Some of the oldest fighting-game franchises still pack a mighty punch today. From *Mortal Kombat* to *The King of Fighters*, these big-shot brawlers aren't to be messed with...

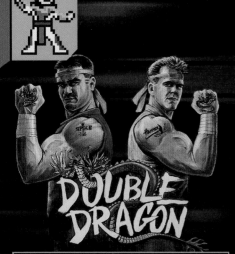

Longest-running fighting game series based on a manga

Many manga series have become popular game franchises, but few have run for as long as Bandai Namco's *Naruto: Ultimate Ninja*. Between its PS2 debut of the same name on 23 Oct 2003 and the *Naruto Shippuden: Ultimate Ninja Storm 4* expansion *Road to Boruto* (below), released on 2 Feb 2017, the series had run for 13 years 102 days. The games offer OTT action with crazy, supernatural powers.

漫
220
画

MILLION
sales of the *Naruto* manga comics, reported in Oct 2015 – the fourth best-selling manga series.

Most ported fighting game

Powering into arcade halls in 1987, Technōs' *Double Dragon* helped kick the martial arts genre into shape. As a mark of its longevity and influence, the co-op brawler has been ported to 24 different platforms over 30 years. More recent ports include the PS4, mobiles and Zeebo.

Best-selling PS4 fighting game

As of 21 Mar 2017, *Mortal Kombat X* (Warner Bros., 2015) had sold 2.95 million copies on PS4, according to VGChartz.

The fantasy hit, infamous for its macabre combatants, including the undead ninja Scorpion (right), is also the **best-selling Xbox One fighter**: 1.46 million units sold.

First beat-'em-up based on a manga series

Sega's 1986 Mark III game *Hokuto no Ken* (*Fist of the North Star*) was based on the Japanese comics of the same name. In the west, it was released for the Master System as *Black Belt*.

First playable female in a fighting game

Unleashed to Japanese arcades in Oct 1985, Taito's *Onna Sanshirou – Typhoon Gal* features a female judo fighter as she tackles a series of male opponents.

Most prolific hack-and-slash meta-series

Including updates and expansions, there have been 74 instalments of Koei Tecmo's *Musou* since 1997. Known as *Warriors* in the west, this Japanese meta-series is made up of the core *Dynasty*, *Samurai* and *Orochi* games, in addition to licensed entries with *Gundam* and *One Piece*.

First digitized fighting game

Before Atari's *Pit-Fighter*, Homedata's relatively obscure *Last Apostle Puppet Show* – aka *Reikai Dōshi: Chinese Exorcist* (1988) – used digitized claymation puppets for sprites. Hardcore Gaming 101 hailed the visuals as "high-end".

MINI-BYTES

The *Mortal Kombat* games feature an in-joke in which sound designer Dan Forden (below right) appears on screen squealing "Toasty!" The long-running gag first appeared in 1993's *Mortal Kombat II* and was triggered by players landing a particularly brutal uppercut.

Longest-running crossover fighting series

The "crossing over" of gaming franchises has been popular ever since the early 1990s, especially so in the fighting genre. SNK's *The King of Fighters* has been flying that flag for 21 years 364 days. Between the release of *The King of Fighters '94* on 25 Aug 1994 and *The King of Fighters XIV* (pictured) on 23 Aug 2016, *KoF* has heralded more than 20 key titles. These predominantly 2D dust-ups reel in heroes from the publisher's other games, including *Fatal Fury* and the military shoot-'em-up *Ikari Warriors*.

WRESTLING

Wrestling's "faces", "heels" and storylines are as important as grapples, holds and throws. And these days the games aren't just about fighting – they're about the whole world that surrounds these hulking lords of the ring.

Most prolific developer of combat sports games

Japanese developer Yuke's has developed 42 combat sports games; from 1995's *Shin Nippon Pro Wrestling: Toukon Retsuden* to, most recently, 2016's *WWE 2K17*.

Their titles also include entries in the *UFC Undisputed* series, 2004's all-female *Rumble Roses* and 2011's robo-boxing movie tie-in *Real Steel*.

First videogame to feature real-life wrestling footage

The select screen for 1993's *WWF Rage in the Cage* (for the Sega CD) featured video clips of all 20 playable wrestlers – including The Undertaker (above right) – and their signature moves.

First licensed wrestling videogame

MicroLeague Wrestling, for the Atari ST and Commodore 64, was licensed by the WWF and released in 1987. With Hulk Hogan (right) taking on Randy Savage in one bout and Paul Orndorff in another, it's the only WWF/WWE title to feature turn-based strategy gameplay.

Most videogames signed by hand

For 2014's *WWE 2K15*, wrestler, actor, TV star and entrepreneur Hulk Hogan (USA) signed 25,000 art cards. These were included in a special "Hulkamania Edition" of the game.

After his wrist-wrecking signing session, he tweeted: "Fried, dyed and laid to the side, brutal!!"

First all-female cast in a fighting game

Cutie Suzuki no Ringside Angel was released for the Mega Drive in 1990.

Exclusive to Japan, it was named after its cover star, pro wrestler Cutie Suzuki, aka Yumi Harashima (JPN). She reappeared in 1994's *JWP Joshi Pro Wrestling: Pure Wrestle Queens*.

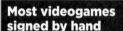

> ## "All the wrestlers play the game... Cody Rhodes is one who plays it a lot."
> *WWE 2K* brand marketing director Bryce Yang

Most prolific wrestler in games

Mark "The Undertaker" Calaway (USA, left) had been playable in 50 of the 65 licensed WWE games as of 10 Apr 2017.

He was first playable in 1992's *WWF Super WrestleMania* and most recently in 2016's *WWE 2K17*. In 2008's *SmackDown vs Raw 2009*, he could turn fellow wrestlers Santino and Finlay into zombie henchmen.

Longest-running wrestling series

After its 1989 debut, the huge-rostered Japanese series *Fire Pro Wrestling* spun out sequels and spin-offs for 23 years.

Its most recent ring romp was 2012's *Fire Pro Wrestling* for Xbox 360, but *Fire Pro Wrestling World* is due in 2017.

First female wrestler in a WWF/WWE game

Gertrude "Luna Vachon" Wilkerson (USA) was playable in the Sega Genesis and Super Nintendo versions of 1994's *WWF Raw*. A glitch meant that she could replicate a move associated with wrestler The 1-2-3 Kid.

Fastest completion of *WWE 2K15* using all Superstars

German gamer "LPer93" grappled through *2K15* using all its Superstars – including The Undertaker (left) – in 3 hr 4 min. The Twitch run on 7 Jul 2015 was verified by Speedrun.com.

At the time, "LPer93" mooted "one more run to figure out what the time would be if the opponent were Santino all the time".

Largest roster in a WWE wrestling game

WWE 2K17 features 156 unique playable wrestlers: 136 on the main game, plus more on DLC. The decades-spanning roster includes legends such as André the Giant and Shawn Michaels, current superstars such as Roman Reigns, and 25 women including Charlotte Flair.

MINI-BYTES

The last WCW game – before the franchise was swallowed by WWF in 2001 – was 2000's *WCW Backstage Assault*, for the PS1 and Nintendo 64. As the game's title implies, all its matches took place outside the ring – a twist that was received poorly by critics and gamers.

Most watched wrestling machinima

"WWE'12: Marvel vs DC Comics" – posted in Jan 2012 by FantasyCaws – had 60,697,126 views on YouTube as of 10 Apr 2017. Using the "Create a wrestler" mode in the *WWE '12* game, it pits heroes and villains from the two comic-book powerhouses against each other.

Fastest *WWE 2K16* victory

Playing in bunny costumes, "oKILL3R JESUSo" and "XxNeroDreXelxX" secured victory in just 15 sec in an extreme-rules tornado tag-team bout. This speedy success – on 7 Nov 2015, on the Xbox One – was posted on WWE Network Gaming's YouTube channel as "WWE 2K16 Online Team Up FASTEST WIN EVER Xbox One Gameplay".

The in-game commentator says that tornado bouts tend to be "fast and furious". No kidding!

COMBAT SPORTS ROUND-UP

Renowned for their technical gameplay, combat sports games are for those who find fantasy fighters a little, well, over the top. Packed with real-life athletes, you can almost feel the shuddering impact of every landing blow.

Most critically acclaimed MMA videogame

Short for "mixed martial arts", MMA lets combatants of multiple fighting styles pit their wits (and brawn) against one another. As of 13 Apr 2017, the PS3 version of THQ's *UFC Undisputed 2010* had a GameRankings score of 87.14%. The game, licensed from the USA's Ultimate Fighting Championship (UFC), was developed by Yuke's – the combat sports kings behind the current *WWE* games.

PRO-FILE: YOUTUBER

MMA GAME

"MMAGAME" (USA)

Subscribers: 51,314

Views: 14,149,426

Trivia: Specializes in tutorials – and comedy videos – based around EA's *UFC* series.

(Info correct as of 13 Apr 2017)

Longest time to find a game Easter egg

On 8 Apr 2016, YouTuber "midwesternhousewives" (USA) found a clue in *Mike Tyson's Punch-Out!!* – 28 years 203 days after the NES game was released on 18 Sep 1987. A spectator nods during a rematch against Piston Hondo, signalling when players should strike.

First hand-held boxing videogame

Inspired by the 1983 arcade hit *Punch-Out!!*, Nintendo's *Boxing* (also released as *Punch-Out!!* in the USA) was a single-screen LED Game & Watch title for up to two players. It was released on 31 Jul 1984.

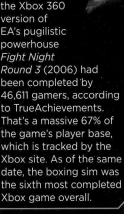

Most completed sports videogame (Xbox)

As of 15 Feb 2017, the Xbox 360 version of EA's pugilistic powerhouse *Fight Night Round 3* (2006) had been completed by 46,611 gamers, according to TrueAchievements. That's a massive 67% of the game's player base, which is tracked by the Xbox site. As of the same date, the boxing sim was the sixth most completed Xbox game overall.

First mixed martial arts videogame

Budokan: The Martial Spirit, developed and published by Electronic Arts in 1989, was a 16-bit game that allowed players to perform four martial arts disciplines: Bo, Karate, Kendo and Nunchaku. It was inspired by tournaments in Japan.

MINI-BYTES

While the premise has very little to do with the actual sport of boxing, the 1984 Acornsoft title *Boxer* is a forgotten gem. It features bizarre bouts during which fighters drop plant pots on each other while dodging dumbbells and collecting balloons – unlike the real thing!

Best-selling UFC videogame

As of 28 Mar 2017, THQ's *UFC 2009 Undisputed* had sold 3.8 million units for the PS3 and Xbox 360, according to VGChartz.

Most game appearances by a real-life martial artist

Jeet Kune Do creator and "godfather of mixed martial arts" Bruce Lee (HKG) had starred in 12 titles as of 13 Apr 2017. This includes the 1984 platformer *Bruce Lee*, a grappling stint in *Virtual Pro Wrestling 64* (1997) and unlockable cameos in *EA Sports UFC* (2014) and *EA Sports UFC 2* (2016).

First arm-wrestling videogame

Released exclusively for the US market in May 1985, Nintendo's coin-operated videogame *Arm Wrestling* was a spin-off of the publisher's earlier boxing hit *Punch-Out!!* The game followed a similar formula, with players battling a series of cartoonish opponents including a sumo wrestler and a spoof of Frankenstein's monster. Both games were made by Nintendo IRD in Japan.

Fastest single-player knockout in *EA Sports UFC 2*

The PS4 players "repalec" (USA) and "DoonIsCool" (UK) have both achieved 4-sec knockouts in EA's 2016 cage-fighter, as verified by Speedrun.com. The former accomplished his speedy success on 20 Mar 2016, while "DoonIsCool" landed a deciding blow on 22 Apr 2016.

First 3D boxing videogame

Teleroboxer, for Nintendo's ill-fated Virtual Boy console, was the first boxing game playable in 3D. Released in Jul 1995, the family-friendly premise suggests that in the future it will be robots fighting for entertainment, but with humans directing the action.

Most critically acclaimed combat sports videogame

The Xbox version of EA's *Fight Night Round 2* (2005) has a GameRankings score of 88.18%, based on 44 reviews. As of 13 Apr 2017, it beat *Fight Night Round 4* (88%) and the 2009 Wii remake of *Punch-Out!!* (87.29%).

189

QUAKECON

Widely dubbed the Woodstock of gaming in reference to the legendary music festival, QuakeCon has evolved into the **longest-running eSports organizer** since its inaugural LAN party in 1996.

Back in those formative days, some 100 people turned up at a hotel in Texas, USA, to play id Software's seminal shooters *Quake* and *DOOM*. Now thousands of FPS fans flock each year to a convention centre in Dallas, USA, to socialize and party, play games, meet the developers and, for the top players, compete in serious tournaments.

QuakeCon's motto has always been "peace, love and rockets". According to id Software's Tim Willits (USA), who has attended each year since 1996, QuakeCon has "grown into a world-class show, but at its heart it is still a grassroots community get-together".

SHANE "RAPHA" HENDRIXSON

Central to each QuakeCon is its Duel Masters championship for competitive players. Following the 2016 QuakeCon, held on 4–7 Aug, the US player Shane "Rapha" Hendrixson had won the **most *Quake* Duel Masters**: five.

What do you attribute your success to?
There are two big factors. First is my mentoring by John "ZeRo4" Hill, who's a former *Quake* world champ. John pushed me from being just a really good player into a champion. Second is my rivalry with Alexey "Cypher" Yanushevsky. We've "flip-flopped" over the years as far as who the best *Quake Live* [2010] player is. It's a good rivalry!

What's your most cherished QuakeCon victory?
In 2009, when I won my first. My dad took me to QuakeCon when I was younger, which introduced me to the whole eSports thing. I was pushed to win in his memory, not for anyone else, but for myself. It was hard to keep composure during the award ceremony, especially with how close I actually came to losing the final. I'll never forget that feeling.

How do you feel about your record of winning the most tournaments?
It's something I've been striving for for a long time and it wasn't easy by any means. So it feels great and I'm proud.

12,381

Largest QuakeCon attendance
QuakeCon 2015

QuakeCon 2016 in numbers

Date:	4–7 Aug 2016
Attendance:	8,600
Volunteers:	319
Volunteer hours worked:	4,918
Exhibitors/sponsors:	41
Prize pool:	$50,000 (£38,235)

Most Duel Masters victories

5	Shane "Rapha" Hendrixson (USA)	(2009, 2011, 2013, 2015, 2016)
4	Alexey "Cypher" Yanushevsky (BLR)	(2008, 2010, 2012, 2014)
3	John "ZeRo4" Hill (USA)	(2000, 2001, 2003)
2	Dan "RiX" Hammans (USA)	(1997, 1998)
2	Johan "Toxjq" Quick (SWE)	(2006, 2007)

Q&A WITH TIM WILLITS, CREATIVE DIRECTOR OF ID SOFTWARE

How did QuakeCon come about?

It grew out of people on the EFnet IRC network, in channel #quake, wishing to meet and game together in person. The original event was held at a hotel a few miles from our office, so everyone at the studio was very excited, and a little curious. Visiting the fans was a great experience. We didn't know what QuakeCon would go on to become then, but the sense of community that *Quake* was creating was very clear.

How involved in the organizing is id Software?

id Software didn't officially start organizing QuakeCon until 1999. Attendances were increasing, and without our full support the event would never be able to reach its full potential. But the event is still coordinated and mostly managed by volunteers and directors.

As the longest-running eSports tournament organizer, has QuakeCon set the blueprint for other events?

All modern competitive tournaments can trace their roots back to QuakeCon. Back in the day, a lot of gamers competed for video cards or free computers, but today prize pools can reach millions of dollars and competitions are watched by millions of fans. That's something I never thought possible 20 years ago, but you can see the ties that link these massive eSports events to what we started at QuakeCon.

Do pro gamers compete at QuakeCon?

About half are North American *Quake* players, while the other half are eSports pros who compete in tournaments around the globe, primarily in Europe. Most of these players are traditionally exclusively *Quake* players, but in the past few years they've begun branching out into other eSports titles. This year Shane "Rapha" Hendrixson [who has won the **most *Quake* Duel Masters**] signed with Team Liquid to compete in *Overwatch* tournaments, joining two Team Liquid *Quake* stars, Tim "DaHanG" Fogarty and Andrew "id_" Trulli.

How do you see eSports and QuakeCon growing?

I don't know how big eSports will eventually get, but it will be exciting to watch, especially knowing how much of an impact QuakeCon had. We're prioritizing eSports for *Quake Champions* [the next game in the *Quake* series] and we hope to help shape the future of [eSports] competition with the franchise that helped start it all. We plan to have *Quake Champions* tournaments, leagues and championships, and QuakeCon will be a big part of that.

Why has QuakeCon lasted so long?

It's down to the volunteers and senior staff of organizers and their passion and love, which makes QuakeCon unique. The event is a true grassroots show, a show that's organized by the community for the community, and we at id Software and [*Quake* publisher] Bethesda are very fortunate to work with them year after year.

SPEEDRUN.COM

Speed-running – the art of completing a game in the fastest time possible – is now an integral part of record-breaking. If players want to know whether they've blasted through *Shovel Knight* or *Resident Evil 7: Biohazard* quicker than their peers, then they turn to Speedrun.com.

Founded in Mar 2014, Speedrun.com is a global leaderboard for the speed-running community. The site currently tracks times in nearly 9,000 games, with fastest completion submissions moderated by a passionate core of experts and players.

Across the following pages you'll find lightning-fast times from the site's leaderboards. If running is your speciality, then getting your name riding high in these charts should be a major goal.

YOSHI'S ISLAND

Q&A WITH SPEEDRUN.COM FOUNDER PETER CHASE

What was the inspiration behind Speedrun.com?
Twitch and speed-running were becoming much more popular, and it was extremely difficult to find the fastest time for a given game. In Dec 2013, a *GoldenEye* speed-runner, Ryan White, spoke about the need for a global leaderboard site, and I just went ahead and made it. The site launched in March 2014.

To a newbie, how would you describe what a speed-run is?
It's an attempt to beat a game as fast as possible for the purposes of entertainment and competition. Any game can be speed-run, and there are usually several categories. Some runs have no restrictions and are usually known as "any%". Other runs may require all levels to be beaten and all items to be collected [often known as 100%]. In the past, speed-running was a niche thing where people would post their best videos online on various websites. But with Twitch, live-streams of speed-runs have become much more popular and accessible, and the bar for competition has been raised substantially over the last few years.

Given the different types of runs, how do you decide on the guidelines for each game that appears on the site?
The rules are primarily decided by the players and moderators of each game. Site staff provide some level of guidance, and help make sure the community consensus is being met.

How big is your team?
The core site team currently consists of seven people from the USA, Europe and Australia. Each game has a set of moderators. Currently, 4,500 people on the site moderate at least one game.

How are runs verified for the leaderboards?
The boards are generally handled somewhat autonomously by the users who request to create them, and other players they choose to add as moderators. Site staff help out when boards don't meet user expectations or when community consensus isn't being met. Videos are submitted by the users via a submission form, which is then accepted by the moderators if it meets the rules and the criteria for the category.

Do most runs traditionally allow for the exploitation of glitches?
Our community has typically favoured tracking a category for fastest completion for games. The absolute fastest you can beat a game is often by using glitches and tricks available to you. Sometimes this results in skipping much of the interesting content within the game, so a category with fewer or no glitches is often defined.

What are the biggest challenges and rewards of running the site?
The biggest challenge is typically handling the community-driven moderation. The reward is that fastest times are easily accessible to the community. Users are now discussing and discovering faster ways to beat games, and many resources are available to learn.

Do you hold any live events or plan to?
Speedrun.com doesn't itself hold events, but community and staff members often attend speed-running marathons. The two best-established marathons are GamesDoneQuick (GDQ), which is a US-based marathon that occurs twice-yearly; the other is the European Speedrunner Assembly (ESA), which is a growing European-based marathon that has a main annual event and appears as part of other events, like DreamHack, throughout the year.

Are you a speed-runner yourself?
I'm more of a fan of watching. I've speed-run *Super Mario Bros.* in the past but my times are nothing to brag about!

What have been some of your favourite runs on the site?
I'm a huge fan of *Yoshi's Island* speed-runs [left], especially the 100% category. The skill required to time every egg shot to collect all of the items is mind-blowing. Among my other favourites are *GTA: Vice City*, *Zelda: A Link to the Past* ("Reverse Boss" order) and *GoldenEye*.

Fancy yourself as a record-breaking speed-runner? Head over to Speedrun.com for details on how to submit your runs. Good luck!

SPEEDRUN.COM IN NUMBERS

As of 10 Mar 2017, there were a massive 8,900 games listed on Speedrun.com, with thousands of runners vying to top their respective leaderboards. Suffice to say, some titles, from platformers to puzzlers, have generated larger competitive player bases than others.

TOP 10 GAMES WITH THE HIGHEST RUN COUNT

The first two 3D *Mario* platformers top an eclectic list of games and genres.

	Title	No. of Runs	Genre	Year
1	Super Mario 64	4,582	Platformer	1996
2	Super Mario Sunshine	4,228	Platformer	2002
3	The Legend of Zelda: Ocarina of Time	3,634	Action-Adventure	1998
4	Diddy Kong Racing	3,297	Racing	1997
5	Super Mario World	2,201	Platformer	1990
6	Portal	2,175	Puzzle	2007
7	Undertale	2,075	RPG	2015
8	The Legend of Zelda: A Link to the Past	1,940	Action-Adventure	1991
9	Super Meat Boy	1,870	Platformer	2010
10	Super Mario Bros.	1,662	Platformer	1985

SUPER MARIO 64

MOST POPULAR PLATFORMS

There are 82 different platforms registered on Speedrun.com, from the 3DO to the X68000. None can touch the PC, though.

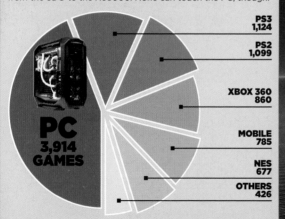

PS3
1,124

PS2
1,099

XBOX 360
860

MOBILE
785

NES
677

OTHERS
426

PC
3,914
GAMES

MOST SPEED-RUN NEW GAMES OF 2016

FPS *SUPERHOT* heads a speed-running craze for indie titles.

	Title	Runs
1	*SUPERHOT* (Superhot Team)	747
2	*Mirror's Edge: Catalyst* (Electronic Arts)	540
3	*Ori and the Blind Forest: Definitive Ed.* (Microsoft)	439
4	*Clustertruck* (tinyBuild Games)	330
5	*Momodora: Reverie Under the Moonlight* (Playism)	294
6	*DOOM* (Bethesda)	287
7	*Furi* (The Game Bakers)	260
8	*Killing Floor 2* (Tripwire Interactive)	227
9	*The Witness* (Thekla, Inc)	211
10	*Ratchet & Clank* (Sony)	210

MIRROR'S EDGE: CATALYST

SPEED-RUNS

The following tables celebrate a small selection of the fastest players in the world, with speedy times recorded in an eclectic mix of games. All data is correct as of 4 Apr 2017. Go... go... GO!

Bastion (2011)
Calamity has struck the city of Caelondia. Can "The Kid" save it? Of course – and in less than 14 sec! Check out helpful videos by speed-runner "valentinoIAN" on the YouTube channel "Synth".

Brawlhalla (2017)
Some games are about subtlety. Some are about strategy. And some are mainly about whacking foes with weapons (oh, and a bit of magic). Enter Brawlhalla! "Look for characters with high defense stats," suggests "ImLogic". "These will be harder to kill."

Game	Category	Place	Player	Time
Assault Android Cactus	Boss Rush	1	SeaJay (AUS)	00:05:08.189
		2	TransparentBlue (FRA)	00:05:10.84
		3	Moonspod (UK)	00:05:43.05
Axiom Verge	Any%; Normal	1	Zecks (FIN)	00:34:57.4
		2	Ryn2075 (USA)	00:35:50.18
		3	BlueyLewis (USA)	00:36:48.11
Barbie: Super Model	Any%; Super Model	1	RantronBomb	00:03:25.9
		2	Deuz (CHL)	00:03:26.23
		3	NerdyNester (USA)	00:03:26.56
Bastion	NG Any%	1	valentinoIAN (USA)	00:13:29
		=2	SomeDude955 (USA)	00:13:34
		=2	HaosEdge (AUT)	00:13:34
The Binding of Isaac: Afterbirth	1 char	1	Grunguiestooth (MEX)	00:01:29
		2	Zamiel (USA)	00:04:13
		3	karolmo (ESP)	00:05:35
Blaster Master	Any% (JP)	1	IluvMario (USA)	00:26:58
		2	Skavenger216 (USA)	00:27:35
		3	feasel (USA)	00:28:04
Brawlhalla	Tournament mode 100%	1	ThStardust (DNK)	00:03:32
		2	ImLogic (USA)	00:03:48
		3	Minayan (FIN)	00:03:55
Bubble Bobble (NES)	Any% (1 player)	1	AND4H (USA)	00:34:18
		2	RottDawg (CAN)	00:40:32
		3	WhenChukAttacks (USA)	00:40:40
Bucky O'Hare	Normal mode	1	callumbal (UK)	00:23:23
		2	dreamofsha (CHN)	00:25:42
		3	nesgoomba (USA)	00:28:21
Bully: Scholarship Edition	Any%	1	Nord (SWE)	02:42:01
		2	SWEGTA (SWE)	02:44:39
		3	The_Metric_System (USA)	02:48:30
Castlevania (NES)	Any%; Normal mode	1	kmac (USA)	00:11:37.964
		2	Baize86 (FIN)	00:11:39.63
		=3	Janthe (FRA)	00:11:46
		=3	DoubleArmory (USA)	00:11:46
		=3	truefalse (CHE)	00:11:46
Cave Story	Best ending	1	PPU (JPN)	00:57:11
		2	magmapeach	00:57:28
		3	draculantern (USA)	00:57:33
Chameleon Twist	Any%	1	qwillinallthefish (USA)	00:12:30
		2	PurpleRupees (USA)	00:12:54
		3	Bingchang (USA)	00:13:00

Game	Category	Place	Player	Time
Chōjin Sentai Jetman	Normal mode	1	m3nt (FIN)	00:09:50
		2	Guhbadoo	00:09:56
		3	BernieLeBof (FRA)	00:11:36
Clustertruck	Any%	1	097Aceofspades (USA)	00:18:57.68
		2	-DarkAngel- (UK)	00:20:16.26
		3	MM4005 (USA)	00:21:49.4
Cornerstone: The Song of Tyrim	Any%; No credits skip	1	Multiwinner (CAN)	00:22:10
		2	DrTChops (CAN)	00:22:42
		3	Savusukka (FIN)	00:23:42
Crash Bandicoot	Any%	1	Kojiroctr (BRA)	00:40:55
		2	WhitePaaws (COL)	00:42:42
		3	Tebt (CAN)	00:43:35
Crash Bandicoot 3: Warped	Any%	1	Kojiroctr (BRA)	00:23:26
		2	PeteThePlayer (DEU)	00:26:27
		3	Jacques (UK)	00:27:48
Defunct	Any%	1	Ikewolf (CHE)	00:13:20
		2	SieniMarsu (FIN)	00:13:43
		3	SwedishCheese (SWE)	00:13:49
Diddy Kong Racing	100%	1	Toufool (USA)	01:50:32
		2	MrsGizamaluke (SWE)	01:50:44
		3	Obiyo (CAN)	01:52:15
Firewatch	Any%	1	Kevbot43 (USA)	01:05:04
		2	snoborder88 (USA)	01:05:12
		3	ZaturnuX (SWE)	01:06:23
Five Nights at Freddy's	Any%	1	flower (RUS)	00:01:09
		2	BlitzPhoenix98	00:01:15.47
		3	EddventureTime58 (UK)	00:01:22

Crash Bandicoot 3: Warped (1998)
A Time Trial mode was among the features introduced to *Crash Bandicoot* with this third instalment. So it would be rude not to speed-run it. Leaderboard numero uno "Kojiroctr" agreed: "What a speedfun!"

Five Nights at Freddy's (2014)
Bears, bunnies, chickens, foxes. Cute, right? Right – except when they're trying to kill you. So one reason to speed-run this cult survival-horror is there's less time for its animatronic antiheroes to give you nightmares for the rest of your life (well, until you watch the incoming movie version).
   Speed-runner "flower" suggests: "If you press the 'New Game' and quickly click the mouse a few times, you will be able to skip the intro!" And here's a tip from us: maybe just get your pizza delivered...

Clustertruck (2016)
Warning: jumping on trucks in this platformer can cause excitement. "DEATHLESS I CANT BELIEVE IT" wrote jubilant speed-runner "097Aceofspades".

For Honor (2017)
Speed is of the essence in Ubisoft's medieval hack-and-slasher – because, when your whole world is on fire and everyone in it wants to kill you, stopping for a cup of tea isn't an option. But before you join the slaughter, ponder this tip by "MealzOnWheals": "You don't need to kill every enemy you meet." (Unless that's the aim. In which case, go nuts.)

Mafia III (2016)
Mixed reviews and a glut of glitches didn't stop *Mafia III* averaging a million sales a month after it emerged in 2016. "Kabalie" set a speed-run record within weeks and joked: "Not glitchy, in any way, shape or form."

Game	Category	Place	Player	Time
For Honor	NG+ Any%	1	Mr.KillshotTV (BLR)	01:26:10
		2	Cropax (DNK)	01:29:00
		3	BranLan (USA)	01:30:55
Furi	Speedrun mode	1	angelym (FRA)	00:30:09
		2	Mrlazyman213	00:31:50
		3	Platypus_Funk (FRA)	00:32:26
Half-Life 2	New Engine	1	deathwingua (UKR)	01:14:11.19
		2	chili_n_such (USA)	01:14:43.92
		3	raintnt (RUS)	01:19:52.78
Harry Potter and the Chamber of Secrets (PC)	Any%	1	turothking (NOR)	00:33:54
		2	Cynaschism (USA)	00:34:42
		3	Respirte (UK)	00:35:11
Harry Potter and the Prisoner of Azkaban (PC)	Any%	1	turothking (NOR)	01:14:30
		2	Cynaschism (USA)	01:14:44
		3	ComplexMonkey (CAN)	01:17:07
Hotline Miami 2: Wrong Number	NG+ Any%	1	Uzikoti (FRA)	00:33:28
		2	Ashmore (FRA)	00:33:42
		3	Jackintoshh (IRL)	00:33:50
Jet Set Radio	Any%	1	Faila (ARG)	00:37:07
		2	aneeslol (USA)	00:38:07
		3	redmogo (USA)	00:38:25
Kirby: Planet Robobot	Any%	1	Yosshi	01:44:02
		2	Kobral (DEU)	01:48:52
		3	Demolition14 (UK)	01:54:28
Leaf Me Alone	Full version – Any%	1	Gyoo (FRA)	00:05:59.94
		2	chunkatuff	00:06:12.08
		3	Alaedar (FRA)	00:06:17.41
The Lion King (SNES)	Any%; Difficult	1	Akiteru (CAN)	00:13:54
		2	TheMexicanRunner (MEX)	00:14:19
		3	AlfredoSalza (CHL)	00:14:47
The Little Mermaid	Any%	1	Angrylanks (USA)	00:06:49.15
		2	McBobX (MAR)	00:06:49.58
		3	JeedUnit (CAN)	00:06:52.79
Mafia II	Any%	1	kdstz (NLD)	03:14:55
		2	Kinfath92 (ITA)	03:18:37.63
		3	Kabalie (FIN)	03:19:57
Mafia III	Any%	1	Kabalie (FIN)	06:23:35
		2	Mattmatt10111 (ATA)	07:24:02
		3	Kinfath92 (ITA)	07:24:07
Mega Man X4	Zero 100%	1	ArielRx (ECU)	00:42:26
		2	Qttsix (TPE)	00:42:32
		3	LoliMetH (USA)	00:42:40

Mirror's Edge: Catalyst (2016)

Glitches are the speedy gamer's friend. In *Catalyst*, kick with one leg in the middle of a wall-run and you'll land on an invisible platform that allows you to reset your falling distance. And that, notes Mirrorsedge.wikia, leads to "the most infamous glitch in all of *Mirror's Edge*... that small platform is completely solid. For three frames, you can jump off that platform, allowing you to double-jump."

Nefarious (2017)

A Kickstarted creation that casts gamers as princess-kidnapping villains, *Nefarious* offers speed-runners a choice of "good ending" or "bad ending". As of 6 Apr 2017, no one had gone for the "good" one. Now that's what we call nefarious.

Nioh (2017)

This hack-and-slasher was in development for a million years – okay, 13 years – before it debuted in Feb 2017. Just four seconds later – okay, four weeks later – Canada's "FaraazKhan" had sliced through it in under two minutes. "All main missions and epilogue," he said triumphantly.

Game	Category	Place	Player	Time
Mighty No. 9	Any%	1	GreenZSaber (USA)	00:32:22.45
		2	mrcab55 (USA)	00:32:55.53
		3	Ryosotis (NLD)	00:33:47.82
Mirror's Edge: Catalyst	Any%	1	alexhxc15 (USA)	01:20:18
		2	MazkuD (FIN)	01:20:40
		3	matchboxmatt (USA)	01:21:22
Momodora: Reverie Under the Moonlight	Any%; Easy	1	LunaArgenteus	00:22:17
		2	Flane (USA)	00:22:43
		3	MisterJack112 (FRA)	00:22:46
Naruto Shippuden: Ultimate Ninja Storm 4	Any%; New Game	1	joystiquebr (BRA)	01:49:17
		2	TrueStorySeamus (UK)	01:49:54
		3	WhathaveIdone (USA)	01:56:49
Nefarious	Any%; Bad ending	1	oreoplaysthings (USA)	00:52:25
		2	Watson690 (UK)	00:53:24
		3	bardninja (USA)	00:59:43
Nioh	Any%	1	FaraazKhan (CAN)	01:51:57
		2	Noir (KOR)	02:20:42
		3	Elajjaz (SWE)	02:32:29
Ori and the Blind Forest: Definitive Edition	All Skills; no OOB; no TA	1	Hetfield90 (USA)	00:31:09
		2	Kydra (CAN)	00:32:02
		3	sigma (CAN)	00:32:08
Overwatch	Tutorial; PC	1	Midnight (PRK)	00:03:50.93
		2	Burchase (USA)	00:03:51.99
		3	nijQ (DEU)	00:03:52.46

Poi (2017)

Missing mid-1990s-style platformers, when Mario going 3D seemed pretty cutting-edge? Then indie adventure *Poi* is for you. "Are you a streamer/ speed-runner?" ask makers PolyKid. "Feel free to record and upload footage to YouTube/ Twitch/etc. and share it with us!" It's a cult game right now, but we think folks will be tempted to beat the times here...

Ratchet & Clank (2016)

Having sprinted to the top of the leaderboard, "nickfredy" played it cool: "Not a bad run." The US gamer has a galaxy of helpful *Ratchet & Clank* tutorials on his YouTube channel "NickFredy".

Prince of Persia: The Sands of Time (2003)

In 2015, Ubisoft's acrobatic actioner acquired traction in the speed-run world, thanks to a newly discovered glitch that allowed the prince to zip through walls and ceilings. Like, as if being able to run along walls and roll *up* stairs wasn't enough for the lovelorn prince! The Czech Republic's "catalyst" showed exactly how it's done in an athletic run likely to unsettle viewers suffering from vertigo. "The champ that runs the camp has returned," the gamer beamed on his YouTube channel.

Game	Category	Place	Player	Time
Poi	Any%; New game	1	Ver (USA)	00:43:56.889
		2	097Aceofspades (USA)	00:45:39.716
		3	Joshmesh (UK)	00:49:15.318
Portal 2	Single player – single segment; Full game	1	PerOculos (LBR)	01:03:58.45
		2	Znernicus (USA)	01:04:01
		3	TheSwagatron (USA)	01:06:41.5
Prince of Persia: The Sands of Time	Any%; Normal	1	catalyst (CZE)	00:37:20
		2	tocaloni1 (DEU)	00:37:49
		3	Vynneve (CAN)	00:41:58
Ratchet & Clank (PS4)	NG+ Any%	1	nickfredy (USA)	00:28:06
		2	doesthisusername (DNK)	00:28:16
		3	Scaff (AUS)	00:28:30
Rayman	Any%; PS1	1	Thextera (BEL)	01:15:02
		2	Arttles (PRT)	01:15:11
		3	fuerchter (DEU)	01:15:33
Rayman 2: The Great Escape	Any%	1	Darnok_PL (POL)	01:56:09
		2	KirbyComment (NLD)	02:00:06
		3	lagpu1 (ESP)	02:05:45

Game	Category	Place	Player	Time
Resident Evil 4	New Game; PC; Professional	1	Morse66 (FRA)	01:29:42
		2	yamatti (JPN)	01:30:33
		3	Pitted (USA)	01:32:08
Salt and Sanctuary	Any%; no OOB	1	Coppie (SVN)	00:11:21
		2	Paerux (TUR)	00:12:36
		3	seanpr (USA)	00:13:04
Sanic Spin 2006	Finish the Game	1	Chadwelli (USA)	00:00:17.71
		2	Xcvazer (FRA)	00:00:17.95
		3	Isla (BLR)	00:00:18.27
Shadow Warrior 2	NG Any%; Easy	1	Raaikken (FIN)	00:46:44
		2	SuccinctAndPunchy (UK)	00:47:30
		3	DemonStrate (USA)	00:50:17
Shantae: Half-Genie Hero	Any%; Shantae Mode; Glitchless	1	Tky619 (UK)	01:04:53
		2	CakeSauc3 (USA)	01:04:58
		3	JTB (USA)	01:07:33
Shovel Knight	Any%; Shovel Knight	1	Smaugy (SWE)	00:42:54
		2	MooMooAkai (USA)	00:43:42
		3	MunchaKoopas (USA)	00:43:54
Silent Hill	NG (Easy)	1	AaronSOLDIER (UK)	00:31:44
		2	SuccinctAndPunchy (UK)	00:32:08
		3	Bawkbasoup (CAN)	00:32:16

Sanic Spin 2006 (2016)
Ever wondered how Sonic jumps and spins without getting sick? Maybe not, but indie title *Sanic Spin* came along to tell us anyway, in a fond but nausea-inducing pastiche of the blue blur. As if speed-running wasn't dizzying enough...

Shadow Warrior 2 (2016)
Guns? Tick. Blades? Tick. Magic? Tick. But if you speed-run *SW2*, ditch the chainsaws. "They effectively lock you in place while sawing," warns TV Tropes, "in a game where standing still on higher difficulties for any length of time is almost certain death."

Shovel Knight (2014)
This tribute to third-gen platformers is a speed-run staple. Gamer "Azoolag" (USA) has even written "Shovel Knight Any% - A Brief History", available at Spadebrigade.com. This charts the ups and occasional downs of our leaderboard champ "Smaugy" in the excellently titled chapter "The Desolation of Smaugy".

Game	Category	Place	Player	Time
Snipperclips: Cut It Out, Together!	World – Any%; Solo	1	ThunderFilms (USA)	00:20:33
		2	MyNameIsMoo (USA)	00:20:44
		3	Nutt (AUS)	00:23:33
Solitaire	Draw One	1	DDos-Dan (AUS)	00:00:08
		2	Strucht DeRügel	00:00:10
		3	Georg Sandner	00:00:11
SOMA	Any%	1	Teravortryx (CAN)	00:59:50
		2	Sychotixx (USA)	01:00:31
		3	amzblk (EST)	01:02:02
Sonic Colors (Wii)	Egg Shuttle	1	CriticalCyd (NLD)	00:41:06.94
		2	DarkspinesSonic (USA)	00:41:32.89
		3	Alluusio (FIN)	00:43:59.9
Splatoon	Any%	1	MoveFishGetOutTheWay (USA)	00:51:34
		2	TonesBalones (USA)	00:51:56
		3	BEAT (JPN)	00:53:01.494
Spyro: Year of the Dragon	Any%	1	jeremythompson (USA)	00:24:57
		2	breakingu (USA)	00:26:11
		3	Dactyly (AUS)	00:26:21
Star Fox 64	Any%	1	Hayate (JPN)	00:22:24
		2	Stivitybobo (USA)	00:22:27
		3	LylatR (CAN)	00:22:29

Snipperclips: Cut It Out, Together! (2017)

One of the points of this Switch launch title (see p.97) is that there are lots of solutions to its puzzles. What could be better than taking the time to explore them? Inevitably, however, speed-runners said: "Yeah, we'll just do it really fast thanks." It's less perilous than running with scissors, after all.

SOMA (2015)

A sci-fi survival-horror puzzler isn't an obvious target for speed-running, but that hasn't stopped dedicated gamers – especially after several skips came to light on its day of release. However, as one Speed Demos Archive user grumbled: "Can we let a game at least get to 2 days old before breaking it?"

Splatoon (2015)

If *Splatoon* doesn't make you smile, you may actually be dead. Is there anything more fun than making a mess? Yes: making a mess really quickly. So it's not surprising that this has one of the more crowded leaderboards, topped (above) by presumed Ludacris fan "MoveFishGetOutTheWay". Runner-up "TonesBalones" points out, for the benefit of multilingual speed-runners, that English is faster than Spanish – and Japanese is faster than both.

Game	Category	Place	Player	Time
SteamWorld Dig	Any%	1	anxest (FRA)	00:22:45
		2	renozealot (FRA)	00:22:57
		3	Berumondo (BEL)	00:23:54
Super Metroid	Any%	1	Oatsngoats (USA)	00:41:56
		2	zoast	00:41:58
		3	kottpower (SWE)	00:42:20
SUPERHOT	Any%; PC	1	Bullets (USA)	00:18:18
		2	Lt_Disco (USA)	00:19:30.63
		3	Ellieceraptor (SWE)	00:19:47.178
The Talos Principle	Any%	1	Kraeft (SWE)	00:10:28
		2	cojosao (USA)	00:10:39
		3	Azorae (USA)	00:11:13
Titan Souls	Any% (Beat The Game); Normal	1	Zic3 (USA)	00:11:47.86
		2	3l3ktr0 (FRA)	00:11:54.28
		3	6oliath (CAN)	00:12:11.88
Titanfall 2	Any%	1	AnAngryAlbino (USA)	01:30:49
		2	Bryonato (USA)	01:33:58
		3	FroobMcGuffin (UK)	01:36:52
Trine	NG+ Any%	1	Evertrn (SWE)	00:29:52
		2	MaximumLeech (USA)	00:30:25
		3	Janmumrik (SWE)	00:33:47
Undertale	Neutral	1	TGH (USA)	00:56:32
		2	xandertje10 (NLD)	00:56:52
		3	Magolor9000 (CAN)	00:57:32
Where's Waldo?	Easy	1	Vexx (CAN)	00:02:02.683
		2	joenome1 (USA)	00:02:03.73
		3	Neerrm (USA)	00:02:05.55
Yoshi's Woolly World	Any% (Classic mode); Normal	1	be_be_be_ (JPN)	02:24:51
		2	Vallu (FIN)	02:25:39
		3	Jolteon92 (UK)	02:32:09
You Have 10 Seconds	Any%	1	Chadwelli (USA)	00:02:55.718
		2	Amoeba (UK)	00:02:59.433
		3	PajamaWarriorJohn (USA)	00:03:08

SteamWorld Dig (2013)
We probably didn't even realize we needed a steampunk platform mining game until this came along. The first run on Speedrun.com, in 2013, lasted just under an hour. Four years on, we're pushing 20 minutes. Check out *Gamer's Edition* in 2021 to see if anyone's got it down to seconds...

Titan Souls (2015)
You've played *The Legend of Zelda* (p.28). You really *should* have played *Shadow of the Colossus* (p.30). So, now, why not play a game that's kind of a mix of the two? It has deliberately simple controls, an old-school top-down design and – as you'd expect from Acid Nerve, developers of the funny *Fruitwolf* – a quirky sense of humour (tip: you need to hit the Yeti where the Sun doesn't shine...).

Titanfall 2 (2016)
The FPS sequel is both crazily over the top and deadly serious (there *are* jokes, but you'll be too busy speed-running – or being killed – to hear them). You can tell how seriously gamers take it because, even when they post fine speed-runs, they say things like: "I had so many errors and pointless deaths. The last boss fight was executed poorly." Cheer up, guys!

YOUR NEW FAVOURITE GAMES

Part 1
Some of the hottest new titles, heading to a gaming platform near you...

RED DEAD REDEMPTION 2

Platforms: PS4, Xbox One
Released in 2010, Rockstar Games' *Red Dead Redemption* was described by many gamers as *"GTA set in the Wild West"*. It's a gun-slinging, horse-riding, open-world action game, which takes place on the American Frontier in the early 1900s. This hotly anticipated sequel promises more thrilling Wild West cowboy action, this time adding online multiplayer.

SUPER MARIO ODYSSEY

Platform: Switch
Mario's first major outing on Nintendo's new console was always going to get excitement levels bubbling, and this platformer looks just as brilliant and imaginative as its predecessors. This time Mario travels beyond the Mushroom Kingdom, with many of the new locations – such as a forest and bustling city – having a semi-realistic feel. The game's unique twist comes in the form of new hats, which grant Mario special powers.

DAYS GONE

Platform: PS4
Days Gone made its debut at E3 in 2016, and its haunting atmosphere instantly impressed as gruff lead Deacon St John scoured a desolate US wilderness. *Days Gone* takes place two years after a global pandemic has obliterated humanity and is billed as an open-world action game with survival-horror elements. It's faintly reminiscent of *The Last of Us*, but hopefully its free-form exploration will give it a strong identity of its own.

GOD OF WAR

Platform: PS4
Sony's series has won accolades for its blistering third-person action and beautiful, bloodthirsty visuals – and the latest instalment looks to feature both in spades. Previous games saw Kratos (right) battling monsters and exploring lands inspired by Greek mythology. His first PS4 outing, however, takes inspiration from Norse myths, giving the series' violent, visceral action a distinct new flavour. And if that wasn't enough, Kratos now has a son to look after.

AGENTS OF MAYHEM

Platforms: PS4, Xbox One, PC
This crazy offering from Volition is best summed up as a spiritual successor to the studio's ridiculously over-the-top *Saints Row* series. Like those games, *Agents of Mayhem* is a colourful, unapologetically daft open-world action extravaganza. It's set in a futuristic version of Seoul, South Korea, and places you at the helm of crime-fighting organization M.A.Y.H.E.M.

DETROIT: BECOME HUMAN

Platform: PS4
Developer Quantic Dream (*Heavy Rain*) is famous for its beautiful, story-driven adventures that feel more like extended interactive movies than traditional games. The studio's latest offering takes on the sci-fi genre, charting the journey of several life-like androids as they escape into the real world. As in previous titles, the choices you make will affect the story, and it's even possible that your actions will cause key characters to die along the way.

> **MORE GREAT NEW GAMES OVERLEAF!**

DRAGON QUEST XI

Platforms: PS4, 3DS, Switch
Square Enix's RPG series isn't overly well known in the West, but it's incredibly popular in Japan – hence its title for **longest-running JRPG series**. Since its 1986 debut, these grandiose games have only ever built on their thirst for big fantasy adventure and turn-based battling. *DGXI* looks atmospheric with a vast world to explore.

DESTINY 2

Platforms: PS4, Xbox One, PC
Destiny was developer Bungie's first major release after leaving the *Halo* series behind, and its frantic, online-focused first-person shooting has been a huge success. Since its release in 2014, the game has received four expansions, but *Destiny 2* is the series' first proper sequel. You'll be able to carry over certain attributes of your Guardian from the first game, and Bungie is promising bigger and better everything this time around.

YOUR NEW FAVOURITE GAMES

Part 2

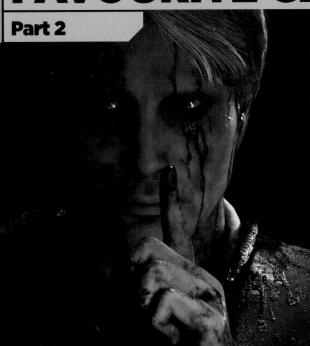

PROJECT CARS 2

Platforms: PS4, Xbox One, PC
Project CARS burst on to the racing-sim scene in 2015, following a hugely successful crowdfunding campaign. Its sequel aims to be bigger and better in every way; it will include over 170 licensed cars, an enormous track roster, plus new vehicle types and motorsports classes. It doesn't end there. Other key features include dynamic time of day, weather and seasonal conditions.

DEATH STRANDING

Platform: PS4
In 2015, *Metal Gear* creator Hideo Kojima split from Konami. His studio's first title as an independent looks like it will be very, very weird indeed. Exclusive to PS4, *Death Stranding* is a unique open-world action game starring *The Walking Dead*'s Norman Reedus. If early promotional material is to be believed, the game has something to do with gloomy beaches, dead crabs, tiny babies and mysterious goo...

SONIC MANIA

Platforms: PS4, Xbox One, Switch, PC
Sonic made his debut on the Mega Drive over 25 years ago. Although his games have grown progressively flashier since then, *Sonic Mania* goes back to basics, returning to the beloved 2D formula of the hedgehog's earliest adventures. The game's familiar side-scrolling platform action features locations inspired by his Mega Drive classics, and its use of 2D sprites and chunky pixels gives the game an authentic '90s look. A nostalgic treat.

XENOBLADE CHRONICLES 2

Platform: Switch
Monolith Soft's epic JRPG *Xenoblade Chronicles* was hugely well received when it was released on Wii in 2010. It shared many elements with other JRPGs, but its dazzling real-time combat and engrossing sci-fi fantasy storyline marked it out as a genre masterpiece. The game did receive a spiritual successor with *Xenoblade Chronicles X* on Wii U, but this Switch outing is its first true sequel. Expect a new lead character and art style, but familiar open-world action.

THE LAST OF US PT II

Platform: PS4

Naughty Dog's post-apocalyptic action-adventure *The Last of Us* melded stealthy action to an emotional storyline – and won lots of awards in the process. This long-awaited sequel is set five years after the 2013 original and sees protagonists Joel and Ellie both returning. But while the first outing told its story from Joel's perspective, *Part II* sees the teenage Ellie taking centre stage. Expect a powerful classic.

STAR WARS: BATTLEFRONT II

Platforms: PS4, Xbox One, PC

EA's rebooted *Battlefront* series is a multiplayer shooter loaded up with vintage Star Wars references. In the original 2015 game, up to 40 players could join in a battle, playing as either Rebel Alliance soldiers or Imperial Stormtroopers, and fight it out in famous locations such as Tatooine and Endor's Forest Moon. The sequel promises more of the same great action, but will focus on elements outside of the original movie trilogy. Most excitingly, it will feature a proper single-player story this time.

SPIDER-MAN

Platform: PS4

Spidey has starred in some great games over the years, but this PS4 exclusive has the potential to be the best yet. It's being developed by Insomniac Games – the team behind *Ratchet & Clank* and *Resistance* – and features plenty of exhilarating acrobatics, with Webhead tearing through a visually impressive New York City. It could well do for Spidey what the *Arkham* series did for Batman.

PSYCHONAUTS 2

Platforms: PS4, Xbox One, PC

Double Fine's delightful platform adventure *Psychonauts* received much praise when it was released in 2005. Playing as Raz, a young boy gifted with psychic powers, players entered the minds of numerous zany characters and explored the strange worlds that existed inside their heads. Now, thanks to a successful crowdfunding campaign, a much-desired sequel is finally on its way.

SUNLESS SKIES

Platform: PC

Sunless Skies is the follow-up to Failbetter Games' *Sunless Sea*, an imaginative exploration game set in the alternative Victorian world of "Fallen London". While the predecessor was a rollicking nautical caper, this takes place among the stars. You'll pilot a space-faring locomotive, battle big sky beasts, meet Empress Victoria beneath a clockwork sun and even murder a planet.

CONTRIBUTORS

MATT BRADFORD

Matt is a Canadian writer and voice actor who has covered the videogame industry for publications and websites since the 1990s. He can be heard across several videogame podcasts, and weekly on Zombie Cast and The NoSleep Podcast.

Which games did you play most this year?
Deux Ex: Mankind Divided, *Uncharted 4*, *XCOM 2* and *Ori and the Blind Forest – Definitive Edition*.
What was this year's most exciting event?
Personally, making the leap to PC gaming. I still love my consoles, but building a PC has absolutely expanded my videogame horizons.

MATTHEW EDWARDS

Matt has written for Eurogamer, *gamesTM* and *Edge*. He now works as a community and eSports manager for Capcom Entertainment Europe. He also co-hosts a weekly stream on CapcomFighters.

Which games did you play most this year?
Street Fighter V, *Resident Evil 7: Biohazard*, *Breath of the Wild* and *Nioh* [right].
What was this year's most exciting event?
The Capcom Pro Tour and getting my Nintendo Switch.

ROBERT CAVE

Robert is a veteran freelance writer and editor who loves videogames, science and pop culture. He has worked on the *Gamer's Edition* since its launch in 2008 and, over the past decade, has visited videogame studios, museums and events on three continents. He also spent far too much time and money playing the 1981 coin-op arcade game *Galaga* on his birthday this year.

Which games did you play most this year?
When I haven't been in the trenches playing *Battlefield 1*, I've been in the far reaches of space playing *Mass Effect: Andromeda* [above right].
What was this year's most exciting event?
The Switch – who doesn't like a new console launch? *The Last of Us Part II* is the game I'm most looking forward to – although when we will get to play it is a matter of great speculation.

DAVID CROOKS

David has written about games for 14 years and has worked on the *Gamer's Edition* since 2009. He contributes regularly to *Retro Gamer*, *gamesTM* and *The Independent*, and has curated two videogame exhibitions.

Which games did you play most this year?
Resident Evil 7: Biohazard freaked me out on the PSVR and it was great to see the return of *Zelda*. A little egg-shaped character from the '80s called Dizzy made a reappearance too.
What was this year's most exciting event?
I can't fail to get excited about a Nintendo launch, so it has to be the Switch.

PAUL DAVIES

Paul has been writing enthusiastically about games since 1992, during which time he became editor of the *Computer and Video Games* magazine and website. He is now a freelance writer and gaming consultant, working closely with developers and publishers.

Which games did you play most this year?
Final Fantasy XV, *Dragon Quest Builders* and *Overwatch* – all brilliant.
What was this year's most exciting event?
I became hopelessly drawn into seasonal events taking place around Blizzard titles!

SAM GOLIN

Sam is a writer, illustrator and comedian who has featured on the TV show *Videogame Nation*. He is half of the nerd-based comedy duo Cult Comics, with Bisha K Ali.

Which games did you play most this year?
Super Smash Bros. 4, *INSIDE* and *Resident Evil 7*.
What was this year's most exciting event?
The release of the Switch, so being able to take *Zelda* on the number 35 bus.

STACE HARMAN

Stace is an author, consultant and co-host of the Indie By Design Podcast. He's frequently looking for exciting new games to play and interesting people to talk to about what goes into making them.

Which games did you play most this year?
Horizon Zero Dawn, *Hearthstone* and *Dead Cells*.
What was this year's most exciting event?
The launch of the Nintendo Switch.

TYLER
HICKS

Tyler is an analyst for professional eSports with Team Liquid's *Halo* team, who finished third at the *Halo* World Championship in Mar 2017.

Which games did you play most this year?
Duelyst, *Halo 5* and *League of Legends* [below].

What was this year's most exciting event?
The *Halo* World Championship.

JORDAN
MAISON

Jordan has written about games for *Pure Nintendo* and StarWars.com, and as the editor of Cinelinx.com. While he loves the newest releases, he's a retro gamer at heart.

Which games did you play most this year?
Deus Ex: Mankind Divided, *No Man's Sky*, *XCOM 2*, *Pokémon Sun* and *Moon*, and *Uncharted 4*.

What was this year's most exciting event?
The hype leading up to the Nintendo Switch was undeniably contagious, and shows potential for the House of Mario.

DAVID
McCOMB

David is a former editor of *Nintendo Official Magazine* and the current editor of *Minecraft Official Magazine*. In the late 1990s he was the UK's "Pokémon King", which involved touring the country and competing against children in quick-fire duels on *Pokémon Red* and *Blue*.

Which games did you play most this year?
Pokémon GO, *Dark Souls III* and *Bloodborne* (again).

What was this year's most exciting event?
Embarking on a new *Legend of Zelda* adventure [right].

BRITTANY
VINCENT

Brittany has been covering videogames, anime and tech for over a decade. Fuelled by horror, rainbow-sugar-pixel-rushes and videogames, she survives on surrealism and ultraviolence. When she's not writing or gaming, she's searching for the perfect successor to the visual novel *Saya no Uta* and walking without rhythm to not attract the worms. Follow her on Twitter @MolotovCupcake and then fire walk with her!

Which games did you play most this year?
Princess Maker Refine, *Rez* VR, *Final Fantasy XV*, *Yakuza 0*, *Shin Megami Tensei: Nocturne*, *System Shock: Enhanced Edition*, *Resident Evil 7* and *Koudelka*. Too many to name.

What was this year's most exciting event?
Finally tearing into *Persona 5* [right] and realizing we're inching ever closer to the *Final Fantasy VII* remake. It's gonna be finished one day.

MATT
WALES

Matt has been writing about games for over a decade, and has contributed words to the likes of IGN, Eurogamer and Kotaku. He's still occasionally amazed to think how fancy games have become since he first played *Manic Miner* on the ZX Spectrum.

Which games did you play most this year?
The Legend of Zelda: Breath of the Wild, *Planet Coaster*, *Persona 5*, *VOEZ*, *Nier: Automata* and *Shovel Knight: Treasure Trove*.

What was this year's most exciting event?
The release of the Switch. Finally, I can play full-fat Nintendo games on the go!

JOHN
ROBERTSON

John has been writing about games for globally focused publications for almost a decade. His first book, *Independent By Design: Art & Stories of Indie Game Creation*, was published in 2016.

Which games did you play most this year?
The Last Guardian, *Reigns* and *Overwatch*.

What was this year's most exciting event?
The Last Guardian finally being released.

INDEX

INDEX

INDEX

PICTURE CREDITS

3 Paul Michael Hughes/GWR; **5** Maltings Partnership; **6** Paul Michael Hughes/GWR, Ryan Schude/GWR, Kevin Scott Ramos/GWR, Ranald Mackechnie/GWR; **7** Paul Michael Hughes/GWR, Kevin Scott Ramos/GWR; **8** Dan Jenkins, Getty; **10** Getty; **11** YouTube, Jynto; **14** Michael Loccisano; **15** Shutterstock, YouTube; **16** iStock; **18** Kevin Scott Ramos/GWR; **20** Shutterstock, Alamy; **21** YouTube; **24** Riot Games; **25** Riot Games, Moby Games; **26** Paul Michael Hughes/GWR, Alamy; **28** Paul Michael Hughes/GWR; **31** Nomadcolossus; **32** YouTube; **38** Carlton Beener; **39** Carlton Beener; **40** Alamy; **41** Moby Games; **42** Alamy; **43** Paul Michael Hughes/GWR; **44** Getty, James Ellerker/GWR; **48** Getty; **49** 123RF; **51** Shutterstock; **54** Kevin Scott Ramos/GWR; **56** Paul Michael Hughes/GWR, Ohio University; **59** Philipp Saedler; **61** Arcade Flyer Archive; **71** Alamy; **72** Paul Michael Hughes/GWR; **73** Red Bull; **74** Alamy, Egmont; **75** Alamy, YouTube; **76** Kevin Scott Ramos/GWR; **78** Shutterstock, Alamy, Getty; **80** Alamy; **81** Heritage Auctions, YouTube, Paul Michael Hughes/GWR; **83** Paul Michael Hughes/GWR, Alamy, James Ellerker/GWR; **84** Kevin Scott Ramos/GWR, Nintendo Today; **86** Alamy, Ryan Dix/GWR; **89** Paul Michael Hughes/GWR, Alamy; **90** Arcade Flyer Archive; **91** Shutterstock; **92** Future Publishing; **93** iStock; **94** Washington Green Fine Art Group, Ak Suggi; **95** Arcade Flyer Archive; **98** Shutterstock; **99** Shutterstock; **100** Kevin Scott Ramos/GWR; **102** Collectibly, Moby Games; **103** Moby Games; **104** Moby Games; **106** Kevin Scott Ramos/GWR; **107** Getty; **108** Getty, Alamy; **109** Shutterstock; **110** Alamy; **112** Reuters; **113** Paul Michael Hughes/GWR; **118** Getty, Moby Games; **119** Luigi Novi; **122** Ranald Mackechnie/GWR, Red Bull; **124** Moby Games, Shutterstock; **125** YouTube, Alamy, Shutterstock; **126** Shutterstock; **127** Shutterstock; **129** Paul Michael Hughes/GWR; **134** Alamy; **135** YouTube; **137** iStock, YouTube; **138** Getty; **139** Alamy; **140** Shutterstock, BBC; **146** Alamy; **152** Shutterstock, Alamy, Ryan Schude/GWR; **153** Getty, Alamy; **154** iStock; **155** Getty, Moby Games; **156** Paul Michael Hughes/GWR; **158** Moby Games, iStock, Shutterstock; **159** Alamy; **160** Getty Images; **161** Ranald Mackechnie/GWR, Getty Images, Moby Games; **162** Moby Games, Alamy; **165** Moby Games; **167** Moby Games, Shutterstock; **173** Shelby Asistio, Arcade Flyer Archive; **174** Alamy; **178** Nelo Hotsuma, Andrew Philippou, Robert Paul, Red Bull; **183** Stephanie Lindgren; **186** Moby Games; **187** Getty; **189** Arcade Flyer Archive; **192** Shutterstock

ACKNOWLEDGEMENTS

Guinness World Records would like to thank the following for their help in compiling *Gamer's Edition 2018*:

22K games (Charley Grafton-Chuck, Gemma Woolnough); Activision Blizzard (Sam Bandah, Emily Woolliscroft, Kevin Flynn, Keith Cox, Jonathan Fargher, Rachael Grant); Phillip Aram; Badland Games UK; Bandai Namco (Ruby Rumjen, Gareth Bagg, Lee Kirton); Sam Barlow; Gonzalo Barrios; Bastion (Luke Karmali, Matthew Bowen); BennyCentral; Bethesda (Mark Robins, Alastair Hatch); Bossa Studios (Poppy Byron); Capcom (Matthew Edwards, Gareth Bagg, Laura Skelly); CCP (Paul Elsy); CD Projekt RED (Robert Malinowski); Julian Checkley and Order 66 Creatures and Effects; Alfie Crook; Cloud Imperium Games (David Swofford, Chris Roberts); Crystal Dynamics; Shirley Curry; Double Fine Productions (James Spafford, David O'Reilly); Sami Cetin; Walter Day; DanTDM; Daybreak Game Company (Raquel Marcelo); Paul Deacon; Dead Good Media (Stu Taylor, Carly Moxey-Kim); Decibel PR (Sam Brace); eSportsearnings.com; Electronic Arts (Bryony Gittins, Shaun White, Tristan Rosenfeldt); Endemol Shine UK (Elspeth Rae); ESL (Anna Rozwandowicz, Chrystina Martel, Christopher Flato); Frontier Developments (Michael Gapper); Gameloft (Jack Wilcock); GameRankings; Anthony Garcia; Gazillion Entertainment (Austin Fong, Chris Baker); Tristen Geren; Global Game Jam (Gorm Lai, Giselle Rosman); GosuGamers (Victor Martyn, Lars Lien, Glen Ainscow, Boris Mihov, Nick D'Orazio); Jace Hall; Harmonix (Criss Burki, Daniel Sussman); Tiffany "iHasCupquake" Herrera; HPS Jardine (Glen Gibson); Joel and Mandy Hopkins; id Software (Tim Willits); Indigo Pearl (Caroline Miller, Ben Le Rougetel, Tom Regan); Isaiah TriForce Johnson; Jelly Media (Mark Bamber); Koch Media (David Scarborough); Konami/Voltage PR (Steve Merrett); Llexi Leon (Phantom Music Management); Lick PR (Kat Osman, Lucy Starvis); Arturo Manzarek Dracul ("the Legend"); MasterOv; Master Overwatch; MCV (Alex Calvin, Seth Barton, Marie Dealessandri); Meagan Marie; MessYourself; Microsoft (Richard Chen, Rob Semsey); Mojang; OP Talent Limited (Liam Chivers); Open World Bionics (Samantha Payne); Overbuff.com; Perfect World Entertainment (Deanna Peter, Narbeh Avanessian, Jayson Gegner); Douglass Perry; Stefano Petrullo; Premier PR (Colette Barr, Will Beckett, Lauren Dillon, Gareth Williams, Yunus Ibrahim, Daniela Pietrosanu); PSNProfiles (Matt Reed); Psyonix (Stephanie Thoensen, Josh Watson); Sonja "omgitsfirefoxx" Reid; Revolution Software (Charles Cecil); Riot Games (Becca Roberts, Jessica Frucht); Rockstar Games (Craig Gilmore, Hamish Brown, Patricia Pucci); Rocksteady Studios (Gaz Deaves); Roll7 (Simon Bennett); Rodrigo Martín Santos; Sega (Sarah Head, Peter Oliver); Shoryuken.com; Dominique "SonicFox" McLean; Sony Computer Entertainment (Hugo Bustillos); Speedrun.com (Peter Chase); Speed Demos Archive; Spencer FC; Sports Interactive (Ciaran Brennan, Neil Brock, Miles Jacobson, Alex Sloane); Square Enix (Ian Dickson); Square in the Air (Andrew Pink); SRK FGC stats (@SRKRanking); StudioMDHR (Ryan Moldenhauer); SuperData (Sam Barberie, Albert Ngo); SwipeRight PR (Kirsty Endfield); Tom "Syndicate" Cassell; Alex "PangaeaPanga" Tan; Jessica Telef; thatgamecompany (Jennie Kong); Think Jam (Ellie Graham, Tom Green); Tommy Tallarico; TrueAchievements (Rich Stone); TT Games; Twin Galaxies; Twitch (Chase); TWiiNSANE; Ubisoft (Oliver Coe, Stefan McGarry); VGChartz; Wargaming (Frazer Nash); Warner Bros. (Mark Ward, Ryan Holloway); Danielle Woodyatt; YouTube Gaming (George Panayotopoulos); Zebra Partners (Beth Llewelyn).

COUNTRY CODES

ABW	Aruba
AFG	Afghanistan
AGO	Angola
AIA	Anguilla
ALB	Albania
AND	Andorra
ANT	Netherlands Antilles
ARG	Argentina
ARM	Armenia
ASM	American Samoa
ATA	Antarctica
ATF	French Southern Territories
ATG	Antigua and Barbuda
AUS	Australia
AUT	Austria
AZE	Azerbaijan
BDI	Burundi
BEL	Belgium
BEN	Benin
BFA	Burkina Faso
BGD	Bangladesh
BGR	Bulgaria
BHR	Bahrain
BHS	The Bahamas
BIH	Bosnia and Herzegovina
BLR	Belarus
BLZ	Belize
BMU	Bermuda
BOL	Bolivia
BRA	Brazil
BRB	Barbados
BRN	Brunei Darussalam
BTN	Bhutan
BVT	Bouvet Island
BWA	Botswana
CAF	Central African Republic
CAN	Canada
CCK	Cocos (Keeling) Islands
CHE	Switzerland
CHL	Chile
CHN	China
CIV	Côte d'Ivoire
CMR	Cameroon
COD	Congo, DR of the
COG	Congo
COK	Cook Islands
COL	Colombia
COM	Comoros
CPV	Cape Verde
CRI	Costa Rica
CUB	Cuba
CXR	Christmas Island
CYM	Cayman Islands
CYP	Cyprus
CZE	Czech Republic
DEU	Germany
DJI	Djibouti
DMA	Dominica
DNK	Denmark
DOM	Dominican Republic
DZA	Algeria
ECU	Ecuador
EGY	Egypt
ERI	Eritrea
ESH	Western Sahara
ESP	Spain
EST	Estonia
ETH	Ethiopia
FIN	Finland
FJI	Fiji
FLK	Falkland Islands (Malvinas)
FRA	France
FRG	West Germany
FRO	Faroe Islands
FSM	Micronesia, Federated States of
FXX	France, Metropolitan
GAB	Gabon
GEO	Georgia
GHA	Ghana
GIB	Gibraltar
GIN	Guinea
GLP	Guadeloupe
GMB	Gambia
GNB	Guinea-Bissau
GNQ	Equatorial Guinea
GRC	Greece
GRD	Grenada
GRL	Greenland
GTM	Guatemala
GUF	French Guiana
GUM	Guam
GUY	Guyana
HKG	Hong Kong
HMD	Heard and McDonald Islands
HND	Honduras
HRV	Croatia (Hrvatska)
HTI	Haiti
HUN	Hungary
IDN	Indonesia
IND	India
IOT	British Indian Ocean Territory
IRL	Ireland
IRN	Iran
IRQ	Iraq
ISL	Iceland
ISR	Israel
ITA	Italy
JAM	Jamaica
JOR	Jordan
JPN	Japan
KAZ	Kazakhstan
KEN	Kenya
KGZ	Kyrgyzstan
KHM	Cambodia
KIR	Kiribati
KNA	Saint Kitts and Nevis
KOR	Korea, Republic of
KWT	Kuwait
LAO	Laos
LBN	Lebanon
LBR	Liberia
LBY	Libyan Arab Jamahiriya
LCA	Saint Lucia
LIE	Liechtenstein
LKA	Sri Lanka
LSO	Lesotho
LTU	Lithuania
LUX	Luxembourg
LVA	Latvia
MAC	Macau
MAR	Morocco
MCO	Monaco
MDA	Moldova
MDG	Madagascar
MDV	Maldives
MEX	Mexico
MHL	Marshall Islands
MKD	Macedonia
MLI	Mali
MLT	Malta
MMR	Myanmar (Burma)
MNE	Montenegro
MNG	Mongolia
MNP	Northern Mariana Islands
MOZ	Mozambique
MRT	Mauritania
MSR	Montserrat
MTQ	Martinique
MUS	Mauritius
MWI	Malawi
MYS	Malaysia
MYT	Mayotte
NAM	Namibia
NCL	New Caledonia
NER	Niger
NFK	Norfolk Island
NGA	Nigeria
NIC	Nicaragua
NIU	Niue
NLD	Netherlands
NOR	Norway
NPL	Nepal
NRU	Nauru
NZ	New Zealand
OMN	Oman
PAK	Pakistan
PAN	Panama
PCN	Pitcairn Islands
PER	Peru
PHL	Philippines
PLW	Palau
PNG	Papua New Guinea
POL	Poland
PRI	Puerto Rico
PRK	Korea, DPRO
PRT	Portugal
PRY	Paraguay
PYF	French Polynesia
QAT	Qatar
REU	Réunion
ROM	Romania
RUS	Russian Federation
RWA	Rwanda
SAU	Saudi Arabia
SDN	Sudan
SEN	Senegal
SGP	Singapore
SGS	South Georgia and South SS
SHN	Saint Helena
SJM	Svalbard and Jan Mayen Islands
SLB	Solomon Islands
SLE	Sierra Leone
SLV	El Salvador
SMR	San Marino
SOM	Somalia
SPM	Saint Pierre and Miquelon
SRB	Serbia
SSD	South Sudan
STP	São Tomé and Príncipe
SUR	Suriname
SVK	Slovakia
SVN	Slovenia
SWE	Sweden
SWZ	Swaziland
SYC	Seychelles
SYR	Syrian Arab Republic
TCA	Turks and Caicos Islands
TCD	Chad
TGO	Togo
THA	Thailand
TJK	Tajikistan
TKL	Tokelau
TKM	Turkmenistan
TMP	East Timor
TON	Tonga
TPE	Chinese Taipei
TTO	Trinidad and Tobago
TUN	Tunisia
TUR	Turkey
TUV	Tuvalu
TZA	Tanzania
UAE	United Arab Emirates
UGA	Uganda
UK	United Kingdom
UKR	Ukraine
UMI	US Minor Islands
URY	Uruguay
USA	United States of America
UZB	Uzbekistan
VAT	Holy See (Vatican City)
VCT	Saint Vincent and the Grenadines
VEN	Venezuela
VGB	Virgin Islands (British)
VIR	Virgin Islands (US)
VNM	Vietnam
VUT	Vanuatu
WLF	Wallis and Futuna Islands
WSM	Samoa
YEM	Yemen
ZAF	South Africa
ZMB	Zambia
ZWE	Zimbabwe

STOP PRESS!

The world of gaming moves faster than Spidey in full swing. Here are a few of our favourite last-minute record-breakers...

Most watched *Pokémon GO* fan video

"Pokemon GO In REAL LIFE", by global film-makers "Shutter Authority", had 59,762,596 views on YouTube as of 8 May 2017. The live-action spoof, involving the pursuit of a cartoon Pikachu, has beaten "POKEMON GO SONG!!! by MISHA (FOR KIDS) [ORIGINAL]" (see p.81).

First gaming "Easter egg"

In Atari's 1977 arcade game *Starship 1*, the message "Hi Ron!" appears on screen and the player wins 10 lives. This was revealed in an interview with engineer Ron Milner, as blogged by a former Xbox executive on 22 Mar 2017.

Longest win streak on *Heroes of the Storm*

According to GosuGamers, South Korea's "MVP Black" won 35 consecutive matches of Blizzard's MOBA from 17 Dec 2015 to 23 May 2016. The team remains the highest-ranked in the game.

Highest-ranked *Mortal Kombat X* player (ever)

US hotshot Dominique "SonicFox" McLean (whose *Injustice* record is on p.101) heads Shoryuken's *Mortal Kombat X* rankings. A career score of 310,065 (from his best 18 tournaments) was over 100,000 more than his nearest rival (the UK's "Foxy Grampa") as of 28 Apr 2017.

"SonicFox" has also won the **most *MKX* tournaments**. His tally of 20 includes three consecutive years as ESL *Mortal Kombat X* Pro League world champion.

Unsurprisingly, "SonicFox" is also the **highest-earning *MKX* player**. As of 28 Apr 2017, he had won an enviable $253,343 (£196,664).

Most original pieces of music in a videogame

As of 12 May 2017, there were 1,163 individual tracks in Jagex's MMO *RuneScape*, ranging from folk songs to full orchestral performances. This tops *Final Fantasy XIV*'s record on p.33.

Most watched videogame tutorial

"New Super Mario Bros. DS – All 18 Secret Exit Locations (Complete Guide)" – posted to YouTube by "packattack04082" (USA) in Sep 2013 – had powered to 58,421,320 views as of 8 May 2017.

With 29.81 million units shifted, *New Super Mario Bros.* (2006) is the **best-selling DS game**.

Most streamed videogame soundtrack on Spotify

The Music of Grand Theft Auto V: Volume 1: Original Music had been streamed 93 million times as of 30 Mar 2017. This beats *Minecraft: Volume Alpha* (63 million), *The Last of Us* (50 million) and *Pokémon X – 10 Years of Pokémon* (42 million). Acts on the album include Yeasayer and Wavves.

Most playable entities in a game

Living up to its name, Double Fine Productions' open-world sim *Everything* (2017) lets you choose from 3,000 playable "things" or entities. These are divided into 56 categories, from aircraft to animals and food to fungus. Programmer David OReilly said: "The initial goal was to make everything a playable character – and take it to the extreme."

Longest marathon on a VR game system

Austrian gamer Johannes Löffelmann played Owlchemy Labs' satirical *Job Simulator* (2016) for 28 hr 43 min 24 sec in his country's capital, Vienna, on 12 Apr 2017. The collaboration with retailer Saturn Austria was undertaken on Sony PlayStation VR. It beat Georgie Barrat's *Minecraft* VR record (see p.89).

Most MLB: The Show cover appearances
Since *MLB 12*, Sony has made alternative covers to promote the baseball game in different markets. *MLB 13* was the first with a cover for Chinese Taipei, and a region-specific version has since been produced every year, as of 8 May 2017. All five star Wei-Yin Chen, who plays for the Miami Marlins but was born in Chinese Taipei.

Most goals scored in a game of *Rocket League*
Not content with smashing the team-of-two record for *Rocket League* (see p.156), India's Shashipreetham Rao Ravella holds the solo top spot too. He scored 66 goals in Aberystwyth, Ceredigion, UK, on 28 Mar 2017, as verified by Twin Galaxies.

Fastest completion of *Yooka-Laylee*
Within days of its release, Playtonic's 3D platformer (about friends Yooka, a chameleon, and Laylee, a helpful bat) had inspired hordes of speed-runners. Canadian PS4 gamer "CGbadass" took the lead on 5 May 2017 with a run of 28 min 58 sec.

Most participants in a game jam (multiple venue)
The 2017 Global Game Jam, on 20–22 Jan, saw 36,397 registered participants jamming from 701 locations in 94 countries, from Algeria to Vietnam. Based on a "waves" theme, 7,258 games were made. Among them were intriguing titles such as *Sputnik Ostrich* and *Mad Anchovy Carnage*.

Most critically acclaimed open-world game
Storming past *GTA IV* and *V* (see p.145), *Zelda* has claimed the top open-world spot on GameRankings. The newcomer *Breath of the Wild* – the veteran franchise's first true open-world title – had 97.3%, from 61 reviews, as of 8 May 2017.

Most watched gaming video on YouTube
"Subway Surfers Trailer Google Play" – uploaded by Denmark's KilooGames in 2012 – had an astonishing 290,408,232 views as of 8 May 2017. The video – about the endless mobile runner – is also the **most viewed trailer**, far eclipsing ones for movies and other games.

Longest time to correct a videogame typo
In the original *The Legend of Zelda* – published in the USA in Jul 1987 – "peninsula" was misspelled "penninsula". This was corrected in the version packaged with the Mini NES console (see p.14), released 29 years 4 months later.

Fastest completion of *Tom Clancy's Ghost Recon: Wildlands*
"BnH247" (USA) blasted through the shooter in 3 hr 24 min 41 sec on 1 Apr 2017. "Decent to good everything but El Muro and Villa Verde," said the PC gamer of his run on the most recent *Ghost Recon* title.

Longest *Overwatch* marathon
Samuel Hibbert, Jay Smith, Tom Leigh and James Williams (all UK) played the shooter for 24 hr 14 sec at GameBlast17 in Hampshire, UK, on 25–26 Feb 2017 – a fundraiser to help people with disabilities play games with adapted consoles.
The **longest *Overwatch* pro win streak** is 59 matches, achieved by USA's Team EnVyUs from 13 Feb to 9 Apr 2016.

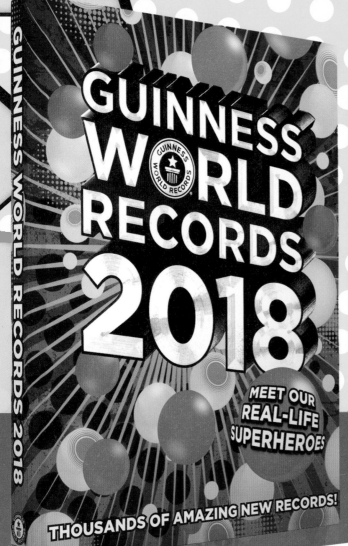
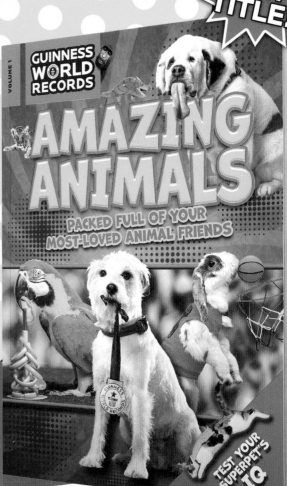